# C·L·A·S·S·I·C
# Baking

Translated by Karen Green, in association with
First Edition Translations, Cambridge

CLB 4423
This title originally published in German under the title
*Backen ist Liebe*
Copyright Südwest Verlag GmbH & Co. KG, München, 1993
This edition published 1995 by Colour Library Books
© 1995 English language translation:
Colour Library Books Ltd, Godalming, Surrey
All rights reserved
Typeset by Dorwyn Ltd, Chichester, Hants
Printed in Belgium by Proost N.V.
ISBN 1-85833-400-4

# C·L·A·S·S·I·C
# Baking

## The Definitive Guide to Recipes and Techniques

**CLB**

*Colour Library Books Ltd*

**Raspberry and pineapple gateau. Recipe on page 37.**

# THE HISTORY OF BAKING

■ Cakes and pastries form an important part of our food culture, and have symbolised our desire for luxury since the early Middle Ages. Representations of the land of milk and honey tempted the tastebuds with images of streets paved with ginger biscuits and shutters made of fragrant gingerbread. Both rich and poor enjoyed sweet cakes and pastries on high days and holidays. Initially they were served when the pangs of hunger had already been assuaged. They were eaten purely for greed and enjoyment, not to quieten a rumbling stomach, and very little has changed today. Among the dearest wishes nowadays of those who have a sweet tooth but who have to count the calories is to be able, just once, to eat their fill of cakes and biscuits. Cakes and pastries should be a feast for the eyes and the palate and, when all is said and done, they should be a treat. Baking itself, stirring, kneading and shaping, is not a duty. Baking is a creative pleasure. Baking is an act of love!

## TRADITION

■ Baking is not a new skill. The Egyptians, Greeks and Romans baked with flour, fruit, honey and spices and wrote about their recipes. The women of ancient Germania sacrificed baked plaits to the gods instead of their own hair. Recipes for gingerbread dating back to the darkest Middle Ages have been found and they had already been mentioned in stories of the saints by the year 1000. A document from as early as 1329 mentions Christmas stollen and we hear of the first Christmas stollen from Dresden in 1528. The traditional Italian Christmas cake, Panettone (recipe page 54) is supposed to have been discovered in the late 15th century by Toni, the owner of the Della Grazia bakery in Milan (thus Pane di Toni – Panettone). By the beginning of the 16th century monks were already preparing the first Baumkuchen (a cake which, when sliced, has a pattern similar to the annual rings of a tree) on the roasting spits of their monastery kitchens (our recipe for Baumkuchen, as a gateau baked in a spring form tin, is on page 46).

In the middle of the 16th century Phillippine Welser, a woman from Augsburg in Germany, wrote, amongst other things, about pear tart and lardy cakes made with flour, sugar and rose-water in her hand-written cookery book.

## GREATER VARIETY

■ The tradition of home baking as we know it first began in the 18th century. This was when millers discovered how to produce fine, white wheat flour without the coarse pieces of bran

**A biscuit mould devised in a monastery cell in the Middle Ages.**

which had previously been unavoidable. The white flour made a completely new range of cakes and pastries possible. The first detailed recipes for the much-loved Christmas stollen start to circulate at this time. (Our modern stollen recipe can be found on page 67.)

## BEAUTIFULLY DECORATED

The women then served gateaux filled with cream, jam, marzipan and fruits at weddings, christenings and other family celebrations. It became customary to separate egg yolks and whites before beating, and the first fatless sponge-type cake went into the oven. The famous Linzer Torte from Austria, made of short-crust pastry, first appeared about this time (our recipe for Linzer Torte is on page 102). The first recipes for meringues (basic recipe page 186) originate from the first half of the 18th century. The first half of the 19th century saw the onset of an era of cakes made from the finest ingredients and of beautifully decorated gateaux. A second major prerequisite for domestic cake baking in the style of today, in addition to white flour, was affordable sugar. In Biedermeier, Germany, the burgeoning industry managed for the first time to produce fine sugar in large quantities and sell it at a reasonable price. Until the middle of the 18th century the sweet crystals were only sold by chemists at high prices as a tonic. People at this time revelled in their domesticity. They invented the coffee morning and no longer invited guests to formal celebratory meals at long tables, but to take a cup of tea, coffee or chocolate in a very civilised manner around the table. In 1832 the Vienna pastry cook Franz Sacher created his famous chocolate gateau, which is still copied today and baked in their own ovens by skilled men and women. (You will find our version on page 34.)

At roughly the same time Josef Karl Dobos, a confectioner from Budapest, was the force behind a totally new light sponge composition containing no fat. (The recipe for Dobos, usually known as fatless sponge is on page 120.)

**Christmas baking at home circa 1890. Coloured wood engraving by Gustav Adolf Kiekebusch.**

# INGREDIENTS AND THEIR PROPERTIES

■ Flour, eggs, sugar and fat are ingredients which are part of almost every cake. It is worth finding out a little about the special properties of these basic ingredients, because if you know how a mixture 'works' you will only be faced with the occasional unpleasant surprise and your cakes will almost always be successful. Baking is in fact much more fun if you are in control.

## FAT

■ Fat is very important in cake mixtures because it combines and enhances the aromas of all the ingredients. It is essential for a good flavour. In addition it makes the mixture crumbly, gives it a melting texture and prevents it from drying out. In some types of baking, such as short-crust pastry for example, fat alone is responsible for the light, delicate texture. The more fat you use, the more crumbly the baking; it melts in your mouth.

The taste and of course the particular recipe determine which type of fat is used in the cake. In the 19th century beef fat was still common. Goose fat and lard were still favoured by some for baking up to the middle of the 20th century. However, such butcher's fat is only used very rarely in modern home baking. Oils also play a lesser role

because they can only be used in special recipes and would make our normal sponge mixtures and short-crust pastry heavy and greasy. Next to butter a good soft margarine is best suited to most recipes because the malleable vegetable fat has a pleasant appearance, becomes creamy and full of air when beaten and combines well with flour in a mixture. When baked it results in a fine, even crumb. The margarine is incorporated without difficulty and is so neutral in taste that it does not predominate but harmonises well with every possible baking ingredient and spice and emphasises their individual tastes. Even rich cream fillings, traditionally known as 'butter cream', are

**Margarine becomes creamy and full of air when beaten.**

very successful when made with margarine and retain their flavour for several days if kept well refrigerated.

## FLOUR

■ In order for cakes, biscuits and gateaux to succeed, the right flour is just as important as the right fat. Our usual extremely finely milled white cake flour absorbs a lot of liquid, egg and fat, and combines the ingredients into an even, malleable mixture. If our recipes simply say flour, then plain flour is always meant. Cake flour is milled from 'soft' wheat. The experts refer to flour which contains little of the rubbery, elastic gluten as soft. A lot of gluten would make delicate cake mixtures tough and dry when baked. Substantial breads, strudels and puff pastry, on the other hand, are more successful with flours made from 'hard' wheat. In those cases the more water the gluten absorbs and the more elastic the framework which the gluten forms in the dough, the better the resulting bake. The so-called 'extra strong' flours and special mixtures for baking bread contain more gluten than normal cake flour. Wholemeal and granary flour containing bran became fashionable in cake baking with the health-oriented wholefood trend because they are richer in roughage and contain more vitamins. Cake mixtures using these types of flour cannot turn out light and airy without extra help because the bran only absorbs liquid slowly and the large particles in such flour do not permit fine textured doughs. On the other hand, freshly milled granary flour lends a pleasant nutty aroma and robust texture to hearty yeast cakes, short-crust pastry rich in fat, bread and rolls.

## SUGAR

■ Sugar not only sweetens cake mixtures, it helps them to rise. Sponge mixtures, for example, lose their fine texture and sink if sweetener is used in the mixture instead of sugar. Without sugar a cake mixture would not develop a brown crust, but would appear pale and yellowish after baking. Furthermore, sugar is yeast's favourite ingredient. Yeast doughs do rise if sweetener is used, but have to work considerably longer because the yeast needs time to convert starch from the flour into sugar. Sugar crystals dissolve when beaten together with butter or margarine, stabilise the mixture and help to retain the air.

The larger the sugar crystals, the longer they take to dissolve in the mixture. For this reason you should primarily use 'caster' sugar for baking – in other words, sugar with very small crystals or icing sugar, which is ground caster sugar – because the finer the sugar, the more quickly it will dissolve. Much also depends on the measure. If the quantity is correct, then sugar makes the cake light. If there is too much sugar in the mixture, then the result will be small, solid and heavy.

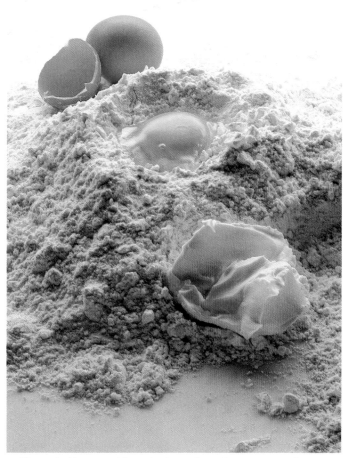

**Fine cake flour combines the ingredients into an even mixture.**

## EGGS

■ Eggs have a three-fold role to play in cake baking. If enough air is beaten into the egg white it lightens the mixture. The emulsifying properties of egg yolk ensure that all the ingredients combine into a smooth mixture. Also, together with flour, eggs stabilise the crumb texture of the baking. The quantity of egg is decisive in the success of fatless sponges and choux pastry. All the recipes in this book are based on size 3 eggs (unless otherwise specified). If you use larger or smaller eggs, this changes the quantity of egg. As a result choux pastry and fatless sponges will have a different composition and sometimes baking will be unsuccessful. Other mixtures are less sensitive. If you don't have enough eggs for a sponge or yeast mixture, you can replace them with the corresponding quantity of water or milk.

# LARGE AND SMALL UTENSILS AND OVENS

### HAND-MIXING MACHINES AND FOOD PROCESSORS

■ Previously it was necessary to rely on strong men's muscle power for stirring cake mixtures. Or the women took it in turns when the recipe said 'Stir the mixture in an anti-clockwise direction, for at least an hour'! Thankfully technology nowadays saves us this waste of time and energy. However, there is not as yet an electric mixer which will mix all mixtures and doughs equally well. Experienced cooks still knead short-crust pastry by hand alone. Yeast doughs and heavy sour doughs for bread are also more successful if they are thoroughly kneaded on the work surface. On the other hand, an electric mixer is indispensable for fatless sponges, sponge mixes and meringues. In a small household a powerful hand mixer with a whisk, dough hook and slicing attachment will fulfil all your baking needs. When it comes to large quantities, heavy tough mixtures and long mixing times, the motor may fail, however, and may even be damaged owing to overheating. This mainly happens if the machine is used for too long, so that the so-called 'consumer use' time is exceeded. Small, compact food processors, with which mixtures are beaten in the bowl by a kind of

blade, are intended for small households, but do not process every kind of mixture as well as a hand mixer. Powerful little food processors with a fixed mixing attachment and dough hook are better at this. They are particularly worth buying for households which bake more than once a week and which have enough room for the equipment to stand on the work

**No one piece of equipment for every type of mixture: mixing spoon, hand mixer and food processor.**

surface, ready for use at any time. If you regularly mix large quantities or heavy mixtures for granary bread, honey cake or yeast baking, you need a large food processor which has room for more than 1 kilo (2lbs 3 oz) of flour in the mixing bowl.

### THE OVEN

■ If you want to buy a new oven, you are spoilt for choice nowadays. There are:
- conduction ovens with heating elements above and below
- fan ovens using hot air
- combination ovens with heating elements above and below and hot air
- combination ovens with built-in microwaves
- gas ovens.

Cake baking shows more clearly than roasting or braising what each individual heating system can achieve. For example, it is not possible to set gas ovens low enough to dry out meringues perfectly. However, these ovens preheat quickly and yeast mixtures and bread usually succeed very well in them. Comparative tests with electric cookers have shown that, depending on the type of baking, either above and below conduction or hot air give the best results. A combination oven is clearly the best choice for baking as by using it all different types of cake turn out as well as possible.

## SHELF POSITIONS

■ In order for heat in the oven to be used to the best advantage, you should position your baking so that the distance from the oven walls is roughly equal on all sides.

### Bottom: Shelf positions 1 and 2

For cakes in deep or medium baking tins, and for cakes in spring form tins which rise very high, such as baked cheesecakes and fatless sponges. Also bread, plaits and stollen.

### Middle: Shelf positions 2 and 3

Good for deep flan bases in spring form tins, but also baking which rises quite a lot on a baking sheet, such as bread rolls, cream puffs, vol-au-vents, croissants, glazed fruit flans, biscuits and flat tartlets.

### Top: Shelf positions 3, 4 and 5

Only dishes which are to be browned should go here – for example, cakes with a meringue topping – because they depend on powerful heat from above.

In fan ovens you can bake on several levels at once. In this case 10-15 cm/4-6 inches space must be left above each tray so that the baking has enough room to rise.

## TEMPERATURE

■ Many tested recipes don't succeed when you follow them because selecting the correct temperature often depends on settings which you know from experience will work, and because oven temperature controls are not standardised. Modern ovens with 10-degree steps on the scale can be set more precisely than older machines. Because the temperature which has been set is usually considerably exceeded when the oven heats up, you should only put baking in if the red light shows that the desired temperature has been reached. If you are using a very old oven, an oven thermometer will help you to test the temperature. By the way, the temperature may vary up or down by 10 percent, even in new ovens. In many of our recipes the recommended temperature is therefore given as a 'margin'. In this way you have a reference value so you can set your oven temperature above or below accordingly. Always start with the lower or middle value. You can then if necessary increase the temperature a

**The skewer test: in order to check whether a cake really is cooked, stick a wooden stick (a kebab skewer, for example) into the middle of the cake. If the wood is clean when pulled out, then the cake is done. If cake mix is stuck to it, the cake must go back into the oven for a few minutes.**

little towards the end of baking time. This way nothing can go wrong. Most failures are caused by the oven being too hot. A lower temperature, especially when baking in a fan oven, produces a more even result.

Electric ovens take from 8 to 20 minutes to preheat to 200°C/400°F. Conduction ovens do not preheat as quickly as ovens which have intensively circulated hot air. Gas ovens are the quickest to reach the required temperature. The table opposite shows a comparison of oven heating system temperatures.

The shelves in fan ovens are often appreciably smaller than others. The reason for this is that grids and air distribution panels which are supposed to exchange heat more effectively take up a lot of space. You may have to reduce your usual recipe quantity and use a smaller baking sheet, or put up with a thicker layer of mixture. If your baking sheet seems to you to be too small for the prepared mixture, use a roasting tin. It also provides enough room for large individual cakes.

| Oven temperatures for various heating systems | | | |
|---|---|---|---|
| Gas oven | Electric oven | | Recommended for |
| | Conduction | Fan | |
| – | 50°C | 50°C | Proving yeast dough. Switch off oven after 5 minutes |
| – | 75°C | 60–80°C | Warming crockery and keeping food warm |
| Mark ½ | 100–120°C | 90–120°C | Drying baking |
| Mark 4 | 170°C | 140–160° | Gateaux with delicate toppings (e.g. curd cheese gateau) |
| Mark 4–5 | 170–190°C | 150–170°C | Sponges, maderia cake, fatless sponges |
| Mark 6 | 200° | 170–190°C | Glazed biscuits, choux pastry |
| Mark 6–7 | 200–225°C | 170–190°C | Biscuits, puff pastry |
| Mark 7–9 | 220–250°C | 200–230°C | Baking which can stand very high heat (e.g. pizza) and grilling |

## BAKING IN THE MICROWAVE

■ A better end result can be achieved for many types of baking in so-called combination microwave ovens. Microwaves quickly and attractively cook the liquid toppings of curd cheese flans, vegetable flans and quiche Lorraine. You no longer get 'soggy layers' because it is easier for the layers of mixture to cook through. On the other hand,

**Not every type of material or dish is suitable for the microwave. Round glass and pottery ones are ideal.**

| What succeeds where? | |
| --- | --- |
| **Microwave oven** | **Conventional oven** |
| Sponges with little flour, but with greater proportions of nuts or fruit | Sponges with a lot of flour, e.g. marble cake, madeira cake |
| Curd cheese cakes or baked cheesecakes on short-crust base | Biscuits which bake quickly, because the microwave doesn't save time |
| Cakes with fruit topping and curd cheese or cream glazes on yeast dough or short-crust pastry | Same applies to: |
| | short-crust pastry flan bases, fatless sponge gateaux, Swiss rolls, choux pastry such as |
| Fruit flan with meringue topping | cream puffs, meringue-type |
| All types of quiches, cheese puffs, onion flan | baking such as macaroons |
| | Yeast plaits or stollen |
| Strudel filled with cream cheese or fruit | Rye bread or granary bread |

sponge cakes with a high proportion of flour are better cooked without a microwave because the reduced baking time, up to 50 percent in combination microwaves, sometimes fails to cook the flour thoroughly so that the cake tastes insipid.

To help you decide, the above summary shows which baking succeeds best in combination microwaves and which it would be better to bake in a conventional oven.

## BAKING DISHES FOR MICROWAVES

■ Round baking dishes with a diameter of approx. 25-30 cm/10-12 inches are best. If square ones are used the cake cooks more in the corners, where the microwave concentrates the heat, and doesn't rise well.

Dishes made from heat-resistant glass, fully glazed pottery and special plastic which can withstand temperatures of 210°C/425F are recommended. Some metal baking tins are especially suitable. Lightweight baking tins made out of tin or aluminium and tins made of reflective materials are not at all suitable. Microwave dishes should not be greased well, as is customary, but should be dusted with breadcrumbs, ground almonds or nuts so the cake doesn't stick. Spring form dishes should be lined with baking parchment.

## BAKING TIMES FOR MICROWAVES

■ Our recipes give baking times and temperatures for conventional ovens. If you want to bake using a microwave combination oven, you can adapt the times and temperatures for microwaves using the following method. Put your cake in the lower third of the oven and select a temperature which is 10 to 20°C higher than stated in the recipe. Switch on the microwave at low power, 150-180 watts, and reduce the baking time by half.

# Classic sponge mixes

American brownies, moist chocolate cake, summery apricot flan and spiced wine triangles for Christmas – sweet temptations which are all based on sponge. These sponge-based mixes are easily controlled with well-balanced ingredients and a dash of verve at every stage of mixing.

Rodon cake. Recipe on page 30.

# HOW TO MAKE A SUCCESSFUL SPONGE CAKE MIXTURE

A luxurious version of the basic Victoria sponge was included in the recipe books of our great-grandmothers' day. The mixture consists of equal parts of fat, sugar, eggs and flour and is made without baking powder or added liquid, simply by beating air into the ingredients. As its German name 'Pfundkuchen' suggests, previously the pound or 'Pfund' measure (500 g) was normally used. If you want to try the recipe today using smaller quantities, it is best to use the weight of the eggs as the measure. Three size 3 eggs weigh just under 200 g, so you will need to weigh out about 200 g/7 oz each of margarine, sugar and flour. Mix the ingredients as shown in steps 1 to 5.

Modern sponge mixtures with baking powder and milk contain only half the fat and less sugar and eggs. This straightforward sponge mixture contains fewer calories and is quicker to make. Here are the ingredients for the simple, reliable basic recipe: 250 g/9 oz margarine, 250 g/9 oz caster sugar, pinch salt, 4 eggs, 500 g/1 lb 2 oz flour, 1 sachet/approx. ½ oz baking powder, about 125 ml/4 fl. oz milk.

When preparing the mixture you can either follow steps 6 and 7 and use a hand mixer, or follow steps 8 and 9 if you want to use a food processor. The result will be just as good.

**1** For the classic Victoria sponge, beat the soft margarine and two-thirds of the sugar with a large balloon whisk – that's how the professionals do it – or use the beaters of a hand mixer, until the sugar has dissolved.

**2** The mixture is right if it is very pale, almost white in colour, and has a light, creamy consistency. Only at this stage should you stir the egg yolks into the fat mixture.

**6** For a cake mixture using baking powder you can add whole eggs one at a time while adding the flour to the fat mixture (as described in step 1). Then gradually pour in the liquid.

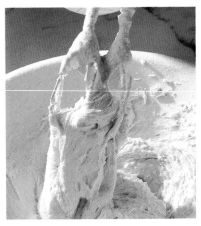

**7** The cake mixture is perfect if it drops slowly off the beaters back into the bowl if you lift up the mixer. If the mixture is too stiff it will cling to the beaters and you will need to add more liquid. If the mixture is too soft it will slip off the beaters and you will have to add more flour.

**3** The egg yolks should be at room temperature so that the fat does not curdle. If this does happen, simply continue beating the mixture. It is important to work as much air as possible into the mixture so that the cake rises when baked.

**4** Sieve the flour into the bowl with the fat and egg mixture and mix. Beat the egg whites with the remaining sugar to stiff peaks and mix some of this in together with the flour so that the mixture becomes smooth.

**5** Fold the remaining egg white carefully into the mixture so that the air is retained. Don't stir in a circle but draw a spoon or a spatula through the cake mixture and egg white from top to bottom in a spiral. Professionals use their hands to do this.

**8** If you are using a food processor, add the fat, eggs and sugar at the same time and switch it to a high speed for about 1 minute. The mixture should have almost doubled in volume and be light and creamy in appearance.

**9** Only then should you add the sieved flour with the baking powder and liquid and mix them briefly on a medium setting. If mixed for too long the gluten in the flour is activated and the mixture quickly becomes heavy.

**10** The following applies whichever method you use: pieces of chocolate or dried fruit are only added to the mixture at the end. These ingredients, which add flavour, are mixed in briefly with a spatula or slotted spoon. If you dust dried fruits lightly with flour they will not sink so easily to the bottom of the cake when baked.

# SPONGE MIXTURE

### THE INGREDIENTS

■ Sponge cakes turn out best if all the ingredients are at room temperature. They then combine perfectly and the mixture becomes creamy and even. You therefore need to take margarine, eggs and milk out of the refrigerator in plenty of time. If the temperatures of different ingredients vary too much, the egg-fat mixture may appear to be curdled and lumpy. This doesn't necessarily mean that the cake will sink when baked, but it won't be as light because the little holes in the curdled mixture allow the carefully beaten – in air to escape faster than an even, creamy layer of fat mixture. Result – the cake turns out more solid. If you want to bring eggs from the refrigerator up to room

**Margarine combines well in a sponge mixture if it is at room temperature.**

temperature quickly, place them in warm water for a short time. You can warm margarine in the microwave for 1 minute (at 600-700 watts).

**Will the mixture fit into my baking tin? Use this simple test to check. Fill the tin with water to check how many litres (pints) will fit into a decorative mould.**

### CORRECT QUANTITIES

■ Figures and decorative shapes such as hearts, snowmen, flowers and rosettes are increasingly popular, but you never know whether the quantity of mixture in the recipe will fit. This little trick will help you determine the correct quantity of mixture for any cake tin. Simply measure how much water your tin will take. Our sponge cake recipes give a litre (pint) measure with the baking tin specification. If the volume of water matches the details, the quantity of mixture is exactly right. If it turns out that there is too much mixture for the

tin you want to use, use an additional smaller tin. If there isn't enough mixture it is best to double the quantity. Cakes baked in tins which are not sufficiently full turn out flat and unattractive.

### GREASING TINS

■ All baking tins, even non-stick ones, should be greased thoroughly with melted margarine so that the cake doesn't stick when turned out. It is easiest to do this with a brush so you can get into all the corners. Baking tins with many sides and edges should be refrigerated for a while after greasing so that the film of grease sets and forms a protective layer on the edge of the tin which will make it easier to turn the cake out later. Melted margarine can combine with the mixture when the tin is being filled, then the non-stick effect is lost. Note: don't use oil to grease a tin. When baked it may form a yellowish film on the edges of the tin which is very difficult to remove later.

One sticky, one light. The cake on the left was made without baking powder and was not mixed thoroughly enough.

Grease round tins well with a brush. Line square tins with baking parchment as well.

## MIX WELL

■ It is obvious that sponge cakes should be spongy. The more thoroughly you mix margarine and sugar together, for example, the more successful your baking will be. Air which is beaten in makes cakes light and soft later. You must be careful when the flour is finally added. If you are mixing by hand, you mustn't clock-watch. But the mixture should only be processed for 3 minutes in a food processor, and for no more than 5 minutes with a hand mixer. In fact, too much mixing changes the structure of flour. Gluten, a component of protein, makes the mixture heavy and the cake won't rise properly. Instead of being fine textured and soft, a cake which has been 'over-stirred' turns out dry, crumbly and stodgy.

## RAISING AGENTS

■ Only sponge mixes containing lots of egg, plenty of sugar and little flour succeed without baking powder; it is essential that fat, sugar and eggs are beaten together thoroughly to incorporate a lot of air. Very experienced cooks sometimes feel confident enough to tackle even very delicate mixtures without baking powder, but light cakes are only guaranteed to turn out light and airy by using baking powder. When the powder comes into contact with moisture in the mixture it produces carbonic acid in the form of millions of tiny bubbles. They cause the cake to rise, making it airy and light. A sponge cake becomes simple and uncomplicated with baking powder, The disadvantage is that the cake may taste slightly of baking powder, which sometimes bothers sensitive palates.

## LEAVE TO REST BRIEFLY

■ The cake should be left in the tin to rest for approximately 3 minutes (no longer!) after baking. The mixture stabilises during this time and a thin layer of air develops between the cake and the tin, making it easier to turn out. Then leave the cake to cool on a rack so that steam can escape and the crust doesn't go soft but stays nice and crisp.

Leave sponge cakes to rest in the tin for a little while, then turn out onto a rack.

# POPPY SEED CAKE WITH CHERRY GLAZE

**Ingredients for a shallow square tin (capacity 2 l/3½ pints)**

**FOR THE MIXTURE:**

250 g/9 oz freshly ground poppy seeds

150 g/6 oz soft margarine

200 g/7 oz caster sugar

3 sachets/approx. 1½ oz vanilla sugar

7 egg yolks

125 g/5 oz ground almonds

2 sachets/approx. 4 oz baking powder

7 egg whites

**FOR THE GLAZE:**

250 g/9 oz cherry jam

12 tsp arrowroot

2 tbsp kirsch

**1** Put the poppy seeds into 200 ml/7 fl. oz of boiling water and leave to swell on the lowest heat setting for 8-10 minutes. Put to one side in a sieve to cool.

**2** Line tin with baking parchment, extending the paper slightly above the edge of the tin.

**3** Beat the margarine, sugar and vanilla sugar together with a balloon whisk or hand mixer until the sugar dissolves. Then add the egg yolks one by one and beat to a cream. Mix the ground almonds with the baking powder and add to the margarine and egg mixture alternately with the cooled poppy seeds. Beat the egg whites until stiff and fold in.

**4** Pour the mixture into the tin and bake in a preheated oven at 175°C/350°F/Gas mark 4 for 30-35 minutes. Leave the cake to cool in the tin.

**5** To make the glaze, purée the jam with the chopping blade of the hand mixer and heat gently. Whisk the arrowroot with the kirsch and stir into the jam. Bring to the boil and spread over cake. Lift cake from tin and remove paper. *Makes 12 pieces.*

# CHOCOLATE CREAM FLAN

**Ingredients for a spring form tin**
**(26 cm diam., 2.5 l capacity/10 inch**
**diam., 4¼ pints capacity)**

**FOR THE MIXTURE:**

120 g/5 oz soft margarine

150 g/6 oz caster sugar

3 eggs

100 g/4 oz good quality plain cooking
chocolate

130 g/5 oz ground almonds

1 tbsp strong black coffee or coffee
essence

40 g/2 oz flour

1 tsp baking powder

**FOR THE TOPPING:**

125 ml/4 fl. oz white wine

3 tbsp dark rum

250 ml/8 fl. oz double cream

1 tsp caster sugar

100 g/4 oz good quality plain cooking
chocolate

1 tsp cocoa powder for dusting

**1** Beat the margarine and sugar together with a balloon whisk or hand mixer until the sugar dissolves. Add the eggs one by one and beat until creamy.

**2** Melt the chocolate in a bowl over hot water. Mix into the margarine and egg mixture with the almonds and coffee. Mix flour and baking powder together, sieve into the bowl and stir in.

**3** Line the base of the spring form tin with baking parchment. Pour the mixture into the tin and bake in a preheated oven at 175°C/350°F/Gas mark 4 for approximately 35 minutes.

**4** Meanwhile mix the white wine and rum and pour over the still warm cake. Beat the sugar and cream together until stiff and spread over the cake. Grate the chocolate or shave into curls with a vegetable peeler and use to decorate the cake. Finally dust with cocoa. *Makes 12 slices.*

VARIATION: If you have children or don't want to use alcohol for other reasons you can replace the white wine with grape juice or possibly cherry juice and omit the rum entirely.

MICROWAVE TIP: The chocolate cream flan takes approx. 20 minutes to bake in a microwave/fan combination oven at 150-180 watts and 150-170°C/300-350°F/ Gas Mark 2-3 or a microwave/ conduction combination oven at 180-200°C/350-400°F/Gas Mark 4-6 respectively.

# ALMOND FLAN

**Ingredients for a spring form tin**
**(24 cm diam., 2 l capacity/9 inches**
**diam., 3½ pints capacity)**

**FOR THE MIXTURE**

250 g/9 oz soft margarine

250 g/9 oz caster sugar

2 eggs

1 egg white

pinch salt

1 tsp ground cinnamon

1 tsp grated lemon zest

250 g/9 oz ground almonds

250 g/9 oz flour

1 tsp baking powder

margarine for greasing

**FOR THE TOPPING**

250 g/9 oz blackcurrant jam

1 egg yolk

2 tbsp flaked almonds

**1** Beat the margarine and sugar together with a balloon whisk or hand mixer until the sugar has dissolved. Then add the eggs, egg white, salt and cinnamon and beat until creamy.

**2** Add the lemon zest and ground almonds. Mix the flour and baking powder together, sieve into the egg and margarine mixture and mix in well.

**3** Put two-thirds of the mixture into the greased tin, smooth until level and spread the blackcurrant jam evenly on top.

**4** Put the rest of the mixture into a piping bag with a plain nozzle. Pipe a border and lattice pattern onto the flan. Brush with beaten egg yolk, scatter flaked almonds on top and bake in a preheated oven for about 75 minutes at 175-200°C/350-400°F/Gas mark 4–6. *Makes 10-12 slices.*

TIP: The aroma of freshly ground almonds is stronger than that of those which are bought pre-packed. You can grind the almonds in a high speed chopper or food processor, but the resulting warmth may cause the oil to seep out and the almonds may become 'greasy'. If you don't have either piece of equipment, but you do a lot of baking, it would be worth buying an almond grinder. In an emergency a coffee grinder will do.

# SPICED WINE TRIANGLES

**Ingredients for 1 baking sheet**

**FOR THE MIXTURE**
250 g/9 oz soft margarine
250 g/9 oz caster sugar
1 sachet/approx. ½ oz vanilla sugar
4 eggs
250 g/9 oz flour
1 sachet/approx. ½ oz baking powder
300 ml/½ pint red wine
1 sachet spiced wine spice, or equivalent
150 g/6 oz grated chocolate

**FOR THE GLAZE**
250 g/9 oz icing sugar

**FOR SPRINKLING**
80 g/3 oz chopped almonds
2 tbsp grated chocolate

1 Beat the margarine, sugar and vanilla sugar together until the sugar has dissolved. Add the eggs one by one and beat until foamy. Mix flour and baking powder together, sieve into the egg and margarine mixture and mix.

2 Heat the red wine with the spices. Measure off 125 ml/4 fl. oz and stir into the mixture together with the chocolate.

3 Line the baking sheet with parchment, spread the mixture on top. Bake in a preheated oven at 175°C/350°F/Gas mark 4 for 25-30 minutes.

4 Mix the remaining spiced wine and icing sugar together and spread over the cold cake. Roast the almonds and sprinkle over cake with the chocolate.
*Makes 32 triangles.*

# CHERRY CRUMBLE CAKE

**Ingredients for 1 baking sheet**

**FOR THE MIXTURE**
200 g/7 oz soft margarine
200 g/7 oz caster sugar
3 eggs
pinch salt
1 tsp grated lemon zest
375 g/13 oz flour
4 tsps baking powder

**FOR THE TOPPING**
125 g/5 oz soft margarine
200 g/7 oz flour
150 g/6 oz caster sugar
25 g/1 oz chopped almonds
½ tsp grated lemon zest
½ tsp cinnamon
2 jars pitted cherries
(370 g/13 oz drained weight)
1 tbsp sugar for sprinkling

1 Beat the margarine and sugar together with a balloon whisk or hand mixer until the sugar dissolves. Add eggs one by one and beat until creamy. Add salt and lemon zest. Mix flour and baking powder together, sieve into egg and margarine mixture and stir in well.

2 Spread the mixture onto the greased baking sheet.

3 Beat the margarine until creamy. Mix in flour, sugar, almonds, lemon zest and cinnamon. Compress to consistency of a crumble.

4 Spread the crumble and drained cherries in diagonal rows on the mixture. Bake in a preheated oven at 200°C/400°F/Gas mark 6 for about 30 minutes. Sprinkle with sugar.
*Makes 16 slices.*

# HUMMELKUCHEN (BUMBLE BEE CAKE)

**Ingredients for 1 baking sheet**
**FOR THE MIXTURE**
150 g/6 oz soft margarine
6 eggs
250 g/9 oz caster sugar
300 g/11 oz flour
1 sachet/approx. ½ oz baking powder
6 tbsp double cream
margarine for greasing
**FOR THE TOPPING**
250 g/9 oz whole almonds
200 g/7 oz soft margarine
200 g/7 oz caster sugar
3 tbsp double cream
60 g/2 oz flour

**1** Blanch the almonds in boiling water, then rinse briefly in cold water. Remove the skins and slice the almonds into flakes or slice finely in a food processor.

**2** Melt the margarine and leave to cool. Beat the eggs and sugar until foaming, add the cool melted margarine first, then stir in the flour, baking powder and double cream in turn.

**3** Spread the mixture on the greased baking sheet and pre-bake in a preheated oven at 200-225°C/400-425°F/Gas mark 6–7 for 15 minutes.

**4** Bring the margarine, sugar, double cream, flour and prepared almond flakes to the boil. Remove pan from the heat and spread the still hot margarine and almond mixture over the prepared sponge base.

**5** Return baking sheet to the oven and bake for a further 10-15 minutes.
*Makes 16 squares.*

# RHUBARB MERINGUE FLAN

**Ingredients for a spring form tin**
**(26 cm diam., 2.5 l capacity/10 inches**
**diam., 4¼ pints capacity)**

**FOR THE MIXTURE**

750 g/1 lb 11 oz rhubarb

125 g/5 oz soft margarine

125 g/5 oz caster sugar

pinch salt

1 sachet/approx. ½ oz vanilla sugar

3 eggs

200 g/7 oz flour

2 tsp baking powder

2 tbsp double cream

margarine for greasing

1 heaped tbsp sugar

**FOR THE MERINGUE TOPPING**

3 egg whites

150 g/6 oz sugar

3 tbsp grated chocolate

1 Wash and prepare the rhubarb and cut into finger-long pieces. Beat the margarine, sugar, salt and vanilla sugar together with a balloon whisk or hand mixer until the sugar dissolves. Add the eggs one by one and beat until foamy. Mix the flour and baking powder together, sieve into the margarine and egg mixture and mix in first the flour and then the double cream by turns.

2 Put the mixture into the greased tin and place the rhubarb on top, sprinkling the sugar over it. Bake the flan in a preheated oven at 175°C/350°F/Gas mark 4 for 35-40 minutes.

3 Beat the sugar and eggs whites until they form stiff peaks. Fold in 2 tsp grated chocolate. Put the mixture into a piping bag with a plain nozzle and pipe over the hot cake. Sprinkle with remaining grated chocolate and bake for a further 15 minutes at 175°C/350°F/Gas mark 4.

# HAZELNUT GATEAU

**Ingredients for a spring form tin**
**(22 cm diam., 1.5 l capacity/8 inches**
**diam., 2½ pints capacity]**

**FOR THE MIXTURE**

125 g/5 oz soft margarine

125 g/5 oz caster sugar

1 sachet/approx. ½ oz vanilla sugar

1 egg

3 egg yolks

160g/6 oz flour

2 level tsp baking powder

2 tbsp dark rum

**FOR THE TOPPING**

3 egg whites

100 g/4 oz caster sugar

150 g/6 oz ground hazelnuts

8 glacé cherries

4 tbsp flaked almonds

3 tbsp apricot jam

1 Beat the margarine with a balloon whisk or hand mixer until creamy. Add the sugar, vanilla sugar, egg and egg yolk and beat until the sugar dissolves. Mix flour and baking powder together, sieve into margarine and egg mixture and stir in. Then add the dark rum.

2 Pour the mixture into a greased or lined tin and bake in a preheated oven at 175°C/350°F/Gas mark 4 for 35-40 minutes.

3 Meanwhile beat the sugar and egg whites until stiff. Stir in the hazelnuts. Put into a piping bag with a star-shaped nozzle and pipe onto the hot cake.

4 Scatter cherries cut into strips and 1 tbsp of almond flakes over the cake. Bake for a further 15 minutes.

5 Dry roast the remaining almond flakes until golden brown. Stir the apricot jam to a smooth consistency with a little water over a low heat and spread over sides of cake. Scatter flaked almonds on sides.

*Makes 8-10 slices.*

# FRUIT CAKE

| Ingredients for a 30 cm/12 inch loaf tin |
| --- |
| 100 g/4 oz dried figs |
| 100 g/4 oz dried apricots |
| 50 g/2 oz glacé cherries |
| 50 g/2 oz candied pineapple |
| 50 g/2 oz dates • 1 tsp flour |
| 100 g/4 oz chopped almonds |
| 50 g/2 oz chopped hazel nuts |
| 100 g/4 oz candied lemon peel |
| 150 g/6 oz raisins |
| 125 g/5 oz soft margarine |
| 125 g/5 oz caster sugar • pinch salt |
| 1 tsp grated lemon zest • 4 eggs |
| 250 g/9 oz flour • 3 tsp baking powder |
| 3 tbsp milk • 1-2 tsp flour |

**1** Dice the fruit and dust with flour. Mix with the chopped almonds, hazelnuts, candied lemon peel and raisins.

**2** Beat margarine, sugar, salt and grated lemon zest together with a balloon whisk or hand mixer until the sugar has dissolved. Add the eggs one by one and beat everything until creamy.

**3** Mix flour and baking powder together, alternately sieve some into egg and margarine mixture and stir, followed by a little milk. Lightly flour the fruit again and also mix in.

**4** Line the tin with baking parchment. Fill with the mixture and bake in a preheated oven at 175°C/350°F/Gas mark 4 for about 75 minutes. *Makes 20 slices.*

**Dried fruits can be chopped easily using a large kitchen knife. Then dust with flour, add to mixture and stir in well.**

# RODON CAKE

| Ingredients for a savarin mould (2 l capacity/3½ pints capacity) |
| --- |
| 200 g/7 oz soft margarine |
| 200 g/7 oz caster sugar |
| 1 sachet/approx. ½ oz vanilla sugar |
| pinch salt • 4 eggs |
| 500 g/1 lb 2 oz flour |
| 1 sachet/approx. ½ oz baking powder |
| approx. 125 ml/4 fl. oz milk |
| 150 g each/6 oz currants and raisins |
| margarine for greasing |
| French toast crumbs for sprinkling |
| 200 g/7 oz icing sugar |
| 2 tsp lemon juice |
| 25 g/1 oz coconut oil |

**1** Beat margarine, sugar, vanilla sugar and salt together with a balloon whisk or hand mixer until the sugar dissolves. Add the eggs one by one and beat until creamy.

**2** Mix flour and baking powder together, then alternately sieve some into egg and margarine mixture followed by some milk.

**3** Mix currants and raisins into mixture. Grease the mould and dust with toast crumbs. Fill mould with mixture and level off.

**4** Bake in a preheated oven at 175-200°C/350-400°F/Gas mark 4–6 for 50 to 60 minutes.

**5** Mix the lemon juice with the icing sugar to make a smooth paste. Melt the coconut oil over a low heat. Mix thoroughly with the sugar and lemon juice mixture. Coat cooled cake in the sugar mixture. *Makes 16 slices.*

# MARBLE CAKE

| Ingredients for a savarin mould |
| --- |
| (2 l /3½ pints capacity) |
| 200 g/7 oz soft margarine |
| 300 g/11 oz caster sugar |
| pinch salt |
| 5 eggs |
| 400 g/14 oz flour |
| 3 tsp baking powder |
| 125 ml/4 fl. oz milk |
| margarine for greasing |
| 100 g/4 oz good quality bitter chocolate |
| 2 tsp cocoa powder |
| 1 sachet/approx. ½ oz vanilla sugar |
| For the glaze |
| 25 g/1 oz coconut oil |
| 1½ tsp cocoa powder |
| 200 g/7 oz icing sugar |

1 Beat margarine, sugar and salt together with a balloon whisk or hand mixer until the sugar dissolves. Then add eggs one by one and beat until creamy. Mix flour and baking powder together, sieve into egg and margarine mixture and stir in with milk.

2 Put half of the mixture into the greased mould. Melt the chocolate in a bowl over hot water, then stir into the remaining mixture with the cocoa powder and vanilla sugar. Pour into the mould. Draw a fork in a spiral pattern through both layers.

3 Bake in a preheated oven at 175-200°C/350-400°F/Gas mark 4–6 for about 80 minutes.

4 In the meantime melt the oil and mix with cocoa powder and sugar as well as 6 tbsp water. Coat the cooled cake in the chocolate mixture.
*Makes 16 slices.*

VARIATION: If children are not going to eat the cake, replace the water with brandy or rum. Use strong black coffee or coffee essence for a mocha glaze.

# MASCARPONE GATEAU

**Ingredients for a spring form tin
(26 cm diam., 2.5 l/10 inches diam., 4¼
pints capacity)**

**FOR THE MIXTURE**

**250 g/9 oz margarine**

**100 g/4 oz caster sugar**

**pinch salt • 6 egg yolks**

**100 g/4 oz good quality white
chocolate**

**250 g/9 oz flour**

**2 level tsp baking powder**

**50 g/2 oz grated chocolate**

**6 egg whites**

**FOR THE FILLING**

**300 g/11 oz mascarpone (Italian cream
cheese)**

**2 egg yolks • 75 g/3 oz caster sugar**

**2 tbsp kirsch • 150 g/6 oz cherry jam**

**1 jar cherries (370 g/13 oz drained
weight)**

**FOR DECORATION**

**250 g/9 oz double cream**

**1 sachet/approx. ½ oz vanilla sugar**

**2 tbsp grated chocolate**

**1** Beat margarine, sugar and salt together with a balloon whisk or hand mixer until the sugar dissolves. Add egg yolks one by one and beat until creamy.

**2** Melt chocolate in a bowl over hot water. Mix flour and baking powder together, sieve into the egg and margarine mixture and stir in. Also stir in melted chocolate and grated chocolate. Beat the egg whites until stiff and fold into mixture.

**3** Line the tin with baking parchment. Fill tin with mixture and bake in a preheated oven at 175-200°C/350-400°F/Gas mark 4–6 for 45 to 50 minutes. Turn out to cool on a cake rack.

**4** Beat the mascarpone, egg yolk, sugar and kirsch together until creamy. Slice the cold gateau into two layers.

**5** Melt jam with a little water over a low heat until smooth. Purée if necessary. Spread half over one of the cake layers and spread the mascarpone cream on top of the jam. Drain the cherries well. Reserve 12 cherries for the garnish and spread the rest over the mascarpone cream.

**6** Place the second cake layer on top of the mascarpone and spread with the remaining jam. Beat cream together with vanilla sugar until stiff. Fill a piping bag with a star-shaped nozzle with the cream and pipe onto the gateau. Decorate with the reserved cherries and grated chocolate. *Makes 12 slices.*

# NUTTY ICE CREAM GATEAU

**Ingredients for a spring form tin
(24 cm diam., 2 l capacity/9 inches
diam., 3½ pints capacity)**
**FOR THE MIXTURE**
150 g/6 oz soft margarine
100 g/4 oz caster sugar
1 sachet/approx. ½ oz vanilla sugar
4 eggs • 200 g/7 oz ground hazelnuts
30 g/1 oz cocoa powder
1½ tsp baking powder
½ tsp ground cloves
margarine for greasing
**FOR THE FILLING**
1 litre vanilla ice cream
1 390 g/14 oz jar cranberries
200 g/7 oz double cream

**1** Beat together margarine, sugar and vanilla sugar with a balloon whisk or hand mixer until sugar dissolves. Add the eggs one by one and beat until creamy. Mix the nuts, cocoa powder, baking powder and ground cloves together and stir into the egg and margarine mixture.
**2** Fill the greased tin with the mixture and bake in a preheated oven at 175°C/350°F/Gas mark 4 for 35-40 minutes.
**3** Turn the cake out to cool on a cake rack and slice into two layers. Place one layer on a cake plate and put the spring form tin, minus base, around the cake. Allow the ice cream to thaw a little, then mix thoroughly and quickly with ¾ of the cranberries.
**4** Pile the ice cream on top of the cake layer and smooth over. Place the second cake layer on top and place the gateau in the freezer for 1-2 hours.
**5** Shortly before serving remove the tin from around the gateau. Beat the cream until stiff, fill a piping bag with a star-shaped nozzle with the cream and pipe all over the gateau. Decorate with the remaining cranberries.
*Makes 10-12 slices.*

# CHOCOLATE CAKE, SACHER STYLE

**Ingredients for a spring form tin
(24 cm diam., 2 l capacity/9 inches
diam., 3½ pints capacity)**

**FOR THE MIXTURE**

140 g/6 oz soft margarine

140 g/6 oz caster sugar

6 egg yolks

300 g/11 oz good quality plain cooking
chocolate

125 g/5 oz flour

1 tsp baking powder

6 egg whites

margarine for greasing

**FOR THE FILLING**

150 g/6 oz apricot jam

**FOR THE COATING**

50 g/2 oz good quality milk chocolate

**1** Beat the margarine and sugar together with a balloon whisk or hand mixer until sugar dissolves. Add the eggs one by one and beat until creamy.

**2** Melt the cooking chocolate in a bowl over hot water. Mix half the melted chocolate into the margarine and egg mixture. Mix together flour and baking powder, sieve into mixture and mix in. Beat the egg whites until stiff and fold into mixture.

**3** Dust the greased tin with flour. Fill tin with mixture, level off and bake in a preheated oven at 175-200°C/350-400°F/Gas mark 4–6 for 60-70 minutes. Turn out and leave to cool.

**4** Slice the cake into two layers. Spread each half with 50 g/2 oz of the jam and layer together. Melt the remaining jam over a low heat, stirring until smooth, then pass through a sieve. Coat the cake with the jam and the remaining cooking chocolate.

**5** Mark 12 slices in the wet coating with the back of a knife. Heat the milk chocolate in a bowl over hot water. Fill a small paper piping bag with the chocolate, snip off the tip to form a nozzle and pipe 'Sacher' in hand-writing onto each slice of cake. *Makes 12 slices.*

# NOUGAT CAKE

**Ingredients for a savarin mould
(1.5 l capacity/2½ pints capacity)**

**FOR THE MIXTURE**

150 g/6 oz nougat

125 g/5 oz soft margarine

200g/7 oz demerara sugar

4 egg yolks

200 g/7 oz ground hazel nuts

4 tbsp milk

1 tsp grated lemon zest

125 g/5 oz wheat flour

2 tsp baking powder

4 egg whites

margarine for greasing

**FOR THE COATING**

50 g/2 oz good quality plain cooking chocolate

**1** Dice the nougat and place in the freezer for approx. 30 minutes. Beat together margarine and sugar with a balloon whisk or hand mixer until sugar dissolves. Stir in egg yolks.

**2** First stir in the hazelnuts, then the milk and lemon zest. Mix flour and baking powder together, sieve into egg and margarine mixture and stir in. Beat the egg white until stiff and fold into the mixture. Then fold in the diced nougat.

**3** Fill the greased mould with the mixture and bake in a preheated oven at 175°C/350°F/Gas mark 4 for 1 hour. Melt the cooking chocolate in a bowl over hot water. Coat the cake with the chocolate. *Makes 16 slices.*

# CHOCOLATE ALMOND SLICES

**Ingredients for 8 slices**

**FOR THE MIXTURE**

150 g/6 oz soft margarine

150 g/6 oz caster sugar

pinch salt

4 egg yolks

125 g/5 oz plain chocolate

50 g/2 oz ground almonds

30 g/1 oz flour

4 egg whites

margarine for greasing

**FOR THE TOPPING**

125 g/5 oz apricot jam

**FOR SPRINKLING**

2 tbsp grated chocolate

1 tbsp icing sugar

**1** Beat together margarine, sugar and salt with a balloon whisk or hand mixer until sugar dissolves. Add eggs yolks one by one and beat everything together until creamy.

**2** Break the chocolate into pieces, pour hot water over the chocolate, leave to stand for 5 minutes, then pour away the water and stir the chocolate into the egg and margarine mixture. Mix the almonds and flour together, sieve into the mixture and mix in as well. Beat the egg whites until stiff and fold in.

**3** Spread the mixture onto a greased baking sheet and bake in a preheated oven at 225°C/ 425°F/Gas mark 7 for 10-15 minutes. Leave to cool.

**4** Slice the cake into three strips. Coat each third in apricot jam and place each strip on top of the other. Sprinkle with grated chocolate and icing sugar and cut into 8 slices.

# RASPBERRY AND PINEAPPLE GATEAU

**Ingredients for a spring form tin**
**(24 cm diam., 2 l capacity/9 inches**
**diam., 3½ pints capacity)**

**FOR THE MIXTURE**

175 g/6 oz soft margarine

50 g/2 oz caster sugar

1 sachet/approx. ½ oz vanilla sugar

5 eggs

1 tsp grated lemon zest

300 g/11 oz flour

2 tsp baking powder

**FOR THE FILLING**

1.5 l/2½ pints whipped cream

3 sachets/approx. 12 oz vanilla sugar

250 g/9 oz raspberries

2 level tsp sugar

6 tinned pineapple rings or ½ fresh
pineapple

**1** Beat together margarine, sugar and vanilla sugar with a balloon whisk or hand mixer until sugar dissolves. First add eggs one by one, then lemon zest, and beat until creamy. Mix flour and baking powder together, sieve into egg and margarine mixture and stir in.

**2** Line the base of the spring form tin with baking parchment, coat with a 2 cm/approx. 1 inch thick layer of mixture and bake in a preheated oven at 200°C/400°F/ Gas mark 6 for 8-10 minutes. Turn out and leave to cool, then bake another 5 layers in the same way.

**3** While the final layer is still warm, cut it into 12 wedges. Beat the cream and vanilla sugar together until stiff. Reserve a few raspberries for decoration, then purée the rest with the sugar and fold into the cream.

**4** Spread a layer of raspberry cream on each of the whole cake layers, and place each on top of the other. Finally place the prepared 'cake wedges' at an angle in the top layer of cream. Decorate with pineapple and raspberries. *Makes 12 slices.*

# BROWNIES

| Ingredients for a square baking tin |
|---|
| **(23 cm x 23 cm/9 x 9 inches)** |
| **FOR THE MIXTURE** |
| 125 g/5 oz soft margarine |
| 175 g/6 oz chocolate bar |
| 225 g/8 oz sugar |
| 1 sachet/approx. ½ oz vanilla sugar |
| pinch salt |
| 2 eggs |
| 125 g/5 oz flour |
| 75 g/3 oz chopped hazelnuts |
| 75 g/3 oz chopped walnuts |
| margarine for greasing |
| **FOR THE TOPPING** |
| 100 g/4 oz nut nougat |
| halved walnuts to decorate |

**1** Melt the margarine over a low heat, then break the chocolate bar into squares and add to the margarine. Melt over a low heat, stirring constantly. When melted, leave to cool.

**2** Add the sugar, vanilla sugar, salt and eggs to the cooled chocolate mixture. Beat with a balloon whisk or hand mixer until the sugar dissolves. Sieve the flour into the margarine and egg mixture and stir in together with the hazelnuts and walnuts.

**3** Fill the greased tin with the mixture, smooth over and bake in a preheated oven at 200-225°C/ 400-425°F/Gas mark 6–7 for 40 minutes.

**4** While the cake is still hot, cut into 12 squares. Melt the nut nougat in a bowl over hot water and place a teaspoonful on each

piece of cake. Decorate each square with a walnut half.
*Makes 12 squares.*

TIP: If you don't have a suitable tin you can bake the mixture in a roasting tin which has been greased well with margarine and reduced to the correct size (approx. 23 cm x 23 cm/approx. 9 inches square) with strips of baking foil. These brownies are best when eaten very fresh, as in America – they should still be a little moist in the middle.

# SPICE CAKE

**Ingredients for a daisy-shaped tin or spring form tin (26 cm diam., 2.5 l capacity/10 inches diam, 4¼ pints capacity)**

**FOR THE MIXTURE**

300 g/11 oz soft margarine

275 g/10 oz caster sugar

pinch salt

6 eggs

4 tsp mixed spice

1 heaped tsp cardamom

1 tsp each of mace, cloves and cinnamon

3 stems crystallised ginger (in syrup in a jar)

375 g/13 oz flour

2 tsp baking powder

2 tbsp double cream

4 tbsp rum

margarine for greasing

**FOR THE GLAZE**

6 tbsp ginger jelly

1 stem crystallised ginger (in syrup from jar)

**1** Beat together margarine, sugar and salt with a balloon whisk or hand mixer until sugar dissolves. Add the eggs one by one and beat until creamy. Add the spices, grate the ginger stems and stir into the mixture together with 1 tbsp of ginger syrup from the jar. Mix flour and baking powder together. First sieve some flour into the egg and margarine mixture, followed by some cream and rum in turn.

**2** Fill the greased tin with the mixture and bake in a preheated oven at 175°C/350°F/Gas mark 4 for approx. 55 minutes.

**3** Melt the ginger jelly over a low heat and stir until smooth, then brush over cake. Slice the ginger root into thin slices and use to decorate spice cake.

*Makes 12 pieces.*

TIP: This cake can also be made in a loaf tin or savarin mould, but it is most important that the tin is large enough. It should be approximately 2.5 l/4¼ pints or the mixture will overflow. The cooking time may change slightly if different tins are used. It is best to test whether the cake is done by using a wooden skewer.

# LEMON CAKE

**Ingredients for a loaf tin (30 cm long, 2 l capacity/12 inches long, 3½ pints capacity)**

| |
| --- |
| **FOR THE MIXTURE** |
| 250 g/9 oz soft margarine |
| 250 g/9 oz caster sugar |
| 5 eggs |
| 250 g/9 oz flour |
| 2 tsp baking powder |
| margarine for greasing |
| 125 ml/4 fl. oz lemon juice |
| 100 g/4 oz icing sugar |
| **FOR DECORATION** |
| 4 tbsp sugar |
| 1 organic lemon |

**1** Beat together the margarine and sugar with a balloon whisk or hand mixer until sugar dissolves. Add the eggs one by one, and beat until creamy. Mix flour and baking powder together, sieve into egg and margarine mixture and stir in.

**2** Fill the greased tin with the mixture. Bake for approx. 75 minutes in an oven preheated to 175-200°C/350-400°F/Gas mark 4–6.

**3** Allow cake to cool a little. Then pierce several times with a knitting needle or skewer. Mix together the lemon juice and icing sugar and drizzle over cake. Leave to cool completely in tin.

**4** Heat sugar with 3 tbsp water until it dissolves. Slice the lemon and add slices to sugar solution, bring to the boil and allow to cool. Decorate lemon cake with lemon slices. *Makes 20 slices.*

# HAZELNUT CAKE

**Ingredients for a savarin mould (2 l capacity/3½ pints capacity)**

| |
| --- |
| margarine for greasing |
| 3 tbsp flaked hazelnuts |
| **FOR THE MIXTURE** |
| 185 g/6 oz soft margarine |
| 300 g/11 oz caster sugar |
| pinch salt • 6 egg yolks |
| 300 g/11 oz ground hazelnuts |
| 75 g/3 oz chopped hazelnuts |
| 6 tbsp milk |
| 185 g/6 oz flour • 3 tsp baking powder |
| 225 g/8 oz nougat |
| 6 egg whites |
| 2 tbsp icing sugar for dusting |

**1** Grease the tin and scatter hazelnut flakes inside. Refrigerate.

**2** Beat together margarine and sugar with a balloon whisk or hand mixer until sugar dissolves. Stir in salt and egg yolks. Add hazelnuts and milk. Mix flour and baking powder together, sieve into egg and margarine mixture and stir in.

**3** Finely dice the nougat and stir into the mixture. Beat the egg whites until stiff and fold into mixture.

**4** Fill the greased tin with the mixture. Bake in a preheated oven at 175-200°C/350-400°F/Gas mark 4-6 for 60 minutes. Turn the cake out to cool onto a cake rack and dust with icing sugar. *Makes 16 slices.*

MICROWAVE TIP: Hazelnut cake can be baked for 25-30 minutes in a fan/microwave combination oven at 150-180 watts and 150-170°C/300-350°F or a conduction/microwave combination oven at 150-180 watts and 180-200°C/350-400°F respectively.

# NUT CAKES WITH CHOCOLATE CREAM FILLING

| Ingredients for 1 muffin tray (cups should be about 5 cm/2 inches deep) |
| --- |
| **FOR THE FILLING** |
| 200 g/7 oz double cream |
| 150 g/6 oz good quality bitter chocolate |
| **FOR THE MIXTURE** |
| 150 g/6 oz soft margarine |
| 125 g/5 oz caster sugar |
| 3 sachets/approx. 12 oz vanilla sugar |
| 3 eggs |
| 150 g/6 oz flour |
| 2 tsp baking powder |
| 150 g/6 oz ground hazelnuts |
| 1 tbsp dark rum |
| margarine for greasing |
| **FOR DECORATION** |
| about 20 whole hazelnuts |

**1** The day before making the cakes, or at least 5 hours before, heat the cream in a saucepan together with the chocolate so that it melts. Stir the mixture, cover and refrigerate.

**2** To make the cake mixture beat margarine, sugar and vanilla sugar with a balloon whisk or hand mixer until sugar dissolves. Gradually stir in the eggs.

**3** Mix together flour, baking powder and hazelnuts and stir into cake mixture. Finally stir in the rum.

**4** Fill the cups of the greased muffin tin with the mixture. Cut the whole hazelnuts into thin slices or chop coarsely and sprinkle over the mixture. Bake for about 25 minutes in an oven pre-heated to 175-200°C/350-400°F/ Gas mark 4–6.

**5** When cooked, ease the nut cakes out of the tin and leave to cool on a wire rack. Beat the well-chilled chocolate and cream mixture with a hand mixer – it should be stiff enough to leave a trail when stirred.

**6** Cut each cake in two, fill with chocolate cream and sandwich together. *Makes 8 cakes.*

# QUARK CAKE/CURD CHEESE CAKE

**Ingredients for a loaf tin (30 cm long, 2 l capacity/12 inches long, 3½ pints capacity)**

**FOR THE MIXTURE**

100 g/4 oz soft margarine

200 g/7 oz caster sugar

pinch salt

1 sachet/approx. ½ oz vanilla sugar

4 eggs

250 g/9 oz low fat quark (curd cheese)

300 g/11 oz flour

1 sachet/approx. ½ oz baking powder

scant 125 ml/4 fl. oz milk

150 g/6 oz sultanas

margarine for greasing

French toast crumbs for scattering

1 tbsp icing sugar for dusting

1 Beat together margarine, sugar, salt and vanilla sugar with a balloon whisk or hand mixer until sugar dissolves. Add eggs one by one and beat until creamy.

2 Press the curd cheese well to drain and add to cake mixture. Mix flour and baking powder together, sieve into egg and margarine mixture. Stir gradually into mixture together with milk. Fold in sultanas.

3 Scatter French toast crumbs into the greased loaf tin. Fill tin with mixture and bake in a preheated oven at 175-200°C/350-400°F/Gas mark 4–6 for about 70 minutes.

4 Leave cake to cool completely on a wire rack, then dust with icing sugar. *Makes 20 slices.*

TIP: If quark cake is to succeed it is important that the quark contains as little liquid as possible. If you have time, place the quark in a fine sieve on top of a bowl, cover with a tea towel and leave to drain overnight.

# MADEIRA CAKE

**Ingredients for a loaf tin (30 cm long, 2 l capacity/12 inches long, 3½ pints capacity)**

**FOR THE MIXTURE**

3 eggs

225 g/8 oz caster sugar

pinch salt

1 tsp grated lemon zest

1-2 tbsp rum or brandy

225 g/8 oz cornflour

225 g/8 oz soft margarine

1 heaped tsp baking powder

2-3 tbsp icing sugar for dusting

**1** Beat together eggs, sugar, salt and lemon zest with a balloon whisk or hand mixer until sugar dissolves. Gradually add the rum or brandy and cornflour while stirring constantly.

**2** Melt the margarine in a pan and stir into egg and margarine mixture while still hot. Finally stir in the baking powder.

**3** Line the loaf tin with baking parchment. Fill tin with mixture and bake in a preheated oven at 175°C/350°F/Gas mark 4 for 50-60 minutes. After baking for about 15 minutes score along the surface of the cake lengthways with a knife.

**4** Leave the cake to cool completely on a cake rack, then dust with icing sugar.

*Makes 20 slices.*

VARIATION: Dusting Madeira cake with sugar is the classic method. However, if you like it can also be coated with chocolate; it will then stay fresh and moist longer. Break 100 g/4 oz good quality milk or plain chocolate into squares and melt in a bowl over hot water. Spread over cake and leave to cool.

TIP: This classic cake gets its fine 'sandy' consistency from being prepared with cornflour. There are many different recipes but most use equal quantities of cornflour and flour.

# APRICOT FLAN

**Ingredients for a spring form tin
(24 cm diam., 2 l capacity/9 inches
diam., 3½ pints capacity)**
**100 g/4 oz soft margarine**
**100 g/4 oz caster sugar • pinch salt**
**2 eggs • 1 tsp grated lemon zest**
**200 g/7 oz flour • 2 tsp baking powder**
**margarine for greasing**
**750 g/1 lb 11 oz apricots**
**30 g/1 oz nibbed almonds**
**1 tbsp crystal sugar for sprinkling**

**1** Beat together margarine, sugar and salt using a balloon whisk or hand mixer until sugar dissolves. Then add the eggs one by one and beat until creamy. Add lemon zest. Mix flour and baking powder together, sieve into egg and margarine mixture and stir in.
**2** Fill the greased tin with the mixture. Wash, halve and pit the apricots. Cut into quarters and press into mixture so pieces are very close together. Scatter nibbed almonds over apricots.
**3** Bake the cake in a preheated oven at 175-200°C/350-400°F/Gas mark 4–6 for 60-75 minutes.
**4** Scatter lump sugar onto the cake while it is still warm.
*Makes 12 slices.*

VARIATION: Instead of apricots this cake can be made with the same quantity of peaches, nectarines, damsons or plums. When fresh fruits are no longer in season, they can be replaced by frozen or bottled fruit.
MICROWAVE TIP: Fruit flan can be baked for 25-30 minutes in a fan/microwave combination oven at 150-180 watts and 160-180°C/325-350°F or a conduction/microwave combination oven at 150-180 watts and 180-200°C/350-400°F respectively.

# BAUMKUCHENTORTE/TREE CAKE

**Ingredients for a spring form tin
(24 cm diam., 2 l capacity/9 inches
diam., 3½ pints capacity)**
**250 g/9 oz soft margarine**
**250 g/9 oz caster sugar**
**5 eggs • 1 tsp grated lemon zest**
**pinch salt • ½ tbsp dark rum**
**80 g/3 oz flaked almonds**
**125 g/5 oz cornflour • 125 g/5 oz flour**
**margarine for greasing**
**200 g/7 oz good quality plain cooking
chocolate**

**1** Beat margarine and sugar together using a balloon whisk or hand mixer until sugar dissolves. Add the eggs one by one and beat until creamy. Add lemon zest, salt, rum and almond flakes.
**2** Mix the flour and cornflour together, sieve into egg and margarine mixture and stir in.
**3** Place 2 tbsp mixture in the greased tin and smooth over base. Bake for 1 to 2 minutes under the grill until pale brown, then spread another tbsp of mixture onto the cake and bake. Continue in the same way until all the mixture has been used up.
**4** Melt the chocolate in a bowl over hot water and use to form a coating on the cooled cake.
*Makes 12 portions.*

**Pour the melted chocolate over the cake and smooth over with a palette knife. We show you how to make chocolate curls (caraque) on page 213.**

# Easy rising in the bakery

Because it reproduces eagerly, dough rises. Tiny bubbles bear witness to the work of the yeast microbes, our smallest helpers. Yeast lends stature to large loaves and plaits. Doughnuts, bread rolls and even pizzas have yeast to thank for their shape. Yeast dough is richly scented proof of living nature, requiring strength and sensitivity for making, cosy warmth and lots of rest for rising.

Raisin plait. Recipe on page 54.

# HOW TO MAKE SUCCESSFUL YEAST DOUGH

There are many ways to make light, fragrant yeast dough, but however you do it, one thing always applies – the dough has to rise! Yeast gets it going, as the light brown cubes of fresh yeast and dried yeast granules contain microbes which, if the yeast is handled carefully, lighten the dough and make it rise. The yeast needs sugar or flour as 'food', a little moisture and time in order for the process to start. The basic ingredients for white bread are 500 g/1 lb 2 oz flour, 1 tsp salt, 250 ml/approx. 8 fl. oz water and 20 g/approx. 1 oz yeast. Cake dough also needs sugar, melted margarine and perhaps egg so that it becomes fine textured and light. A reliable, versatile Basic recipe for yeast cake requires 20 g (about ½ cube)/approx. 1 oz fresh yeast or 1 sachet dried yeast, a generous 250 ml/8 fl. oz tepid milk, 500 g/1 lb 2 oz flour, 40 g/approx. 2 oz sugar, a pinch of salt and 60 g/2 oz margarine.

If you also want to use an egg, add it to the measuring jug when measuring out the quantity of milk. This ensures that the correct proportion of flour to liquid is maintained.

**1** To make the dough, make a well in the flour. Mix crumbled fresh yeast with a pinch of sugar and a little tepid milk into the well. Leave in a warm place for 15 minutes, or wait until dough has doubled in size if keeping it at room temperature.

**2** This is how the professionals make dough without sugar: dissolve the yeast in the full quantity of liquid. This method is practical if you are using a food processor, or if dough is prepared cold and left in the refrigerator overnight.

**6** By using the dough hook of a hand mixer or a food processor, yeast dough can be kneaded in 5 to 10 minutes. If you are using a mixing spoon, it will take twice as long and require a lot of effort. The dough is ready when it looks smooth and silky, forms a ball shape by itself and comes away from the sides of the bowl.

**7** Remove the dough from the bowl and knead well by hand on a floured work surface. The best way to do this is to push the dough away from you with a gliding movement and then bring it back towards you.

**3** Dried yeast is convenient. It can be mixed with flour and stirred straight into the dough. However, better and more reliable results are produced by moistening the dried granules first with a little milk or water and adding a spoonful of sugar to start them working.

**4** Regardless of whether fresh or dried yeast is used, you can tell from the air bubbles whether the yeast is working well. The length of time required for the yeast to reach this stage depends on the temperature. You will get the quickest results by leaving the yeast in a warm place to work. If left at room temperature or cooler, it will need longer.

**5** Knead the yeast mixture together with the remaining ingredients to form a smooth dough. If you are in a hurry you can omit leaving the yeast to work by simply adding the dried yeast or fresh yeast dissolved in liquid to the flour and kneading even more thoroughly. You must allow more time for the dough to rise.

**8** Now the dough has to rise and double in size. At room temperature it will rise evenly and well. It will rise more quickly if placed next to a source of heat, such as in an airing cupboard. You can also wrap the dough loosely in cling film and leave it in the refrigerator; it will then take several hours to rise.

**9** When the dough has doubled in size, it must once more be kneaded thoroughly and 'knocked back'. This is important as it removes large air bubbles, ensuring that the bread will have a fine, even texture.

**10** Shortly after kneading the dough should be as stretchy as a rubber band. Before rolling out or shaping it should be covered and left for a few minutes so it can relax, otherwise it will continually contract and change shape.

# YEAST DOUGH

### DISASTER RECOVERY

■ Many people are in awe of yeast dough. Here is a short check-list to help you ensure nothing goes wrong either with preparation or when kneading. *If the dough doesn't rise ...*

... it may be because salt came into direct contact with the yeast. Salt quickly removes moisture from the yeast cells, they dry out and then can't help the dough to rise.

... melted fat may also have come into contact with the yeast. Fat encases the yeast cells so they can no longer reproduce.

... perhaps the dough got too hot. The hard-working yeast microbes are much more sensitive to heat than they are to cold. The maximum temperature they can stand is 38°C/100°F. Milk and fat may have accidentally been heated to too great a temperature, for example, or the yeast may have died off when rising because the temperature next to a heat source or in a bain-marie reached 40°C/104°F or more.

... perhaps the yeast is too cold. Then the microbes only work in slow motion. The ideal temperature for yeast to work is between 25 and 28°C/77 and 82°F. You should place the bowl near to a source of heat, but not directly on top of it.

... perhaps the dough is too stiff and the yeast needs a little more moisture to make the dough rise.

... the dough may have been kneaded for too long in a food processor. The dough is then known as 'machine dead'. Watch the dough during kneading and switch the processor off after about 5 minutes. Large quantities of dough mixture will be ready after 10 minutes at most in a food processor.

### VARIATIONS

■ At the very least you can easily bake different types of bread rolls using a basic yeast dough (basic recipe page 50)! For example, you can knead dried herbes de Provence, thyme or oregano into the prepared dough, or you can spice it up with coriander, caraway or aniseed. Chopped sunflower seeds, linseed and raisins are also suitable.

### HOW MUCH YEAST?

■ A cube of yeast (42 g)/2 oz is sufficient for 500 g/1 lb 2 oz flour, but only 20 to 30 g/approx. 1 oz yeast is needed if the dough contains little or no fat. Complex doughs with lots of fat, raisins and nuts can use up to 50 g/2 oz of fresh yeast. A sachet containing 7 g/approx. ¼ oz dried yeast corresponds to 25 g/1 oz fresh yeast.

**For attractive bread rolls, brush the dough with milk and dust with flour (top), or brush with salted water and sprinkle sesame, poppy or caraway seeds on top (centre). If you like, you can make a cross in the dough, brush with beaten egg and scatter cereal flakes, crystal sugar or nibbed almonds over the rolls (bottom).**

Yeast dough can also rise too much. If it is left to rise in a warm place for too long, it will not rise later in the oven.

## CONVECTION OVENS

■ If you have a convection oven you can bake several trays of bread dough at once. Put the shaped dough into the cold convection oven without letting it rise for the last time, and bake for approximately 5 minutes longer than usually required.

## FOR CREATIVE COOKS

■ Yeast dough can be cut with scissors to form attractive shapes. The resulting smooth edges still look perfect when baked. This method is particularly suited to free-form cakes and pastries. Roll out a basic yeast dough (recipe on page 50) until about 2 cm/1 inch thick. Place a paper pattern on top or cut out the shape free-hand. Gingerbread men shapes are quick and easy to cut out (see photo on right). Before baking brush the shape with beaten egg and decorate with strips of dough, crystal sugar, raisins and almonds.

Cut the dough with scissors – this is the way to make baked shapes which can be given as presents.

## FRUIT CAKES

■ In Germany the epitome of a luscious fruit cake is one made of freshly baked yeast dough, straight from the oven, thickly layered with fresh seasonal fruits. Apple and damson cake are amongst the most popular of all. Ripe, sharp apples are best for this, such as Russet, Cox and Reinette. Jonathan, Golden Delicious and Gloucester are less suitable. The best damson cake is made from firm fleshed, late ripening varieties.

## LEAVE TO COOL

■ Yeast also 'works' in the refrigerator, but at a snail's pace. However, you can use this to your advantage and make life easier for yourself if, for example, you want freshly baked rolls for breakfast on Sunday morning. Make the dough the previous evening with cold milk and eggs and only warm the margarine until it just melts. Don't leave the dough to rise but put it straight into the refrigerator covered with polythene. Then all you have to do next morning is knead and shape it. Allow the shaped dough to rise as usual before placing in a preheated oven.

Juicy fruit goes well with yeast dough. It is best to bake the cake in a deep roasting pan so the juice doesn't run out into the oven.

# RAISIN PLAIT

| Ingredients for 1 plait (approx. 24 slices) |
| --- |
| 30 g/approx. 1 oz yeast |
| 1 tsp sugar |
| 250 ml/8 fl. oz lukewarm milk |
| 500 g/1 lb 2 oz flour |
| 50 g/2 oz caster sugar |
| 1 sachet/approx. 2  oz vanilla sugar |
| pinch salt • 1 tsp grated lemon zest |
| 100 g/4 oz soft margarine • 1 egg yolk |
| 100 g/4 oz chopped candied peel |
| 100 g/4 oz raisins |
| 50 g/2 oz chopped glacé cherries |
| 25 g/1 oz chopped pistachio nuts |
| margarine for greasing |
| flour for shaping |
| 1 egg yolk for glaze |

1 Dissolve crumbled yeast and sugar in milk. Leave to work in a warm place for 10 minutes.
2 Place flour, sugar, vanilla sugar, salt and lemon zest in a mixing bowl. Melt margarine. Add egg yolk, yeast mixture and margarine to flour and sugar mixture. Knead to a smooth ball with a food processor or the dough hook of a hand mixer. Cover and leave in a warm place to rise to double the size. Knead in the remaining ingredients.

3 Grease a baking sheet. With floured hands make 3 long sausages out of the dough, then plait together. Place on baking sheet, leave to rest for a further 15 minutes. Mix egg yolk with 1 tbsp water, brush plait with egg mixture and bake in a preheated oven at 200-225°C/400-425°F/Gas mark 6–7 for 35-40 minutes until golden brown.

# PANETTONE

| Ingredients for a deep, round tin (approx. 2.5 l capacity/approx. 4¼ pints capacity) |
| --- |
| 600 g/1 lb 5 oz flour |
| 150 g/6 oz caster sugar |
| 250 ml/8 fl. oz milk |
| 1 cube/2 oz fresh yeast |
| 200 g/7 oz soft margarine |
| 3 eggs |
| 2 egg yolks |
| 1 tsp salt |
| 1 pinch nutmeg |
| 1 tsp grated lemon zest |
| 100 g/4 oz candied lemon peel |
| 100 g/4 oz candied orange peel |
| 50 g/2 oz chopped glacé cherries |
| 150 g/6 oz raisins |
| margarine for greasing |
| 2 tbsp icing sugar for dusting |

1 Mix flour and sugar in a mixing bowl. Make a well in the centre. Warm the milk. Dissolve the crumbled yeast in 4-5 tbsp of warmed milk, pour into flour well, cover and leave to work in a warm place for 15 minutes.
2 Melt margarine in remaining warm milk. Beat together eggs, egg yolks and spices with a balloon whisk or hand mixer and add to flour and yeast mixture. Knead to a smooth dough using a food processor or the dough hook of a hand mixer. Cover and leave to rise in a warm place until doubled in size.

3 Knead the lemon peel, orange peel, glacé cherries and raisins into the dough. Grease tin well (e.g. a pan or a bowl with tall, straight sides), place dough in the tin and leave to rest for a further 25 minutes.
4 Cut a cross in the surface of the dough with a knife. Bake for 1½ hours in a preheated oven at 175°C/350°F/Gas mark 4. Remove cake from tin, leave to cool and dust with icing sugar.
*Makes 16 slices.*

# POPPY RING

**FOR THE DOUGH**

| |
|---|
| ½ cube/1 oz fresh yeast |
| 1 tsp sugar |
| 125 ml/4 fl. oz lukewarm milk |
| 60 g/2 oz soft margarine |
| 375 g/13 oz flour |
| 80 g/3 oz caster sugar |
| pinch salt |
| 1 egg |

**FOR THE FILLING**

| |
|---|
| generous 125 ml/4 fl. oz milk |
| 80 g/3 oz soft margarine |
| 250 g/9 oz freshly ground poppy seeds |
| 150 g/6 oz caster sugar |
| ½ tsp grated lemon zest |
| 50 g/2 oz currants |
| margarine for greasing |
| 1 egg yolk for glaze |

1 Dissolve crumbled fresh yeast and sugar in milk. Cover and leave to work in a warm place for 10 minutes.

2 Melt margarine, and place in a bowl with flour, sugar, salt and egg. Add the yeast mixture. Knead dough to a smooth ball using a food processor or the dough hook of a hand mixer. Cover and leave to rise in a warm place until doubled in size.

3 Bring milk and margarine to boil and pour over poppy seeds. Leave to steep, then stir in sugar, lemon zest and currants.

4 Roll out the dough to form a rectangle (approx. 35 x 50 cm/14 x 20 inches). Spread poppy seed mixture on the dough in two long strips and divide dough in two lengthways. Starting from the long side, roll up each sheet of dough to form a sausage shape and then twist together to form a rope.

5 Grease a baking sheet, place dough on sheet and form into a tight ring. Using kitchen scissors, cut into surface of dough in a zig-zag pattern.

6 Bake in a preheated oven at 200-225°C/400-425°F/Gas mark 6–7 for 30 minutes. Mix together egg yolk and 1 tbsp water. Brush over the ring after it has been in the oven for 15 minutes.

*Makes approx. 16 portions.*

**Spread the poppy seed mixture on the dough in two long strips. Then cut the sheet of dough in half and roll up.**

# DANISH TURNOVER

**FOR THE DOUGH**
| |
|---|
| 1 cube/2 oz fresh yeast |
| 60 g/2 oz caster sugar |
| scant 125 ml/4 fl. oz lukewarm milk |
| 50 g/2 oz soft margarine |
| 375 g/13 oz flour |
| ½ tsp salt |
| 2 eggs |

**FOR THE FILLING**
| |
|---|
| 100 g/4 oz light coloured jam (e.g. apricot) |
| 50 g/2 oz sultanas |
| 50 g/2 oz chopped almonds |

**To brush on**
| |
|---|
| 1 egg yolk |
| 1 tbsp sugar |

**For sprinkling**
| |
|---|
| 3 tbsp chopped almonds |

1 Dissolve crumbled yeast with 1 tsp sugar in the milk. Cover and leave to work in a warm place for 10 minutes.

2 Melt margarine. Place in a mixing bowl with flour, remaining sugar, salt and eggs and add yeast mixture. Knead dough to a smooth ball with a food processor or the dough hook of a hand mixer. Cover and leave to rise in a warm place until doubled in size.

3 Roll out dough into a rectangle approx. 1 cm/2 inch thick. Mark 3 sections of equal size lengthways on the dough. First coat centre section with jam, then spread with sultanas and chopped almonds.

4 Make diagonal cuts 2 cm/1 inch apart in the 2 outer sections and fold in to centre. Line a baking sheet with baking parchment. Lay turnover on top and leave to rest for 20-30 minutes.

5 Mix egg yolk with 1 tbsp water and brush over turnover. Bake for 30-40 minutes in a preheated oven at 200-225°C/400-425°F/ Gas mark 6–7.

6 Bring sugar to boil with 1 tbsp water and brush onto turnover 10 minutes before end of baking time. Finally, scatter the chopped almonds over the turnover.
*Makes 24 slices.*

# APRICOT FLAN

**Ingredients for a flan dish or pizza plate (28 cm/11 inches diam.)**

**FOR THE DOUGH**

½ cube/1 oz fresh yeast

2 tbsp caster sugar

125 ml/4 fl. oz lukewarm milk

250 g/9 oz flour

pinch salt

30 g/1 oz soft margarine

margarine for greasing

**FOR THE TOPPING**

50 g/2 oz French toast

2 tbsp soft margarine

2 eggs

5-6 tbsp double cream

1 kg/2 lb 3 oz apricots, stones removed

1 tbsp icing sugar for dusting

**1** Dissolve yeast and sugar in the milk. Cover and leave in a warm place to rise.

**2** Place flour and salt in a bowl. Melt margarine and add to bowl with yeast mixture. Knead to a smooth ball of dough. Leave in a warm place to rise until doubled in size. Crush the French toast in a strong polythene bag (a freezer bag is ideal).

**3** Grease the tin. Press dough out to line the tin, drawing the dough up the sides of the tin. Scatter French toast crumbs over the dough base. Dot margarine over the base. Beat together eggs and double cream and pour over base. Cover with apricot halves. Bake in a preheated oven at 200-225°C/400-425°F/Gas mark 6–7 for 30 minutes. Dust with icing sugar. *Makes 12 slices.*

# FRUIT SAVARIN

**Ingredients for a savarin or ring mould (2.5 l capacity/4¼ pints capacity)**

**FOR THE DOUGH**

1 cube/2 oz fresh yeast

500 g/1 lb 2 oz flour

60 g/2 oz caster sugar

250 ml/4 fl. oz lukewarm milk

150 g/6 oz soft margarine

5 eggs

pinch salt

margarine for greasing

150 g/6 oz caster sugar

375 ml/12 fl. oz rum

5-6 tbsp apricot jam for glazing

**FOR THE FILLING**

400 g/14 oz strawberries

150 g/6 oz each raspberries, blackberries and blueberries

**1** Dissolve crumbled yeast in milk with 2 tbsp flour and sugar. Cover and leave to work in a warm place for 10 minutes.

**2** Melt margarine, place in a bowl with eggs and salt. Add yeast mixture. Sieve flour into bowl. Cover and leave in a warm place to work for 30 minutes.

**3** Knead all ingredients into a smooth ball of dough. Grease the tin, fill with dough and leave to rest a further 30 minutes. Bake in a preheated oven at 175°C/350°F/Gas mark 4 for 50-60 minutes.

**4** Bring sugar to boil with 375 ml/12 fl. oz water, leave to cool, then stir in rum. Turn the savarin out onto a deep plate. Pour sugar and rum mixture over savarin.

**5** Warm jam over a low heat, stirring until it achieves a smooth consistency. Brush jam over the cake, then fill cake with fruit. *Makes 10-12 portions.*

# ALMOND PLAIT

| Ingredients for 1 plait (about 16 slices) |
|---|
| **FOR THE DOUGH** |
| ½ cube/1 oz fresh yeast |
| 1 tsp sugar |
| 125 ml/4 fl. oz lukewarm milk |
| 80 g/3 oz soft margarine |
| 375 g/13 oz flour |
| 75 g/3 oz caster sugar |
| pinch salt • 1 egg |
| **FOR THE FILLING** |
| 250 g/9 oz unpeeled almonds |
| 100 g/4 oz caster sugar |
| 1 egg |
| scant 125 ml/4 fl. oz double cream |
| 1 small apple |
| egg yolk to glaze |
| margarine for greasing |
| 1 tbsp apricot jam |

**1** Dissolve crumbled yeast in milk with sugar. Cover and leave to work for 10 minutes in a warm place.

**2** Melt margarine, place in a bowl with flour, sugar, salt and egg. Add yeast mixture and knead to a smooth dough with a food processor or the dough hook of a hand mixer. Cover and leave in a warm place to rise until doubled in size.

**3** Meanwhile grind the unpeeled almonds. Mix together with egg, sugar and double cream. Peel the apple, grate finely and mix into almond mixture.

**4** Knead the dough thoroughly, roll out into a rectangle (approx. 40 x 50 cm/approx. 16 x 20 inches) and cover with filling.

**5** Roll up dough, starting from longest side. Brush the edge with beaten egg yolk and crimp together. Cut the roll in half lengthways with a sharp knife and twist the two strips into a rope pattern. Place on a greased baking sheet and leave to rest.

**6** Warm apricot jam and brush over plait. Bake in an oven pre-heated to 175-200°C/350-400°F/ Gas mark 4–6 for 25-30 minutes.

# APPLE CREAM FLAN

| Ingredients for a roasting tin or 2 spring form tins (each 26 cm/10 inches diam.) |
| --- |
| **FOR THE DOUGH** |
| ½ cube/1 oz fresh yeast |
| 1 tsp sugar |
| 200 ml/7 fl. oz lukewarm milk |
| 50 g/2 oz soft margarine |
| 375 g/13 oz flour |
| 30 g/1 oz caster sugar |
| salt · margarine for greasing |
| **FOR THE TOPPING** |
| 1.5 kg/34 lb apples (e.g. Cox] |
| 1 organic lemon |
| 100 g/4 oz caster sugar |
| 50 g/2 oz currants · 3 eggs |
| 375 g/13 oz cream or crème fraiche |
| 1 tbsp icing sugar for dusting |

**1** Dissolve crumbled yeast with sugar in milk. Cover and leave in a warm place to work.

**2** Melt margarine. Place in a bowl with flour, sugar and salt. Add yeast mixture and knead to a smooth ball of dough. Cover and leave to rise until doubled in size. Grease tin, press out dough in tin, drawing the dough up the sides of the tin.

**3** Peel apples if liked, quarter, and remove cores. Finely grate lemon zest. Squeeze lemon. Mix everything together with the sugar and 50 g/2 oz currants. Spread over dough and bake for 20 minutes in an oven preheated to 200°C/400°F/Gas mark 6.

**4** Beat eggs together with the cream and remaining sugar and pour over the flan. Bake for a further 30 minutes. Dust with icing sugar.

Baked in a roasting tin.

# CRUMBLE CAKE

| Ingredients for 1 baking sheet |
| --- |
| ½ cube/1 oz fresh yeast |
| 1 tsp sugar |
| generous 250 ml l/8 fl. oz lukewarm milk |
| 60 g/2 oz soft margarine |
| 500 g/1 lb 2 oz flour |
| 40 g/2 oz caster sugar |
| salt |
| margarine for greasing |
| FOR THE CRUMBLE TOPPING |
| 250 g/9 oz flour |
| 250 g/9 oz chopped almonds |
| 150 g/6 oz caster sugar |
| 250 g/9 oz soft margarine |

1 Dissolve crumbled yeast and sugar in the milk. Cover and leave to work for 10 minutes in a warm place.

2 Melt the margarine, add to a bowl with flour, sugar and a little salt. Add yeast mixture and knead to a smooth dough with a food processor or the dough hook of a hand mixer. Cover and leave to rise in a warm place until dou-bled in size, then knead well again.

3 Grease the baking sheet. Roll out dough, lay it on the sheet and leave to rest for a further 30-40 minutes.

4 For the crumble, rub together flour, almonds, sugar and cubed margarine by hand until it resem-bles bread crumbs. Press into small clumps and spread over the dough.

5 Bake in an oven preheated to 200-225°C/400-425°F/Gas mark 6–7 for 25-30 minutes.
*Makes 16 squares.*

# SUGAR CAKE

| Ingredients for 1 baking sheet |
| --- |
| FOR THE DOUGH |
| ½ cube/1 oz fresh yeast |
| 1 tsp sugar |
| generous 250 ml/8 fl. oz lukewarm milk |
| 60 g/2 oz soft margarine |
| 500 g/1 lb 2 oz flour |
| 80 g/3 oz caster sugar |
| salt |
| FOR THE TOPPING |
| 200 g/7 oz soft margarine |
| 150 g/6 oz slivered hazelnuts |
| 150 g/6 oz caster sugar |
| 1 tsp cinnamon |

1 Dissolve the crumbled yeast and sugar in the milk. Cover and leave to work for 10 minutes in a warm place.

2 Melt margarine. Place in a bowl with flour, sugar and salt and add yeast mixture. Knead to a smooth dough using a food processor or the dough hook of a hand mixer. Leave to rise until doubled in size in a warm place.

Knead again and roll out onto baking sheet.

3 Using the index and middle fingers, make depressions in the dough until you reach the baking sheet but the dough is not pierced.

4 For the topping, dot margarine across the depressions. Scatter the hazelnut slivers over the dough. Mix sugar and cinnamon togeth-er, place in a fine sieve and spread evenly over the cake.

5 Bake for 15-20 minutes until golden brown in an oven pre-heated to 200°C/400°F/Gas mark 6.

*Makes 16 squares.*

# DAMSON CAKE

**Ingredients for 1 baking sheet**

**FOR THE DOUGH**

½ cube/1 oz fresh yeast

1 tsp sugar

125 ml/4 fl. oz lukewarm milk

60 g/2 oz soft margarine

375 g/13 oz flour

75 g/3 oz caster sugar

pinch salt

½ tsp grated lemon zest

1 egg

**FOR THE TOPPING**

2 kg/4½ lb damsons

margarine for greasing

**FOR SCATTERING**

2-3 tbsp sugar

1-2 tsp cinnamon

**1** Dissolve crumbled yeast and sugar in milk. Cover and leave to work in a warm place for 10 minutes.

**2** Melt margarine. Place in a bowl with flour, sugar, salt, lemon zest and egg. Add yeast mixture and knead to a smooth dough using a food processor or the dough hook of a hand mixer. Cover and leave to rise in a warm place until doubled in size.

**3** Meanwhile wash damsons, halve and remove stones. Grease baking sheet. Roll out the dough, lay on the baking sheet and draw up the edges of the dough. Spread halved damsons on the dough. Bake in a preheated oven at 225°C/425°F/Gas mark 7 for about 30 minutes.

**4** Mix together sugar and cinnamon and place in a fine sieve. Sieve over the cake 10 minutes before the end of cooking time. *Makes 16 squares.*

TIP: Late varieties of damson are best for this cake. They have more flavour, are sweeter and don't lose as much juice when baked as earlier varieties do.

# BEE STINGS

**Ingredients for 1 baking sheet**

**FOR THE DOUGH**

½ cube/1 oz fresh yeast

1 tsp sugar

good 250 ml/8 fl. oz lukewarm milk

60 g/2 oz soft margarine

500 g/1 lb 2 oz flour

40 g/2 oz caster sugar

salt

margarine for greasing

**FOR THE TOPPING**

50 g/2 oz soft margarine

5 tbsp sugar

100 g/4 oz double cream

4 tbsp honey

300 g/11 oz flaked almonds

**1** Dissolve crumbled yeast and sugar in milk. Cover and leave to work in a warm place for 10 minutes.

**2** Melt margarine. Place in a bowl with flour, sugar and salt. Add yeast mixture and knead to a smooth dough. Cover and leave to rise until doubled in size. Knead again.

**3** Grease baking sheet. Roll out the dough and lay on top of baking sheet. Prick all over with a fork. Leave to rest.

**4** Bring the margarine, sugar, cream and honey to a fast boil. Stir in flaked almonds and leave to cool. Spread over the dough. Bake for 25 minutes in an oven preheated to 200°C/400°F/Gas mark 6. *Makes 16 slices.*

# ROSE CAKE

**Ingredients for a spring form tin (26 cm/10 inches diam.)**

**FOR THE DOUGH**

15 g/approx. ½ oz yeast

1 tsp sugar

generous 125 ml/4 fl. oz lukewarm milk

30 g/1 oz soft margarine

250 g/9 oz flour

20 g/1 oz caster sugar

salt • 1 egg yolk

**FOR THE FILLING**

200 g/7 oz marzipan mix

200 g/7 oz double cream

2 sachets/approx. 1 oz vanilla sugar

1 tsp grated lemon zest

75 g/3 oz each currants and raisins

100 g/4 oz chopped almonds

margarine for greasing

2 tbsp milk for glazing

2 tbsp apricot jam

**1** Dissolve the crumbled yeast and the sugar in milk. Cover and leave to work for 10 minutes in a warm place.

**2** Melt margarine, knead to a smooth dough with the remaining dough ingredients and leave to rise until doubled in size.

**3** Roll out the dough into a rectangle measuring 40 x 50 cm/16 x 20 inches. Mix together marzipan and cream and spread over the dough. Mix together remaining ingredients, except milk and jam, and spread on top of dough. Now roll up the dough from the longest side and divide the roll into 12 equal portions.

**4** Grease the tin. Position dough rolls in tin with cut surfaces uppermost and brush with milk. Leave to rest for 20 minutes. Bake for 30 minutes in an oven preheated to 200°C/400°F/Gas mark 6. Melt jam over a low heat until smooth and brush onto the cake whilst still warm.

# GUGELHUPF

**Ingredients for a gugelhupf tin/savarin mould (2 l capacity/3½ pints capacity)**

30 g/1 oz yeast

1 tsp sugar

scant 125 ml/4 fl. oz lukewarm milk

250 g/9 oz soft margarine

500 g/1 lb 2 oz flour

250 g/9 oz caster sugar

pinch salt

1 tsp grated lemon zest

4 tbsp lemon juice

4 eggs

25 g/1 oz candied peel or candied orange rind

125 g/5 oz chopped almonds

150 g/6 oz raisins

50 g/2 oz currants

margarine for greasing

1 tbsp icing sugar for dusting

**1** Dissolve crumbled yeast and sugar in milk. Cover and leave to work in a warm place for 10 minutes.

**2** Melt margarine. Place in a bowl with flour, sugar, salt, lemon zest and juice, as well as the eggs. Add the yeast mixture and knead to a smooth dough using a food processor or the dough hook of a hand mixer.

**3** Chop the candied peel or candied orange peel. Knead into dough together with 100 g/4 oz chopped almonds, the raisins and currants. Cover and leave to rise in a warm place until doubled in size.

**4** Grease the tin and dust with remaining almonds. Place dough in the tin, leave to rest for a fur-ther 30 minutes and bake in a preheated oven at 175-200°C/350-400°F/Gas mark 4–6 for about 60 minutes. After turning out dust with icing sugar. *Makes 16 slices.*

VARIATION: Coat the gugel-hupf in icing made from 250 g/9 oz icing sugar and 3-4 tbsp lemon juice and scatter with nibbed almonds.

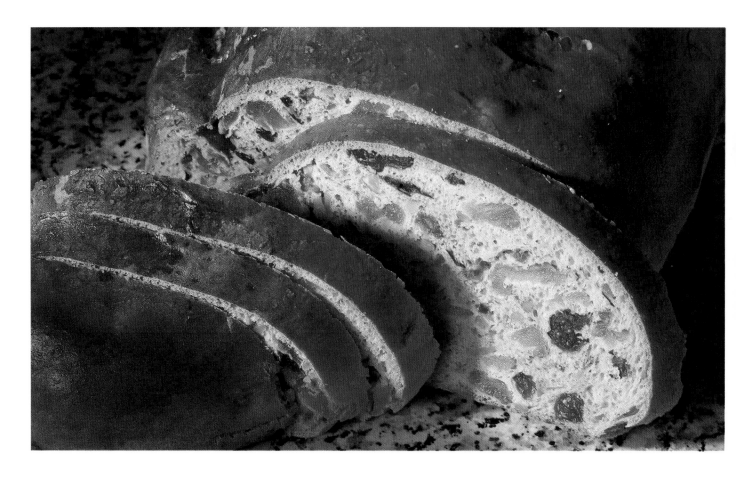

# FRUIT BREAD

| Ingredients for 1 loaf (approx. 20 slices) |
| --- |
| 750 g/1 lb 11 oz dried pears |
| 100 g/4 oz dried apricots |
| 100 g/4 oz dried plums, stones removed |
| 75 g/3 oz candied orange peel |
| 100 g/4 oz dates |
| 150 g/6 oz walnuts |
| 30 g/1 oz yeast |
| 1 tsp sugar |
| 30 g/1 oz margarine |
| 1 kg/2 lb 3 oz flour |
| 1 heaped tsp salt |
| 100 g/4 oz sultanas |
| 100 g/4 oz caster sugar |
| ½ tsp grated lemon zest |
| ½ tsp each ground cloves and ginger |
| 1 tsp cinnamon |
| 1 tsp cardamom |
| 2 tbsp kirsch |
| 1 egg yolk for glazing |

1 Dice the pears, apricots, plums, orange peel and dates; chop the walnuts.

2 Dissolve the crumbled yeast and sugar in a good 125 ml/4 fl. oz lukewarm water. Cover and leave to work in a warm place for 10 minutes.

3 Melt margarine. Mix flour and salt and put everything in a bowl with the yeast mixture. Knead to a smooth dough using a food processor or the dough hook of a hand mixer. Cover and leave to rise in a warm place until doubled in size.

4 Remove ⅓ of the dough and reserve. Mix together sultanas, sugar, lemon zest, spices and kirsch. Knead diced fruit and nuts into ⅔ of the dough. Form the fruit dough into a bloomer shape.

5 Roll out reserved dough and wrap around the loaf. Line a baking sheet with baking parchment. Place bread on baking sheet with the seam underneath. Mix egg yolk with 1 tbsp water and brush onto bread. Prick top of loaf several times with a fork. Leave to rest for 30 minutes.

6 Bake in a preheated oven at 175-200°C/350-400°F/Gas mark 4–6 for approx. 75 minutes.

MICROWAVE TIP: Fruit bread is particularly moist if you first place the dried fruit in a large bowl with 1 cup of water or wine, cover and simmer for 8-10 minutes at 600-700 watts, stirring once briefly during cooking. Then continue as described in recipe.

# CHRISTSTOLLEN

| Ingredients for 2 stollen |
| --- |
| 1 cube/approx. 2 oz fresh yeast |
| 1 tsp sugar |
| 250 ml/8 fl. oz lukewarm milk |
| 375 g/13 oz soft margarine |
| 1 kg/2 lb 3 oz flour |
| 150 g/6 oz caster sugar |
| ½ tsp salt |
| 100 g/4 oz chopped almonds |
| 100 g/4 oz diced candied lemon peel |
| 50 g/2 oz diced candied orange peel |
| 375 g/13 oz sultanas |
| 125 g/5 oz currants |
| ½ tsp grated lemon zest |
| margarine for greasing |
| 125 g/5 oz soft margarine for coating |
| icing sugar for dusting |

**1** Dissolve the crumbled yeast and sugar in the milk. Cover and leave to work for 10 minutes in a warm place.

**2** Melt margarine. Place in a bowl with flour, sugar and salt. Add yeast mixture and knead to a smooth dough with a food processor or the dough hook of a hand mixer. Cover and leave to rise for 1 hour at room temperature.

**3** Knead in the almonds, lemon peel, orange peel, sultanas, currants and lemon zest. Cover and leave to rise in a warm place until doubled in size.

**4** Shape 2 stollen from the dough. Grease a baking sheet, place 1 stollen on sheet and bake for about 60 minutes in an oven preheated to 175-200°C/350-400°F/Gas mark 4–6. Melt half of the margarine and brush onto the warm stollen. Dust with icing sugar. Bake second stollen in the same way.

*Makes approx. 20 slices per stollen.*

**To form a stollen: shape dough into a bloomer and make a depression with the rolling pin along the dough. Slightly fold half of dough over rolling pin.**

# APPLE DOUGHNUTS

**Ingredients for 16 doughnuts**
**500 g/1 lb 2 oz flour**
**100 g/4 oz caster sugar**
**125 ml/4 fl. oz lukewarm milk**
**1 cube/2 oz fresh yeast**
**75 g/3 oz soft margarine**
**2 eggs**
**300 g/11 oz sharp apples**
**75 g/3 oz candied orange peel**
**50 g/2 oz sultanas**
**50 g/2 oz currants**
**vegetable oil for cooking**
**sugar for dredging**

**1** Place sugar and flour in a bowl. Make a well in the centre. Mix half of the milk with crumbled yeast and pour into well. Cover and leave to work in a warm place for 15 minutes.
**2** Melt the margarine in remaining milk, add beaten eggs and pour into the yeast mixture.

Knead to a smooth dough using a food processor or the dough hook of a hand mixer. Cover and leave to rise in a warm place until doubled in size.
**3** Peel and dice the apples. Finely chop the orange peel and knead into the dough with the chopped apple, sultanas and currants. Leave to rest again for 15 minutes.
**4** Heat the oil in a deep fat fryer to 175°C/350°F. Using 2 tablespoons, form little balls of dough and drop one by one into the hot fat. Cook for about 4 minutes until golden brown, turning once. Remove from fryer, drain and dredge with sugar.

# DOUGHNUTS

**Ingredients for 16 doughnuts**
**30 g/1 oz fresh yeast • 1 tsp sugar**
**scant 125 ml/4 fl. oz lukewarm milk**
**60 g/2 oz soft margarine**
**500 g/1 lb 2 oz flour**
**40 g/2 oz caster sugar • pinch salt**
**1 egg • vegetable oil for frying**
**½ jar plum preserve or**
**200 g/7 oz cherry jam**
**sugar for dredging**

**1** Dissolve crumbled yeast and sugar in milk. Cover and leave to work in a warm place for 10 minutes.
**2** Melt margarine. Place in a bowl with flour, sugar, salt and egg. Add yeast mixture and knead to a smooth dough using a food processor or the dough hook of a hand mixer. Cover and leave to rise until doubled in size.
**3** Once more knead dough thoroughly and shape into a

sausage. Cover and leave to rise for a further 5 minutes. Cut the dough sausage into 16 equal portions and shape each one into a ball. Place dough balls on a floured surface and leave to rest for 15 minutes.
**4** Heat oil in a deep fat fryer to 175°C/350°F. Put 2-4 balls at a time in the oil, cover and fry for 3 minutes. Turn doughnuts and fry for a further 3 minutes uncovered, until cooked. Drain on absorbent kitchen paper.
**5** Place plum preserve in a piping bag with an extra long nozzle. Prick a hole in the doughnut and fill it with plum preserve. Dredge with sugar.

# NUT CROISSANTS

| Ingredients for 15 croissants |
| --- |
| **FOR THE DOUGH** |
| 1 cube/2 oz fresh yeast |
| 50 g/2 oz caster sugar |
| 500 g/1 lb 2 oz flour |
| 250 ml/8 fl. oz milk |
| 60 g/2 oz soft margarine |
| 1 egg |
| pinch salt |
| **FOR THE FILLING** |
| 50 g/2 oz whole hazelnuts |
| 50 g/2 oz whole walnuts |
| 1 tbsp sunflower seeds |
| 100 g/4 oz caster sugar |
| 100 g/4 oz double cream |
| 75 g/3 oz rum-soaked raisins |
| margarine for greasing |
| 1 egg yolk and 1 tbsp milk for glazing |

**1** Dissolve the crumbled yeast in the milk together with a pinch of sugar and 3 tbsp flour. Cover and leave to work in a warm place.

**2** Melt margarine and place in a bowl with remaining flour, egg, salt and yeast mixture. Knead to a smooth dough, cover and leave to rise in a warm place until doubled in size.

**3** Chop the whole nuts finely. Melt sugar in a pan over a low heat, then caramelise sugar over a medium heat and remove from stove. Add cream and cook until cream sours. Stir in nuts and raisins.

**4** Roll out dough into a rectangle. Cut into 3 equal strips lengthways, then cut strips into triangles. Divide nut mixture amongst the triangles, then roll up the dough,

encasing nut mixture, to form crescent shapes. Grease a baking sheet, place croissants on sheet and leave to rest for 10 minutes.

**5** Beat together egg yolk and milk and brush onto croissants. Bake for 15 minutes in an oven preheated to 225°C/425°F/Gas mark 7.

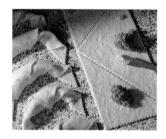

**First cut out 3 strips of dough using a pastry wheel, then cut out 15 triangles. Place a small amount of the nut mixture on each triangle. Roll up into crescents**

# APPLE CAKE WITH FLAKED ALMONDS

**Ingredients for a flan tin or spring form tin (28 cm/11 inches diam.)**

**FOR THE DOUGH**

| |
|---|
| 300 g/11 oz flour |
| 50 g/2 oz caster sugar |
| 1 sachet/approx. ½ oz vanilla sugar |
| pinch salt |
| ½ cube/1 oz fresh yeast |
| 150 ml/¼ pint lukewarm milk |
| 1 egg yolk |
| 40 g/2 oz soft margarine |
| margarine for greasing |

**FOR THE TOPPING**

| |
|---|
| 2 tbsp apricot jam |
| 700 g/1 lb 9 oz cooking apples |
| 60 g/2 oz caster sugar |
| 2 tbsp flaked almonds |
| 30 g/1 oz soft margarine |

**1** Knead together flour, sugar, vanilla sugar, salt, crumbled yeast, milk, egg yolk and margarine to a smooth dough in a food processor or using the dough hook of a hand mixer. Cover and leave to rise until doubled in size.

**2** Grease the tin. Knead dough once more, roll out and press into tin.

**3** Warm 1 tbsp jam over a low heat, stirring until smooth, then spread over dough base. Peel, quarter and core apples and cut into slices. Arrange on dough in a rosette shape, working from the edge of the tin in towards centre.

**4** Sprinkle sugar and flaked almonds on top of apple and dot margarine over the cake. Bake for 25-30 minutes in an oven preheated to 225°C/425°F/Gas mark 7.

**5** Melt remaining jam together with 2 tbsp hot water and brush over edge of cake. *Makes 16 slices.*

TIP: Apple cake can also be baked on a baking sheet. Simply double the quantity of dough and apples. Treble the quantities of jam and flaked almonds.

# SWABIAN POTATO CAKE

**Ingredients for a spring form tin (28 cm /11 inches diam.)**

| |
|---|
| 750 g/1 lb 11 oz potatoes |
| salt |
| 80 g/3 oz margarine |
| 375 g/12 oz plain flour |
| ½ cube/1 oz fresh yeast |
| 125 ml/4 fl. oz lukewarm milk |
| 2 tsp caraway seeds |
| ½ tsp salt |
| 100 ml/3 fl. oz butter milk or skimmed milk |
| 200 g/7 oz sour cream |
| 4 egg yolks |
| pepper |
| nutmeg |
| 4 egg whites |
| margarine for greasing |
| 3 tbsp ground almonds |
| 50 g/2 oz soft margarine, cubed |
| 3 tbsp chopped herbs |

**1** Cook the potatoes in salted water, drain and leave to cool.

**2** Melt margarine. Place in a mixing bowl with flour, crumbled yeast, milk, caraway and 2 tsp salt and knead to a smooth dough. Cover and leave to rise until doubled in size.

**3** Mash the potatoes. Mix together with butter milk, sour cream and egg yolks and season to taste. Beat egg whites until stiff and fold into potato mixture.

**4** Grease tin. Roll out the dough until thin and line tin well with dough. Scatter almonds across dough base, then fill with potato mixture.

**5** Dot butter across top of cake and bake in a preheated oven at 200°C/400°F/Gas mark 6 for 60 minutes. Scatter chopped herbs on baked cake. *Makes 16 portions.*

# ONION FLAN

**Ingredients for a spring form tin (26 cm/10 inches diam.)**

| |
|---|
| **FOR THE DOUGH** |
| ½ cube/1 oz fresh yeast |
| 1 tsp sugar |
| 60 g/2 oz margarine |
| 250 g/9 oz flour |
| 1 tsp salt |
| For the topping |
| 1.5 kg/3¼ lb onions |
| 20 g/1 oz soft margarine |
| 3 eggs |
| caraway |
| salt, pepper |
| 150 g/6 oz sour cream |
| margarine for greasing |
| 150 g/6 oz streaky bacon |

**1** Dissolve crumbled yeast and sugar in 125 ml/4 fl. oz lukewarm water. Cover and leave to work in a warm place.

**2** Melt margarine, place in a mixing bowl with flour and salt. Add yeast mixture and knead to a smooth dough. Cover and leave to rise until doubled in size.

**3** Peel onions, cut into rings and fry gently in margarine until transparent. Season with caraway, salt and pepper.

**4** Stir eggs and sour cream into onions and adjust seasoning. Leave onion mixture to cool. Grease the tin, roll out dough and use to line tin, drawing dough up the sides of the tin.

**5** Fill tin with onion mixture. Finely dice streaky bacon and scatter over onions. Bake in a preheated oven at 200°C/400°F/ Gas mark 6 for 60 minutes. *Makes 12 portions.*

# SAVOURY GUGELHUPF

| Ingredients for a gugelhupf tin/savarin mould (2 l capacity/3½ pints capacity) |
| --- |
| 400 g/14 oz streaky bacon |
| 60 g/2 oz yeast |
| 1 tsp sugar |
| 150 g/6 oz soft margarine |
| 600 g/1 lb 5 oz flour |
| 1 tsp salt |
| 2 eggs |
| 125 g/5 oz chopped hazelnuts |
| 2 tsp chopped rosemary |
| margarine for greasing |

1 Finely dice bacon and fry until crisp in a pan without any fat. Drain on absorbent kitchen paper.

2 Dissolve the crumbled yeast and sugar in 400 ml/approx. 14 fl. oz warm water. Cover and leave to work in a warm place.

3 Melt margarine. Place in a bowl with flour, salt and eggs. Add yeast mixture and knead to a smooth dough in a food processor or using the dough hook of a hand mixer. Finally knead in 100 g/4 oz nuts, bacon and rosemary.

4 Cover and leave to rise in a warm place until doubled in size. Grease the tin and scatter remaining nuts around the tin. Fill tin with dough and leave to rest for a further 15 minutes. Bake in a preheated oven at 200°C/400°F/ Gas mark 6 for 50-60 minutes. *Makes 16 slices.*

TIP: This cake stands or falls depending on the quality of bacon used. It is preferable to use dry cured bacon, You can identify this bacon by its solid, robust texture.

# CHEESE STRAWS

| Ingredients for 35 straws |
| --- |
| 350 g/12 oz flour |
| 25 g/1 oz yeast |
| 1 tsp sugar |
| 1 tsp salt |
| 125 g/5 oz soft margarine |
| 125 ml/4 fl. oz lukewarm milk |
| 2 egg yolks |
| 100 g/4 oz Emmental cheese |
| caraway |
| paprika or salt |

1 Knead the flour, crumbled yeast, sugar, salt, margarine and milk to a smooth dough in a food processor or using the dough hook of a hand mixer. Cover and leave to rise in a warm place until doubled in size.

2 Roll out the dough into a 4 mm/⅛ inch thick rectangle. Mix egg yolk with 2 tbsp water and brush over half the sheet of dough. Reserve some of the egg mixture.

3 Finely grate cheese and scatter over dough which has been brushed with beaten egg. Reserve 2 tbsp cheese for sprinkling. Fold other half of dough over the cheese, and roll out again until 4 mm thick. Cut into strips approx. 2.5 cm/1 inch wide and 15 cm/6 inches long.

4 Brush the straws with remaining egg, sprinkle with remaining cheese, caraway, paprika or salt. Twist into spirals.

5 Grease a baking sheet, place straws on sheet and bake in an oven preheated to 225°C/425°F/ Gas mark 7 for 15-20 minutes.

TIP: These cheese straws taste best straight from the oven. They freeze well.

# MINCED PORK PASTIES

| Ingredients for 20 pasties |
| --- |
| 1 cube/2 oz yeast, 1 tsp sugar |
| 250 ml/8 fl. oz milk |
| 100 g/4 oz margarine |
| 500 g/1 lb 2 oz flour • ½ tsp salt |
| 1 egg • 200 g/7 oz streaky bacon |
| 200 g/7 oz leeks • 1 clove garlic |
| 100 g/4 oz mushrooms |
| 2 eggs • 2 small onions |
| 200 g/7 oz spicy pickled gherkins |
| 2 sprigs dill |
| 500 g/1 lb 2 oz minced pork |
| salt • pepper • 1 egg yolk • 2 tbsp milk |

1 Dissolve crumbled yeast and sugar in the milk. Cover and leave to work in a warm place.

2 Melt margarine. Place in a bowl with flour, salt and egg. Add yeast mixture and knead to a smooth dough. Cover and leave to rise until doubled in size.

3 Dice bacon and render down. Wash leeks, slice into fine rings and gently fry in bacon fat. Crush garlic, clean mushrooms and slice, and combine everything with the leeks.

4 Hard boil and shell eggs. Peel onions, drain gherkins. Chop eggs, onions and gherkins into small dice, finely chop dill. Mix the above ingredients with the minced pork, season with salt and pepper and add to the leek mixture.

5 Thoroughly knead dough again, roll out into a large rectangle, and cut out circles with a diameter of 10 cm/4 inches. Place 2 tbsp filling on each circle. Brush edges of dough circle with water. Fold over dough and crimp edges together. Leave to rest for a further 10 minutes.

6 Mix egg yolk with milk. Brush pasties with egg mixture. Grease a baking sheet, place pasties on it and bake for 40-45 minutes in an oven preheated to 200°C/400°F/ Gas mark 6.

# BACON ROLY-POLY

| Ingredients for 2 roly-polys |
| --- |
| ½ cube/1 oz fresh yeast |
| 1 tsp sugar |
| good 250 ml/8 fl. oz warm milk |
| 50 g/2 oz soft margarine |
| 500 g/1 lb 2 oz flour |
| 2 tsp salt |
| 400 g/14 oz bacon |
| 2 sprigs parsley |
| margarine for greasing |
| 1 egg yolk for glaze |

1 Dissolve crumbled yeast and sugar in milk. Cover and leave to work in a warm place for 10 minutes.

2 Melt margarine. Place in a bowl with flour and salt. Add yeast mixture and knead to a smooth dough. Cover and leave to rise in a warm place until doubled in size.

3 Dice bacon finely, and cook in a non-stick frying pan, without fat, until transparent. Chop parsley and cook briefly with bacon. Leave to cool.

4 Roll out dough into a rectangle measuring 30 x 50 cm/12 x 20 inches and spread bacon on dough. Cut through the dough diagonally and roll up each half starting from cut side. Grease a baking sheet and lay roly-polys on sheet. Leave to rest for 15 minutes.

5 Mix egg yolk with 1 tbsp water and brush over roly-polys. Prick roly-polys all over with a fork. Bake in a preheated oven at 200-225°C/400-425°F/Gas mark 6–7 for approx. 20 minutes.

MICROWAVE TIP: You can also cook the bacon until crisp in a microwave. Put the diced bacon in a moderately deep, open dish. Cook for 8-10 minutes at 600-700 watts, stirring once.

# PETERLING

| Ingredients for 1 baking sheet |
| --- |
| FOR THE DOUGH |
| 375 g/13 oz flour |
| 30 g/1 oz yeast |
| 1 tsp sugar |
| 1 tsp salt |
| 100 g/4 oz soft margarine |
| FOR THE TOPPING |
| 4 bunches flat-leaved parsley |
| 150 g/6 oz bacon |
| 400 g/14 oz double cream |
| 2 eggs · salt · pepper |
| margarine for greasing |

1 Put the flour, crumbled yeast, sugar, 150 ml/¼ pint warm water, salt and margarine in a bowl. Knead to a smooth dough in a food processor or using the dough hook of a hand mixer. Cover and leave to rise in a warm place until doubled in size.
2 Coarsely chop parsley. Finely dice bacon. Beat cream and eggs together, season with salt and pepper.

3 Knead dough again. Grease a baking sheet, roll out dough and line baking sheet with it. Scatter ⅔ of parsley over dough and pour egg and cream mixture on top. Spread bacon evenly over the egg mixture. Bake in a pre-heated oven at 200°C/400°F/Gas mark 6 for 25-30 minutes. Garnish with parsley. *Makes 16 slices.*

TIP: Only chop the parsley just before it is needed. The aroma begins to disperse after just 5 minutes and the rich vitamin C

# LEEK WAFFLES

| Ingredients for 12 waffles |
| --- |
| FOR THE DOUGH |
| ½ cube/1 oz yeast |
| 1 tsp sugar |
| 250 ml/8 fl. oz lukewarm milk |
| 100 g/4 oz soft margarine |
| 300 g/11 oz flour |
| 1 tsp salt |
| 3 egg yolks |
| 100 g/4 oz leeks |
| 3 egg whites |
| margarine for greasing |
| AS AN ACCOMPANIMENT |
| 200 g/7 oz smoked salmon |
| 200 g/7 oz trout roe |
| 400 g/14 oz crème fraiche |
| 1 bunch dill |

1 Dissolve the crumbled yeast and sugar in the milk. Cover and leave to work in a warm place for 10-15 minutes.
2 Melt margarine, place in a bowl with flour, salt and egg yolks. Add yeast mixture and knead to a smooth dough in a food processor or using the dough hook of a hand mixer. Cover and leave to rise in a warm place until doubled in size.
3 Slice leeks into fine rings, beat egg whites until stiff. Fold both into dough. Preheat waffle irons, grease with margarine. Place 2-3

tbsp dough in a waffle iron and bake. Continue in this way to produce 11 more waffles.
4 Serve the waffles with smoked salmon, trout roe, crème fraiche and dill.

TIP: If you are expecting a lot of guests you can cook the waffles 1-2 hours in advance and put them to one side wrapped in foil. Reheat for 5 minutes in a pre-heated oven at 200°C/400°F/Gas mark 6. They will taste just as good as freshly made waffles.

# PIZZA PRIMAVERA

| Ingredients for a baking sheet |
| --- |
| **FOR THE DOUGH** |
| ½ cube/1 oz yeast |
| 1 tsp sugar |
| 100 g/4 oz soft margarine |
| 375 g/13 oz flour |
| 1 tsp salt |
| **FOR THE TOPPING** |
| 400 g/14 oz cottage cheese |
| 100 g/4 oz low fat curd cheese or quark |
| 1 bunch chives |
| 3 cloves garlic, salt, pepper |
| 1 bunch spring onions |
| 1 kg/2 lb 3 oz tomatoes |
| margarine for greasing |
| 3 tbsp capers |
| 3 tbsp olive oil |
| 5-8 bay leaves |

**1** Dissolve crumbled yeast and sugar in 200 ml/approx. 7 fl. oz warm water. Cover and leave to work in a warm place.

**2** Melt margarine. Put in a bowl with flour and salt. Add yeast mixture and knead to a smooth dough. Leave to rise in a warm place until doubled in size.

**3** Mix together the cottage cheese and curd cheese. Chop chives. Press garlic cloves in a garlic press and mix into cheese mixture with chives. Season with salt and pepper. Clean spring onions and chop into rings. Wash tomatoes and slice.

**4** Grease a baking sheet. Roll out dough and place on baking sheet, drawing dough up sides of sheet. Spread cheese mixture over dough. Arrange onions and tomatoes on top of cheese.

**5** Leave pizza to rest for a further 15 minutes. Scatter capers over pizza, drizzle with olive oil and bake in an oven preheated to 225°C/425°F/Gas mark 7 for 30-40 minutes.

**6** Chop basil leaves into strips and scatter over pizza.
*Makes 16 slices.*

# NEAPOLITAN PIZZA

**Ingredients for a spring form tin (26 cm/10 inches diam.)**

**FOR THE DOUGH**

| |
|---|
| ½ cube/½ oz yeast |
| 1 tsp sugar |
| 125 g/5 oz flour |
| pinch salt |
| 30 g/1 oz soft margarine |

**FOR THE TOPPING**

| |
|---|
| 1 small tin peeled tomatoes (250 g/9 oz drained weight) |
| 1 onion |
| 1 clove garlic |
| 1 tsp each thyme and oregano |
| salt, pepper |
| margarine for greasing |
| 2 tomatoes |
| 150 g/6 oz mozzarella cheese |
| 12 black olives |
| 1 jar anchovies (25 g)/1 oz) |
| thyme for sprinkling |

**1** Dissolve crumbled yeast and sugar in 4 tbsp warm water. Cover and leave to work in a warm place.

**2** Put flour, salt and margarine in a bowl. Add yeast mixture and knead to a smooth ball in a food processor or using the dough hook of a hand mixer. Cover and leave to rise in a warm place until doubled in size.

**3** In the meantime, reduce the tinned tomatoes and juice over a high heat. Peel onion, and dice finely. Crush garlic. Add both to tomatoes with oregano and thyme. Cook mixture briefly. Season with salt and pepper and put to one side.

**4** Grease tin. Knead dough again, roll out and press into tin. Spread tomato mixture over dough.

**5** Slice tomatoes and mozzarella and arrange on pizza with olives and anchovies. Scatter thyme over pizza and bake for 30-40 minutes in an oven preheated to 200-225°C/400-425°F/Gas mark 6–7.

TIP: If possible, use fresh thyme rather than dried; it is much more aromatic.

# HERB BREAD

**Ingredients for a loaf tin (30 cm long, 2 l capacity/12 inches long, 3½ pints capacity)**

**FOR THE DOUGH**

1 cube/2 oz yeast

1 tsp sugar

50 g/2 oz soft margarine

500 g/1 lb 2 oz flour

salt • 1 egg

**FOR THE FILLING**

1 clove garlic • 1 tbsp oil

margarine for greasing

100g/4 oz mixed herbs (e.g. chives, parsley, thyme, lovage, bay leaves)

evaporated milk for brushing

**1** Dissolve crumbled yeast and sugar in 250 ml/8 fl. oz warm water. Cover and leave to rise.

**2** Melt margarine. Place in a bowl with flour, 1 tsp salt and egg. Add yeast mixture and knead to a smooth dough. Cover and leave to rise until doubled in size. Knead well once again.

**3** Roll out dough into a rectangle approx. 30 x 40 cm/12 x 16 inches. Leave to rest for 15 minutes. Crush garlic, mix with oil and pinch of salt. Coat dough with garlic mixture.

**4** Grease tin. Chop herbs and spread over dough. Fold dough over to form a roll and place in tin. Using a knife make a deep incision along the dough, brush with evaporated milk. Bake in an oven preheated to 200°C/400°F/ Gas mark 6 for 50-60 minutes.

# ITALIAN PIZZA BREAD

**Ingredients for 12 flat cakes**

**FOR THE DOUGH**

½ cube/1 oz yeast

1 tsp sugar

500 g/1 lb 2 oz flour

½ tsp salt

30 g/1 oz soft margarine

**FOR THE TOPPING**

2 cloves garlic

6 tbsp cold pressed olive oil

1 sprig fresh or 2 tsp dried rosemary

**1** Dissolve the yeast and sugar in 300 ml/½ pint warm water. Mix flour and salt together. Knead into a smooth dough with melted margarine and yeast mixture. Cover and leave to rise for 15 minutes until dough has doubled in size.

**2** Knead dough, roll into a sausage shape, divide into 12 portions and roll out into oval cakes. Place on a baking sheet lined with baking parchment and make indentations in dough with a spoon handle.

**3** Crush garlic and mix with oil. Brush over dough cakes and sprinkle rosemary on top. Leave to rest for 15 minutes and bake in a preheated oven at 200-225°C/ 400-425°F/Gas mark 6–7 for 15-20 minutes until golden brown.

# PROSCIUTTO PIZZA

| Ingredients for 1 pizza (28 cm/11 inches diam.) |
| --- |
| 400 g/14 oz flour |
| 1 tsp salt |
| ½ tsp sugar |
| 30 g/1 oz yeast |
| 30 g/1 oz soft margarine |
| 500 g/1 lb 2 oz tomatoes |
| 2 cloves garlic |
| 4 onions |
| 50 g/2 oz soft margarine |
| salt · pepper |
| margarine for greasing |
| 50 g/2 oz tomato puree |
| ½ tsp each oregano, thyme, rosemary |
| 4 slices parma ham |
| 4 slices salami |
| 200 g/7 oz pickled artichoke hearts |
| 8-10 black olives |
| 300 g/11 oz mozzarella |
| 4 tbsp olive oil |
| sprigs of rosemary |

1 Knead flour, salt, crumbled yeast, 200 ml/approx. 7 fl. oz warm water and margarine to a smooth dough in a food processor or using the dough hook of a hand mixer. Cover and leave to rise until doubled in size.

2 Blanch tomatoes in boiling water and remove skins. Crush garlic, peel and dice onions. Fry together in margarine until transparent. Leave to cool, season with salt and pepper. Knead the dough again.

3 Grease a baking sheet. Roll out dough into a round and place on baking sheet. Spread tomato purée over dough. Sprinkle with oregano, thyme and rosemary. Spread diced onion over pizza.

4 Top with tomato slices, ham, salami, halved artichoke hearts and olives. Slice mozzarella, arrange on pizza and drizzle with olive oil. Bake for about 30 minutes in an oven preheated to 200°C/400°F/Gas mark 6. Scatter sprigs of rosemary on top.
*Makes 12 slices*

# BREAD ROLLS

| Ingredients for 10 rolls |
| --- |
| 200 ml/approx. 7 fl. oz milk |
| 4 tbsp soft margarine |
| 500 g/1 lb 2 oz flour |
| 1 cube/2 oz yeast |
| ½ tsp salt |
| 2 egg yolks |
| 2 tsp sugar |
| evaporated milk |
| sesame seeds, poppy seeds and large oat flakes for sprinkling |

**1** Warm together the milk, 3 tbsp water and margarine. Put the flour, crumbled yeast, salt, egg yolk and sugar in a bowl. Add the milk and margarine mixture and knead to a smooth dough in a food processor or using the dough hook of a hand mixer. Cover and leave to rise for 30 minutes in a warm place.

**2** Make 10 round bread rolls out of the dough and leave to rest for a further 15 minutes.

**3** Brush with evaporated milk and decorate some rolls with sesame seeds, some with poppy and the rest with oat flakes. Bake in a preheated oven at 200°C/400°F/Gas mark 6 for 15 minutes.

VARIATION: You can also add finely chopped herbs or very finely diced, lightly fried onions to the bread dough.

TIP: For party-sized rolls the dough should be divided into 20 portions to make smaller rolls. The baking time is then reduced by about 5 minutes.

# SALT PRETZEL

| Ingredients for 14 pretzels |
| --- |
| 1 cube/2 oz yeast |
| 1 tsp sugar |
| 500 g/1 lb 2 oz flour |
| 1 tbsp salt |
| 2 tbsp bicarbonate of soda |
| 2 tbsp sea salt for sprinkling |

**1** Dissolve the crumbled yeast with the sugar in 375 ml/12 fl. oz warm water. Cover and leave to work in a warm place for 10 minutes.

**2** Mix the flour and salt together in a bowl. Add the yeast mixture, stirring constantly. Knead to form a smooth dough. Cover and leave to rise until doubled in size.

**3** Bring 1.5 2½ pints water to boil in an enamel or glass saucepan. Add bicarbonate of soda and keep at a rolling boil for 10 minutes.

**4** Knead dough again, shape into a sausage and divide into 14 sections. Roll out each piece and shape into a pretzel.

**5** Immerse the pretzels one by one in the boiling soda for 20 seconds each, using a skimming spoon. Drain and sprinkle with sea salt.

**6** Line a baking sheet with baking parchment. Place the pretzels on the sheet and bake for 20 minutes in an oven preheated to 200°C/400°F/Gas mark 6.

Roll out each piece of dough into a 40 cm/16 inch long strand. The middle should be thicker than the ends. Form into pretzels and immerse one by one in the boiling soda.

# Ultimately delicate, essentially strong

Short-crust pastry serves as a crispy base for multi-layered gateaux and a delicious envelope for savoury pasties, while biscuits and cookies are short-crust pastry in its purest form. It likes cool conditions and deft, skilled fingers which knead flour and fat together in a perfect combination. All that is needed finally is a quick trip to the oven and short-crust pastry becomes the superstar of quality patisserie.

Fruit tartlets. Recipe on page 94.

# HOW TO MAKE SUCCESSFUL SHORT-CRUST PASTRY

Throughout the Western world, short-crust pastry features in good home cooking. This is hardly surprising since it is quick and straightforward to make and can be used in an amazing variety of different ways. However, methods and recipes vary so much that very different pastries can result. Nevertheless, because of their crisp, delicate and somewhat crumbly texture they can all be classed as true short-crust pastry. Typical short-crust pastry contains twice as much flour as fat, generally speaking, and is just as successful when made in a food processor as it is if traditional methods involving chopping up or rubbing in are used (steps 1 to 3 and 4 to 6). A tried and tested BASIC RECIPE for short-crust pastry requires 250 g/9 oz flour, 125 g/5 oz margarine, 60 g/2 oz caster sugar, pinch salt and 1 egg. If you want hearty pastry you can simply omit the sugar.

PASTRY FOR TARTS AND FLANS is wonderfully short, but contains a lot of fat and very little or no sugar. Take 200 g/7 oz flour, 150 g/6 oz margarine, a pinch of salt and 1 egg yolk and work the ingredients together with a knife or the dough hook of a hand mixer.

PASTRY FOR PIES is much firmer and is made without egg. You will need 250 g/9 oz flour, 100 g/4 oz margarine, 1 tsp each of salt and vinegar and a scant 125 ml/4 fl. oz water. The best way is to mix the ingredients for this pastry according to steps 7 to 9.

Each kind of short-crust pastry must be left to rest for about half an hour in the refrigerator before you shape and bake it.

**1** CHOPPED DOUGH: Put the flour into a large bowl in a mound, or simply heap it on the work surface. Cut the chilled margarine into cubes and add to the flour. Scatter caster sugar around the edge of the flour and break the egg into the centre.

**2** If the ingredients are in a bowl as shown, cut them into each other using two knives in criss-cross fashion until the mixture forms pea-sized crumbs. If you are working directly on the work surface, use a large palette knife instead of two knives.

**6** Now you can use your hands again. Knead the pastry crumbs into a dough and shape into a ball. Be careful not to knead the pastry too vigorously.

**7** PIE PASTRY: Put the flour in a bowl and scatter the cubes of chilled margarine in a circle, Then pour very cold water (iced water) in the middle.

**3** Quickly press the resulting crumbs together by hand to make a dough. It is better not to knead it at this stage, otherwise the fat will melt and the dough will become heavy.

**4** PASTRY USING RUB-BING-IN METHOD: For this method you don't cut the ingredients with a knife, but 'rub' the flour and chilled margarine with your fingertips until the texture resembles even-sized bread crumbs. Take a small quantity at a time between your fingers and work it quickly so the fat doesn't melt.

**5** Beat the egg thoroughly and pour into the middle of the pastry crumbs. Mix all the ingredients together briefly with a fork. Some of the individual ingredients should still be distinguishable.

**8** Mix the ingredients with a fork or with your fingers. This should be done as quickly as possible and not too evenly. The irregular pieces of fat will make the pastry airy.

**9** Pie pastry and other types of short-crust pastry with a high proportion of fat can be processed further to make a light, flaky quick puff pastry. To do this roll out the dough into a rectangle, fold one-third over into the middle, then fold the other section over the top and roll out again. Repeat the process two or three times.

**10** Short-crust pastry is particularly successful if you use a hand mixer and soft margarine. Put all the ingredients together in a bowl. Mix as briefly as possible using the dough hook. Then place the dough on a work surface and shape into a ball with your hands.

# SHORT-CRUST PASTRY

## KNEADING PASTRY

Nothing can really go wrong with short-crust pastry. If it does, you have been working in a kitchen which is too hot, you have used ingredients which are not cool or you have kneaded the pastry too vigorously and for too long. These are the mistakes which occur most frequently. Heat and intensive kneading make the pastry 'burnt', in other words it breaks up and becomes crumbly. If you are using the dough hook on a hand mixer or a food processor, and following a recipe which uses little fat, then the danger of this happening is especially great. For this reason you should always use well-chilled ingredients, and only work the pastry until it just holds together, irrespective of which

method you are using. If in spite of everything disaster strikes, first aid is at hand. Add one or two tablespoons of ice-cold water and knead again briefly. Unfortunately in such cases the pastry often shrinks a bit when baked.

## LINING THE TIN

Most filled pies have a short-crust pastry base with deep sides. So that the pastry is of even thickness all over, and to avoid it becoming 'stressed', first roll out the pastry thinly, drape over a rolling pin and place on the base of a spring form tin which has been separated from the sides. Place the closed sides of the tin on top of the pastry. In this way you will easily be able to remove the excess pastry. Close the tin. Out of pastry make a thick sausage shape which is long enough to go round the inside of the tin, position it around the sides and using your hands draw the pastry up the sides of the tin to form an even edge.

## WHAT DOES THE EGG DO?

Fat is not the only thing responsible for making short-crust pastry delicate enough to melt in the mouth. Eggs also have a role to play. The egg yolk gives the pastry its attractive appearance and acts as an emulsifier because of the lecithin it contains. This makes the dough shorter and more even textured. In contrast

**To make the base roll out the pastry until thin. Shape the sides with your hands.**

egg white makes the dough firmer, and a bit tougher, but this is exactly what you want for short-crust pastry flan bases! Short-crust pastry which contains whole eggs keeps its shape much better than pastries which are very delicate and crumbly, which are made without any egg at all or just with egg yolk.

**Compare the short-crust pastry on the left which was kneaded for too long and has become 'burnt' with that on the right, which is perfect.**

## BE SPARING WITH FLOUR

▓ Flour is dusted onto the work surface to prevent pastry sticking when it is rolled out, but the more you roll out the pastry, especially if you're making biscuits, the more flour it takes up and it thus becomes tougher. It is possible to roll out pastry without flour by rolling on baking parchment or foil. The pastry won't stick and the last biscuit will taste as good as the first.

## BAKING BLIND

▓ Thin short-crust pastry bases are ideally suited to filling with fresh cream, crème or custards and fruit. Before baking, dried pulses or rice are used as a temporary filling so that the pastry retains its shape and the sides don't collapse. The blind filling can be removed either after baking or, even better, halfway through the cooking time if the pastry is firm enough, so that the pastry base browns during the remaining cooking time. If you are using a small, deep tin, the pastry base will cook more evenly if you don't use paper under the filling. Instead of using rice when baking blind, fill the pastry case itself with large dried beans and remove halfway through cooking time.

## FIRM BASE

▓ Because short-crust pastry bases are smooth and firm, they are often used as a base for delicate fatless sponge gateaux, which can then be sliced more easily. If used in this way, short-crust pastry should be rolled out to about 0.5 cm/⅕ inch thick. Place a spring form tin which equals the size of the sponge base on top of the pastry and cut out the pastry base. Prick the pastry base all over with a fork so that it doesn't bubble during baking. Brush pastry with melted jam or cooking chocolate when baked, place the sponge base on top and press down lightly with your hand so they stick together.

**Tartlet tins are quick and easy to line. Place the tins close together. Drape the rolled out pastry over a rolling pin and roll out across top of tins. Push the pastry down into the sides of the tins using a brush. Then run the rolling pin across the tops of the tins so that the pastry is cut off around the edges of the tins.**

## DARK SPOTS

▓ Your short-crust pastry was easy to knead, rolled out beautifully and was straightforward to bake. It tastes good too, but you are left with the visual problem of tiny dark brown spots throughout the pastry. What went wrong? The answer is that you almost certainly used sugar which was too coarse. When baking you should use the finest caster sugar, but if you want to make absolutely sure, make your short-crust pastry with icing sugar – then the problem of spotty pastry will be solved.

**When baking blind, place greaseproof paper or baking parchment on top of the pastry base before you fill it with rice. Dried beans can go straight on top of pastry. If some beans still stick to the pastry when baked, they can easily be removed.**

# CHERRY CHEESECAKE

| Ingredients for a spring form tin (24 cm/9 inches diam.) |
| --- |
| 250 g/9 oz flour |
| ¼ tsp baking powder |
| 125 g/5 oz margarine |
| 65 g/3 oz sugar • 1 egg |
| 2 jars cherries, (drained weight 740 g/1 lb 11 oz each) |
| 50 g/2 oz cornflour |
| 2-3 tbsp ground almonds |
| 75 g/3 oz margarine |
| 750 g/1 lb 11 oz low fat curd cheese or quark |
| 200 g/7 oz caster sugar |
| 1 sachet/approx. ½ oz vanilla sugar |
| 1 tsp grated lemon zest |
| 2 tbsp lemon juice • 5 eggs |
| 1 tbsp flour • 1 egg yolk |
| 2 tbsp apricot jam |
| 3 tbsp flaked almonds |
| 3 tbsp icing sugar for dusting |

1 Mix the flour with baking powder, margarine, sugar and egg to form a smooth dough. Using your hands shape into a ball, wrap in cling film and refrigerate for 30 minutes.

2 Drain cherries, reserve syrup. Mix cornflour to a smooth paste with 3 tbsp cherry syrup. Bring remaining syrup to the boil, stir in cornflour paste and simmer for a further 30 seconds, stirring continually. Stir in cherries.

3 Roll out pastry and use to line tin. Spread cherries and almonds on base. Melt margarine and leave to cool. Mix margarine together with curd cheese, sugar, vanilla sugar, lemon zest, eggs and flour.

4 Spread cheese mixture over the cherries. Bake for 50 minutes in an oven preheated to 175°C/350°F/Gas mark 4. Beat egg yolk with a little water and brush over cheesecake. Bake for another 10 minutes. Leave to cool, then remove from tin.

5 Brush side of cheesecake with jam. Brown almond flakes in a frying pan without fat until golden brown and press into edge of cheesecake. Finally dust cheesecake with icing sugar.
*Makes 10-12 slices.*

# FILLED ALMOND SLICE

| |
| --- |
| 300 g/11 oz flour |
| 200 g/7 oz icing sugar |
| 200 g/7 oz ground almonds |
| few drops almond essence |
| 2 tsp cocoa powder |
| 200 g/7 oz margarine |
| 1 egg • 5 leaves white gelatine |
| 600 g/1 lb 5 oz double cream |
| 3 tbsp orange liqueur (Cointreau or similar) |
| 2 sachets/approx. 1 oz vanilla sugar |
| 5 tbsp flaked almonds |
| 1 tbsp icing sugar for dusting |

1 Mix flour, icing sugar, almonds, almond essence, 1½ tsp cocoa powder, margarine and egg to a smooth dough. Shape into a ball, wrap in cling film and refrigerate for 1 hour.

2 Line a baking sheet with baking parchment. Divide pastry into 4 portions and roll out on baking sheet to form a rectangle. Bake each pastry base in a preheated oven at 200°C/400°F/Gas mark 6 for 12-15 minutes.

3 Leave bases to cool, remove carefully from baking parchment and trim edges while bases are still warm. Leave to cool on a wire rack.

4 Soften gelatine in cold water, drain and melt over a low heat. Beat the cream, liqueur and vanilla sugar together until stiff. Fold in gelatine and leave until semi-set. Fold in 2 tbsp flaked almonds.

5 Spread cream over base and edges of pastry and place one on top of the other. Refrigerate the almond slice for 2-3 hours. Toast the remaining almonds until golden brown and scatter over the slice. Mix remaining cocoa with the icing sugar and dust over cake.
*Makes 6-8 slices.*

# ENGADINE NUT PIE

**Ingredients for a spring form tin (28 cm/11 inches diam.)**

**FOR THE FILLING**

350 g/12 oz caster sugar

300 g/10 oz whole walnuts

100 g/4 oz double cream

**FOR THE PASTRY**

350 g/12 oz flour

200 g/7 oz margarine

150 g/6 oz caster sugar

pinch salt

1 egg

1 Melt sugar in a pan over a low heat until liquid and pale yellow. Coarsely chop walnuts, add to sugar and remove from heat. The walnuts should not turn brown. Add 1 tbsp water and cream. Mix well and refrigerate.

2 Meanwhile mix flour, margarine, sugar, salt and egg to a smooth dough. Shape into a ball, wrap in cling film and refrigerate for 30 minutes.

3 Divide pastry into 3 portions. Roll out 1 portion into a circle and use to cover base of the spring form tin. Form a sausage shape out of the second portion and use to line the sides of the tin. Spread nut and cream mixture over the pastry base.

4 Roll out remaining pastry into a circle and use to make a lid for the pie, covering the nut filling. Crimp edges tightly together.

5 Bake in a preheated oven at 200-225°C/400-425°F/Gas mark 6–7 for 45 minutes. When baked, run a knife around the edge of the tin immediately to prevent any filling which may have escaped from sticking. Leave pie to cool in tin.

*Makes 10 slices.*

# DUTCHMAN'S TART

**Ingredients for a spring form tin
(24 cm/9 inches diam.)**

**FOR THE PASTRY**

| | |
|---|---|
| 300 g/11 oz flour | |
| 125 g/5 oz margarine | |
| 75 g/3 oz caster sugar | |
| pinch salt | |
| 1 egg | |
| 1 tbsp milk | |

**FOR THE FILLING**

| | |
|---|---|
| 75 g/3 oz margarine | |
| 100 g/4 oz caster sugar | |
| 1 sachet/approx. ½ oz vanilla sugar | |
| 3 eggs | |
| 1 tsp grated lemon zest | |
| 150 g/6 oz ground almonds | |
| 30 g/1 oz flour | |
| ¼ tsp baking powder | |
| 50 g/2 oz apricot jam | |
| 3 tbsp flaked almonds for sprinkling | |

1 Mix flour, margarine, sugar, salt, egg and milk to a smooth dough. Shape into a ball, wrap in cling film and refrigerate for 30 minutes.

2 Roll out 4/5 of pastry and use to line base and sides of spring form tin. Prick base all over with a fork and bake blind for 15 minutes in an oven preheated to 225°C/425°F/Gas mark 7.

3 Meanwhile beat together margarine, sugar, vanilla sugar and eggs until creamy. Add almonds and lemon zest. Mix together flour and baking powder, stir into margarine and egg mixture.

4 Spread baked pastry base with the apricot jam and top with the almond mixture. Roll out remaining pastry until thin, cut out strips using a pastry wheel and place on top of the tart in a pinwheel pattern.

5 Scatter flaked almonds over tart and bake in a preheated oven at 175-200°C/350-400°F/Gas mark 4–6 for 40-45 minutes.
*Makes 12 slices.*

**It is easy to cut short-crust pastry with a pastry wheel. For the Dutchman's tart, lay the strips of pastry on top of the filling in a pinwheel pattern.**

# FRUIT TARTLETS

| Ingredients for 6 brioche moulds (approx. 12 cm/5 inches diam.) |
| --- |
| **FOR THE PASTRY** |
| **300 g/11 oz flour** |
| **200 g/7 oz margarine** |
| **100 g/4 oz caster sugar • 3 egg yolks** |
| **dried pulses for baking blind** |
| **FOR THE FILLING** |
| **750 g/1 lb 11 oz berries or** |
| **1 kg/2 lb 3 oz seasonal orchard fruit (cherries, plums)** |
| **3 tbsp caster sugar** |
| **250 ml/8 fl. oz white wine or grape juice** |
| **1 sachet/approx. ½ oz clear tart glaze or arrowroot** |

1 Mix flour, margarine, sugar and egg yolks to a smooth dough. Shape into a ball, wrap in cling film and refrigerate for 30 minutes.
2 Roll out the pastry until 0.5 cm/¼ inch thick. Grease brioche tins and line with pastry. Place pulses in pastry case and bake blind in a preheated oven at 200°C/400°F/Gas mark 6 for 10 minutes.

3 Remove pulses from pastry cases, leaving any beans which stick to pastry. Return to oven and bake for a further 10-15 minutes. Remove remaining beans and remove pastry case from tin.
4 Clean fruit, chop into small pieces, sprinkle with 1 tbsp sugar and leave for 10 minutes to draw the juices. Drain fruit and make juice up to 250 ml/8 fl. oz with wine or grape juice.
5 Fill pastry cases with fruit. Prepare glaze according to directions on packet. If using arrowroot, dissolve in a small quantity of juice and mix to make a smooth paste. Gently heat the wine or fruit juice in a pan and bring to boil. Stir in arrowroot and continue to cook briefly until glaze is clear. Allow to cool, then drizzle glaze over tartlets.

# BERRY TART WITH ALMOND CREAM

| Ingredients for a spring form tin (26 cm/10 inches diam.) |
| --- |
| **FOR THE PASTRY** |
| **300 g/11 oz flour** |
| **125 g/5 oz margarine** |
| **75 g/3 oz caster sugar** |
| **pinch salt • 1 egg • 2 tbsp rum** |
| **margarine for greasing** |
| **FOR THE TOPPING** |
| **750 g/1 lb 11 oz berries (e.g. blackberries)** |
| **750 ml/1¼ pints blackcurrant or grape juice** |
| **3 sachets tart glaze or approx. 1½ oz arrowroot** |
| **75 g/3 oz caster sugar** |
| **200 g/7 oz double cream** |
| **3 tbsp almond liqueur** |

1 Mix flour, margarine, sugar, salt, egg and rum to a smooth dough. Cover and refrigerate for 30 minutes.
2 Roll out pastry and use to line greased spring form tin. Prick all over with a fork and bake in a preheated oven at 225°C/425°F/Gas mark 7 for about 15 minutes. Leave to cool on a wire rack.
3 Wash and drain berries. Bring fruit juice to boil with glaze mix, or arrowroot mixed to a smooth paste with a little juice, and 50 g/2 oz sugar.
4 Place a plastic or metal flan ring on the pastry base. Fill with fruit and pour hot glaze over top of fruit. Leave to cool until glaze sets.
5 Beat cream together with remaining sugar until stiff and fold in almond liqueur. Run a knife around the edge of the flan ring to loosen and remove from tart. Serve the almond cream with the tart. *Makes 12 slices.*

# APPLE AND CRANBERRY ROLL

| Ingredients for approx. 10 slices |
| --- |
| **FOR THE PASTRY** |
| **200 g/7 oz flour** |
| **80 g/3 oz margarine** |
| **½ tsp salt** |
| **FOR THE FILLING** |
| **6 apples (approx. 750 g/1 lb 11 oz weight)** |
| **4 slices French toast** |
| **1 jar cranberry compote (375 g/13 oz)** |
| **1 egg white** |
| **1 egg yolk** |
| **crystal sugar for sprinkling** |

1 Mix flour, margarine, salt and 5 tbsp cold water to a smooth dough. Shape into a ball, wrap in cling film and refrigerate for 30 minutes.

2 Meanwhile peel, halve and core the apples and slice thinly. Place French toast in a freezer bag and crush to fine crumbs using a rolling pin. Mix with the sliced apple and the cranberry compote.

3 Roll out pastry to form a rectangle 30 x 40 cm/12 x 16 inches. Heap the filling in a strip down the centre of the pastry, then fold over the sides to form a roll. Brush edges of pastry with egg white and crimp together. Brush pastry with beaten egg yolk.

4 Bake in a preheated oven at 225-250°C/425-475°F/Gas mark 7-9 for 40 minutes and sprinkle with crystal sugar while still hot.

**The perfect roll – lift one side of the baking parchment up so that the pastry folds over the filling. Continue to lift paper carefully so that the roll forms by itself.**

# GATEAU MIGNON

| Ingredients for a spring form tin (24 cm/9 inches diam.) |
| --- |
| FOR THE PASTRY |
| 375 g/13 oz flour |
| 225 g/8 oz margarine |
| 180 g/6 oz sugar |
| 3 egg yolks |
| pinch salt |
| FOR THE FILLING |
| 250 ml/8 fl. oz lemon juice |
| 250 ml/8 fl. oz white wine |
| 100 g/4 oz caster sugar |
| 2 packets vanilla flavoured blancmange powder |
| 5 egg yolks |
| 100 g/4 oz marzipan |
| 85 g/3 oz icing sugar |
| 1 tbsp lightly beaten egg white |
| 2 tbsp apricot jam |
| 3 tbsp flaked almonds |

1 Mix flour, margarine, sugar, egg yolk and salt to a smooth dough. Shape into a ball, wrap in cling film and refrigerate for 1 hour.
2 Divide pastry into 6 portions and roll each one out between cling film to fit spring form tin base. Trim edges. Bake pastry bases in a preheated oven at 200°C/400°F/Gas mark 6 for 10-12 minutes.
3 Bring lemon juice, white wine and sugar to boil with 250 ml/8 fl. oz water. Mix blancmange powder with 7 tbsp water and add to white wine mixture. Simmer for 3 minutes. Remove blancmange mixture from heat.

Beat egg yolk and stir into blancmange. Strain into a bowl through a sieve and leave to cool.
4 Layer pastry bases and lemon custard within spring form ring. Refrigerate for 2-3 hours.
5 Roll out marzipan until thin between cling film, cut out a circle which matches size of gateau and place on top of lemon mixture.
6 Beat icing sugar together with egg white and spread evenly over gateau. Brush sides of gateau with warm jam. Toast flaked almonds without fat until golden brown and use to decorate sides of gateau.
*Makes 10-12 slices.*

# APPLE PIE

| Ingredients for a spring form tin (24 cm/9 inches diam.) |
| --- |
| FOR THE PASTRY |
| 375 g/13 oz flour |
| 2 tsp baking powder |
| 125 g/5 oz caster sugar · pinch salt |
| 1 tsp grated lemon zest |
| 200 g/7 oz margarine · 2 eggs |
| FOR THE FILLING |
| 1.5 kg/3¼ lbs apples |
| 5 tbsp white wine or water |
| 75 g/3 oz sugar |
| 1 tsp grated lemon zest |
| 2 sachets/approx. 1 oz vanilla sugar |
| 75 g/3 oz raisins |
| 2 tbsp ground almonds |
| 1 tbsp flaked almonds |
| 125 g/5 oz icing sugar for dusting |

1 Mix flour, baking powder, sugar, salt, lemon zest, margarine and eggs to a smooth dough. Shape into a ball and refrigerate for 30 minutes.
2 In the meantime peel the apples, halve, core and slice into 8 pieces. Simmer for 10 minutes in the white wine or water, sugar, lemon zest and vanilla sugar. Stir in the raisins. Pour into a sieve and leave to cool.

3 Roll out ⅔ of pastry between cling film and use to line base and sides of spring form tin. Scatter almonds over pastry base, spread apples on top of almonds. Roll out remaining dough in a circle large enough to cover the tin. Cover apple with pastry, crimp edges tightly together. Cut decorative shapes out of left-over pastry.
4 Bake in an oven preheated to 175-200°C/350-400°F/Gas mark 4–6 for 45-50 minutes. While the pie is still warm, dust with icing sugar. *Makes 10-12 slices.*

MICROWAVE TIP: The apples can be simmered in a microwave for about 5 minutes at 600-700 watts.

# PEAR PIE

| | |
|---|---|
| **Ingredients for a pie dish (26 cm/10 inches diam.)** | |
| **FOR THE PASTRY** | |
| 125 g/5 oz flour | |
| pinch salt | |
| 25 g/1 oz icing sugar | |
| 60 g/2 oz margarine | |
| 1 egg (size 4) | |
| **FOR THE FILLING** | |
| 5 very ripe pears (e.g. William) | |
| 2 tbsp apricot jam | |
| 3 tbsp pear brandy or kirsch | |
| ½ tsp cinnamon | |
| 25 g/1 oz chopped pistachio nuts | |
| 1 egg yolk | |

1 Mix flour, salt, icing sugar, margarine and egg to a smooth dough. Shape into a ball, wrap in cling film and refrigerate for 30 minutes.

2 Meanwhile peel, halve and core pears. Place pear halves in dish. Mix together apricot jam, pear brandy and cinnamon and pour over pears. Scatter pistachio nuts on top.

3 Roll out the pastry thinly, put the dish on top and cut around the dish leaving a 15 cm/6 inch 'allowance'. Cover the dish with pastry and press down the edges, using a fork to produce a pattern.

4 Knead the remaining pastry, shape into a sausage and press around edge of dish. Beat egg yolks with a little water and brush over pastry.

5 Bake the pie in a preheated oven at 200-225°C/400-425°F/Gas mark 6–7 for 45-50 minutes. Serve when still warm. *Makes 12 slices.*

**The pastry must be cut to allow room for it to expand during baking. As a guideline, put your dish on the sheet of pastry and cut around it, leaving a margin of about 15 cm/6 inches from the dish.**

# RHUBARB CUSTARD TART

**Ingredients for a square tin (about 26 x 26 cm/10 x 10 inches)**

**FOR THE PASTRY**

| |
|---|
| 200 g/7 oz flour |
| 1 tsp baking powder |
| 100 g/4 oz caster sugar |
| 1 egg |
| 125 g/5 oz margarine |
| **FOR THE TOPPING** |
| 1 kg/2 lb 3 oz rhubarb |
| 150 g/6 oz double cream |
| 1 sachet vanilla blancmange powder |
| 3 tbsp white wine |
| 100 g/4 oz caster sugar |
| 1 sachet/approx. ½ oz vanilla sugar, |
| 2 eggs |
| 100 g/4 oz slivered hazelnuts |

1 Mix the flour, baking powder, sugar, egg and margarine to a smooth dough. Shape into a ball, wrap in cling film and refrigerate for 30 minutes.

2 Meanwhile clean the rhubarb and cut into pieces. Simmer for 2 minutes over a low heat with 1 tbsp water. Leave to cool.

3 Beat cream until stiff. Mix blancmange powder to a smooth paste with the white wine, Stir into the cream together with the sugar, vanilla sugar and eggs.

4 Line tin with pastry, leaving a border above the edge of the tin. Prick the pastry base all over with a fork and sprinkle with slivered hazelnuts, reserving 3 tbsp for the topping.

5 Put the rhubarb on top of the pastry and pour over egg custard. Sprinkle remaining hazelnuts on top. Bake in a preheated oven at 225°C/425°F/Gas mark 7 for 30-35 minutes. *Makes 12 slices.*

TIP: If you don't have a suitable tin, the tart can be baked in a roasting tin.

**Freshly made rhubarb custard tart tastes best when the pastry is still crisp.**

# RICE CAKE

| Ingredients for a baking sheet |
| --- |
| **FOR THE PASTRY** |
| **500 g/1 lb 2 oz flour** |
| **pinch baking powder** |
| **125 g/5 oz icing sugar** |
| **pinch salt** |
| **250 g/9 oz margarine** |
| **2 eggs** |
| **FOR THE FILLING** |
| **750 ml/approx. 1¼ pints milk** |
| **pinch salt** |
| **200 g/7 oz long grain rice** |
| **50 g/2 oz apricot jam** |
| **125 g/5 oz double cream** |
| **4 egg whites** |
| **100 g/4 oz margarine** |
| **125 g/5 oz caster sugar** |
| **4 egg yolks** |
| **100 g/4 oz ground almonds** |
| **½ tsp grated lemon zest** |
| **2 tbsp icing sugar for dusting** |

1 Mix flour, baking powder, icing sugar, salt, margarine and eggs to a smooth dough. Shape into a ball, wrap in cling film and refrigerate for 30 minutes.

2 Bring milk to the boil with the salt. Add rice. Simmer in a pan with the lid on for 20 minutes.

3 Roll out dough on baking sheet. Prick all over with a fork. Bake in an oven preheated to 175-200°C/350-400°F/Gas mark 4–6 for 15 minutes. Spread with jam.

4 In separate bowls first beat cream until stiff, then egg whites. Beat together margarine, sugar and egg yolks until creamy. Stir rice mixture, almonds and lemon zest into margarine mixture. Fold in cream and egg whites. Spread the mixture over the pastry base. Bake for 40 minutes at 175-200°C/350-400°F/Gas mark 4–6. Dust with icing sugar.
*Makes 16 slices*

# BREAD PUDDING WITH PLUMS

| Ingredients for a small baking sheet (about 35 x 25 cm/14 x 10 inches) |
| --- |
| **FOR THE PASTRY** |
| **250 g/9 oz flour** |
| **125 g/5 oz margarine** |
| **65 g/2 oz caster sugar** |
| **pinch salt** |
| **1 egg yolk** |
| **1 tbsp milk** |
| **FOR THE TOPPING** |
| **100 g/4 oz cranberry jam** |
| **1 jar yellow plums** |
| **(drained weight 370 g/13 oz)** |
| **5 eggs** |
| **1 egg white** |
| **180 g/6 oz caster sugar** |
| **160 g/6 oz stale white bread** |
| **160 g/6 oz desiccated coconut** |
| **¼ tsp cinnamon** |
| **1 tsp grated lemon zest** |
| **¼ tsp baking powder** |
| **1 tsp icing sugar for dusting** |

1 Mix together flour, margarine, sugar, salt, egg yolk and milk to form a smooth dough. Shape into a ball, wrap in cling film and refrigerate for 30 minutes

2 Roll out the pastry on the baking sheet, drawing pastry up 1 cm/½ inch above edge of sheet. Bake in an oven preheated to 225°C/425°F/Gas mark 7 for 10 minutes. Spread with cranberry jam. Drain plums and spread over pastry base.

3 Beat together eggs, egg white and sugar until thick and creamy. Finely grate the white bread. Combine with desiccated coconut, cinnamon, lemon zest and baking powder. Stir slowly into the egg and sugar mixture. Spread over the pastry base and bake in a preheated oven at 175°C/350°F/Gas mark 4 for 40 minutes or until done. Dust with icing sugar. *Makes 16 slices.*

# NUT LAYER GATEAU

**Ingredients for a gateau 20-22 cm/8-9 inches diam.**

**FOR THE PASTRY**

| |
|---|
| 300 g/11 oz flour |
| 200 g/7 oz icing sugar |
| 100 g/4 oz ground walnuts |
| 100 g/4 oz ground hazelnuts |
| 1 tbsp brandy |
| 200 g/7 oz margarine |
| flour for rolling out |

**FOR THE FILLING**

| |
|---|
| 1 sachet/approx. ½ oz vanilla sugar |
| 700 g/1 lb 9 oz double cream |

**FOR DECORATION**

| |
|---|
| 2-3 tbsp icing sugar |
| 3 tbsp flaked hazelnuts |

1 Mix flour, icing sugar, nuts, brandy and margarine to a smooth dough. Shape into 5 balls, wrap in cling film and refrigerate for 30 minutes.

2 Roll out each ball of pastry on baking parchment dusted with a little flour into a circle. Lay a dinner plate (20-22 cm diam./8-9 inches diam.) on each pastry circle and cut round it using a knife. Knead together pastry cuttings, refrigerate once more for a little while, then roll out again to form a sixth pastry circle.

3 Line a baking sheet with baking parchment. Place 1-2 pastry circles on baking sheet, removing paper on which they were rolled out.

4 Bake pastry circles in an oven preheated to 175°C/350°F/Gas mark 4 for 10-12 minutes until golden brown. Remove from baking sheet with baking parchment and leave to cool completely on a wire rack. Bake all 6 pastry circles in this way.

5 For filling, add vanilla sugar to cream and beat until stiff. Fill a piping bag with a large nozzle with cream. Pipe cream onto pastry circles. Layer cream and pastry alternately, finishing with a layer of cream.

6 Refrigerate gateau for 2-3 hours. Decorate with icing sugar and toasted flaked hazelnuts. *Makes 12 slices.*

# LINZER TARTLETS

**Ingredients for 8 individual tarts (250 ml capacity/approx. 2 pint capacity each)**

**FOR THE PASTRY**

350 g/12 oz unshelled almonds

350 g/12 oz flour

½ tsp grated lemon zest

½ tsp cinnamon

pinch ground cloves

200 g/7 oz caster sugar

2 egg yolks

250 g/9 oz margarine

margarine for greasing

commercial bread crumb mix for sprinkling

**FOR THE FILLING**

200 g/7 oz raspberry jam

1 egg yolk

2 tbsp icing sugar for dusting

1 Grind the almonds, mix with flour, lemon zest, cinnamon, cloves and sugar. Add egg yolk and margarine and knead to a smooth dough. Shape into a ball, wrap in cling film and refrigerate for 2 hours.

2 Grease tins and sprinkle with bread crumbs. Roll out ⅔ of dough and use to line tins. Spread raspberry jam on base of pastry.

3 Make thin sausages out of remaining dough, press flat, and lay over tarts in a lattice pattern. Beat the egg yolk and brush over pastry lattice.

4 Bake for 45-50 minutes in a preheated oven at 175°C/ 350°F/ Gas mark 4. Leave to cool slightly in the tins, then remove and leave to cool completely on a wire rack. Dust with icing sugar.

# SWISS VICARAGE TART

**Ingredients for a spring form tin (26 cm/10 inches diam.)**

**FOR THE PASTRY**

250 g/9 oz flour

125 g/5 oz margarine

60 g/2 oz caster sugar

1 egg

**FOR THE FILLING**

3 egg yolks • 150 g/6 oz caster sugar

1 tbsp lemon juice • 1 tbsp rum

5 apples (approx. 750 g/1 lb 11 oz)

3 egg whites • 30 g/1 oz flour

¼ tsp baking powder

200 g/7 oz ground almonds

margarine for greasing

1 tbsp icing sugar for dusting

1 Mix flour, margarine, sugar and egg. Shape into a ball, wrap in cling film and refrigerate for 30 minutes.

2 Roll out pastry. Line base and sides of tin. Bake at 225°C/425°F/ Gas mark 7 in a preheated oven for 15 minutes. Meanwhile beat the egg yolks and sugar until thick and creamy. Add lemon juice and rum. Peel 1 apple, halve, core and grate into egg mixture.

3 Beat egg whites until stiff. Fold into egg mixture with flour, baking powder and almonds, and spread mixture over pastry base. Peel, halve and core remaining apples, and cut each half into a fan shape. Arrange on almond mixture. Melt margarine and brush over tart. Bake for 60 minutes in a preheated oven at 175-200°C/350-400°F/Gas mark 4–6. Dust with icing sugar while still hot. *Makes 12 portions.*

# YOGHURT CREAM SLICES

| Ingredients for a square tin |
|---|
| (approx. 26 x 26 cm/10 x 10 inches) |
| 150 g/6 oz flour |
| 80 g/3 oz ground almonds |
| ½ tsp baking powder |
| 150 g/6 oz margarine |
| 80 g/3 oz caster sugar |
| pinch salt |
| 1 egg |
| 300 g/11 oz frozen raspberries |
| 450 g/1 lb yoghurt |
| 150 g/6 oz caster sugar |
| pinch salt |
| 1 tsp grated lemon zest |
| 75 ml/3 fl. oz lemon juice |
| 2 tbsp raspberry brandy |
| 6 leaves white gelatine |
| 250 g/9 oz double cream |
| 125 ml/4 fl. oz raspberry juice |
| ½ sachet clear glaze or ¼ oz arrowroot |

1 Mix the flour, almonds, baking powder, margarine, sugar, salt and egg to a smooth dough in a food processor or using the dough hook of a hand mixer. Shape into a ball, wrap in cling film and refrigerate for 1 hour.

2 Roll out pastry between cling film to size of tin, and use to line

base and sides of tin. Bake for 25 minutes in a preheated oven at 200°C/400°F/Gas mark 6.

3 Thaw the raspberries. Mix together yoghurt, sugar, salt, lemon zest, lemon juice and raspberry brandy. Soften gelatine in cold water, drain and melt over a low heat, then stir into yoghurt mixture. Beat cream until stiff and fold into yoghurt. Spread ⅔ raspberries over the pastry base, spread yoghurt crème over raspberries. Decorate the slices with remaining raspberries. Make a glaze from the raspberry juice and glaze mix or arrowroot and use to decorate slices. *Makes 16 slices.*

# SUMMER GATEAU

| Ingredients for a spring form tin |
|---|
| (24 cm /9 inches diam.) |
| 50 g/2 oz hazelnuts |
| 150 g/6 oz flour |
| 100 g/4 oz cornflour |
| pinch salt |
| 50 g/2 oz icing sugar |
| 150 g/6 oz margarine |
| 2 egg yolks |
| 65 g/2 oz caster sugar |
| 2 egg whites |
| 50 g/2 oz flour |
| 25 g/1 oz cornflour |
| 4 tbsp blackcurrant jelly |
| 750 g/1 lb 11 oz seasonal berries |
| 50 g/2 oz sugar |
| 1 sachet instant raspberry jelly |
| 150 ml/¼ pint white wine |
| 50 g/2 oz sugar |
| 150 g/6 oz crème fraiche |
| 250 g/9 oz double cream |
| 1 sachet/approx. ½ oz vanilla sugar |
| 4 tbsp flaked almonds |

1 Toast and grind hazelnuts, mix with flour and cornflour. Add salt, icing sugar and margarine and knead to a smooth dough. Shape into a ball, wrap in cling film and refrigerate for 30 minutes.

2 Roll out dough and line base of tin. Bake in a preheated oven at 200°C/400°F/Gas mark 6 for 10-12 minutes. Meanwhile, beat egg yolks, 2 tbsp warm water and sugar until thick and creamy. Beat the egg whites until stiff and fold into egg yolk mixture. Mix the flour and cornflour and sieve onto egg mixture. Fold in.

3 Mix the blackcurrant jelly with 1 tsp hot water until smooth and brush over pastry base while still warm. Put the egg mixture onto the base and bake for a further 12-15 minutes at 200°C/400°F/Gas mark 6.

4 Sprinkle sugar over berries. Prepare the jelly mix with white wine, 150 ml/¼ pint water and sugar according to instructions on packet. Leave to thicken slightly. Take 150 ml/¼ pint from jelly mixture and mix with crème fraiche. Spread over base and allow to set. Mix the berries with the remaining jelly and spread over gateau.

5 Beat the cream with the vanilla sugar until stiff. Spread over sides of gateau. Toast the flaked almonds until golden brown and scatter over sides of gateau.

*Makes 10-12 slices.*

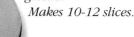

# CREAMY CHEESECAKE

| Ingredients for a spring form tin (24 cm/9 inches diam.) |
| --- |
| **FOR THE PASTRY** |
| **150 g/6 oz flour** |
| **75 g/3 oz margarine** |
| **30 g/1 oz caster sugar** |
| **pinch salt** |
| **1 egg yolk** |
| **1 tbsp milk** |
| **FOR THE FILLING** |
| **3 egg yolks** |
| **150 g/6 oz caster sugar** |
| **1 sachet/approx. ½ oz vanilla sugar** |
| **500 g/1 lb 2 oz 20% fat curd cheese or quark** |
| **8 leaves white gelatine** |
| **4 egg whites** |
| **250 g/9 oz double cream** |
| **200 g/7 oz berries (e.g. blueberries and whitecurrants)** |
| **1 tbsp ground pistachio nuts** |

1 Mix flour, margarine, sugar, salt, 1 egg yolk and milk to a smooth dough. Shape into a ball, wrap in cling film and refrigerate for 30 minutes.

2 Roll out dough and place on tin base. Cut round edge. Bake in a preheated oven at 200-225°C/400-425°F/Gas mark 6–7 for 20 minutes. Leave to cool, place on a cake plate and place sides of spring form tin on top.

3 Beat egg yolks, sugar and vanilla sugar until frothy. Fold in curd cheese. Soften gelatine in cold water, drain, melt over a low heat and stir into cheese mixture.

In separate bowls beat egg whites and cream until stiff and fold into cheese mixture.

4 Pour the mixture onto the pastry base and leave to set in refrigerator. Before serving, use a knife to loosen the cheesecake from the sides of the tin and remove tin. Cover top of cheesecake with fresh fruit and decorate sides with ground pistachio nuts.

*Makes 10-12 slices.*

# CINNAMON CAKE

| Ingredients for a spring form tin (26 cm/10 inches diam.) |
| --- |
| FOR THE PASTRY |
| 250 g/9 oz flour |
| 65 g/2 oz caster sugar |
| pinch salt |
| 125 g/5 oz margarine |
| FOR THE FILLING |
| 3 eggs |
| 125 g/5 oz double cream |
| 125 ml/4 fl. oz milk |
| 4 slices French toast |
| 50 g/2 oz candied lemon peel |
| 150 g/6 oz caster sugar |
| pinch salt |
| 200 g/7 oz ground almonds or hazelnuts |
| 1½ tbsp cinnamon |
| 1½ tsp baking powder |
| FOR SPRINKLING |
| 1 tbsp each cinnamon and icing sugar |
| 2 tbsp flaked hazelnuts |

1 Mix flour, sugar, salt and margarine to a smooth dough. Shape into a ball, wrap in cling film and refrigerate for 30 minutes.

2 Roll out pastry and use to line tin. Prick all over with a fork and bake in a preheated oven at 175-200°C/350-400°F/Gas mark 4–6 for 10 minutes.

3 Whisk together eggs, cream and milk. Put French toast in a freezer bag and crush to bread crumbs with a rolling pin. Finely chop the candied lemon peel and mix into egg and cream mixture with rest of ingredients.

4 Pour the filling over the pastry base. Bake in a preheated oven at 175-200°C/350-400°F/Gas mark 4–6 for a further 40 minutes. Sprinkle cinnamon, icing sugar and flaked nuts over cake. *Makes 12 slices.*

# BAKED CHEESE CAKE

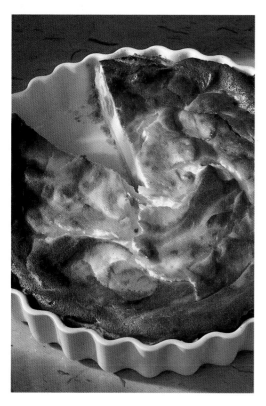

| Ingredients for a pie dish or spring form tin (26 cm/10 inches diam.) |
| --- |
| FOR THE PASTRY |
| 250 g/9 oz flour |
| pinch salt |
| 50 g/2 oz icing sugar |
| 125 g/5 oz margarine |
| 1 egg |
| 150 g/6 oz dried pulses for baking blind |
| FOR THE FILLING |
| 50 g/2 oz margarine |
| 750 g/1 lb 11 oz curd cheese or quark (20% fat) |
| 200 g/7 oz caster sugar |
| ½ tsp grated lemon zest |
| 2 tbsp lemon juice |
| 3 egg yolks |
| 75 g/3 oz dried apricots |
| 40 g/2 oz cornflour |
| 3 egg whites |

1 Mix together flour, salt, icing sugar, margarine and egg to form a smooth dough. Shape into a ball, wrap in cling film and refrigerate for 30 minutes.

2 Roll out pastry and use to line tin. Lay baking parchment over pastry and spread dried pulses over paper, Bake blind in a preheated oven at 200-225°C/400-425°F/Gas mark 6–7 for 10 minutes. Then remove pulses and bake for a further 5 minutes.

3 Melt margarine. Mix together with curd cheese, sugar, lemon zest, lemon juice and egg yolks. Chop the apricots into small pieces, mix with cornflour and stir into cheese mixture. Beat the egg whites until stiff and fold into cheese.

4 Pour over pastry base and bake for 55 minutes in an oven preheated to 175°C/350°F/Gas mark 4. When baking time is complete, turn off oven and leave cheesecake in oven with the door open for about 10 minutes, then take out of oven and leave to cool in tin. *Makes 12 slices.*

# FRENCH APPLE TART

**Ingredients for a flan tin or spring form tin (26 cm/10 inches diam.)**

**FOR THE PASTRY**

200 g/7 oz flour

1 tsp caster sugar

pinch salt

150 g/6 oz margarine

1 egg yolk

**FOR THE TOPPING**

500 g/1 lb 2 oz cooking apples

margarine for greasing

1 egg yolk

3 tbsp apricot jam

1 Mix flour, sugar, salt, margarine and egg yolk to a smooth dough. Shape into a ball, wrap in cling film and refrigerate for 30 minutes.

2 Meanwhile peel, halve and core apples and slice thinly. Grease flan tin or spring form tin with margarine. Roll out dough and use to line tin.

3 Position the apple slices in overlapping layers on the pastry, working in a circle from the centre to edge of the tin. Brush the tart with egg yolk and bake in a preheated oven at 200°C/400°F/ Gas mark 6 for 50-60 minutes.

4 Mix the apricot jam with 1 tbsp water until smooth and warm slightly. About 10 minutes before the tart is cooked, brush with jam and continue baking. *Makes 12 slices.*

MICROWAVE TIP: The apricot jam can be warmed up in the microwave for 30 seconds at 600-700 watts.

TIP: Tart and flan pastry is so short it melts in the mouth, and it can also easily crumble when removing the tart from the tin. For this reason special flan tins have a loose base.

# ALMOND SHORTBREAD BISCUITS

| Ingredients for about 60 biscuits |
| --- |
| 100 g/4 oz almonds |
| 200 g/7 oz flour |
| pinch salt |
| 100 g/4 oz icing sugar |
| 125 g/5 oz margarine |
| 2 egg yolks |
| 1 drop almond essence |
| flour for rolling out |

1 Pour boiling water over the almonds, leave to stand for a few minutes, tip into a sieve and blanch with cold water. Remove kernels from shells, spread out and leave to dry. Finally, grind very finely in an almond mill or food processor.

2 Place almonds, flour, salt, icing sugar and margarine in a bowl. Mix the egg yolks with the almond essence, add to the flour and knead everything to a smooth dough. Shape into a ball, wrap in cling film and refrigerate for 30 minutes.

3 Line a baking sheet with baking parchment. Divide the dough into portions and roll out on a lightly floured surface to the thickness of the back of a knife. Cut out biscuits and place on baking sheet.

4 Bake in a preheated oven at 200°C/400°F/Gas mark 6 for 10-12 minutes. Leave to cool on a wire rack. To keep the biscuits fresh, store in a tin.

VARIATION: The pastry can easily be flavoured with a little grated orange or lemon zest.

# ORANGE COOKIES

**Ingredients for approx. 40 cookies**

**FOR THE DOUGH**

125 g/5 oz margarine

75 g/3 oz caster sugar

2 egg yolks

2 tsp grated orange zest

1 tbsp orange juice

pinch salt

250 g/9 oz flour

¼ tsp baking powder

margarine for greasing

**FOR THE ICING**

100 g/4 oz icing sugar

1 tsp grated orange zest

1-2 tbsp orange juice

1 Beat the margarine, sugar and egg yolks until creamy. Add orange zest, orange juice and salt. Mix the flour and baking powder and sieve into egg mixture. Knead everything into a smooth dough. Shape into a ball, wrap in cling film and refrigerate for 30 minutes.

2 Grease a baking sheet with margarine. Roll out dough until about 3 mm thick/approx. ¼ inch. Cut out cookies, place on baking sheet and bake in a pre-heated oven at 200°C/400°F/Gas mark 6 for 10-12 minutes.

3 To make the icing, mix together the icing sugar, orange zest and orange juice. Spread over warm cookies.

VARIATION: Lemon cookies can also be made using this recipe. Orange zest and juice are simply replaced by lemon zest and lemon juice.

TIP: The pastry should be kneaded and worked very quickly, otherwise the pastry will easily tear when you are cutting out the cookies because it will be too soft and warm.

# NOUGAT SANDWICH BISCUITS

**Ingredients for 10 biscuits**

**FOR THE PASTRY**

200 g/7 oz flour

50 g/2 oz ground hazelnuts

½ tsp ground ginger

½ tsp grated lemon zest

60 g/2 oz caster sugar

pinch salt

125 g/5 oz margarine

1 egg

**FOR THE FILLING**

400 g/14 oz nut nougat creme (Nutella or similar)

1 tbsp chopped pistachio nuts

10 whole hazelnuts

1 Mix the flour with the ground hazelnuts, ginger, lemon zest, sugar, salt, margarine and egg to a smooth dough. Shape into a ball, wrap in cling film and refrigerate for 1 hour.

2 Meanwhile heat the nougat in a bain-marie until smooth and creamy. Remove from heat and leave to cool.

3 Roll out pastry on baking parchment to just 3 mm/approx. ¼ inch thick, and cut out 20 rounds 8 cm/approx. 3 inches in diameter. It is best to use a metal pastry cutter for this, but you can also use a glass or cup.

4 Line a baking sheet with baking parchment. Place the biscuits on the sheet. Bake in a preheated oven at 225°C/425°F/Gas mark 7 for 10-12 minutes. Leave to cool on a wire rack.

5 Put the nougat in a piping bag with a star-shaped nozzle. Reserve some nougat for decoration and pipe the rest onto half of the biscuits, topping the nougat with another biscuit. Pipe a nougat star onto the top of each sandwich. Decorate with sprinkled pistachio nuts and a whole hazelnut.

TIP: Children love cakes which they can hold in their hands to eat. You can also fill the sandwich biscuits with jam, jelly, apple or nut purée. Whatever the filling the sandwich biscuits will keep for up to 3 weeks in the refrigerator if wrapped in cling film.

# MADEIRA BISCUITS

| Ingredients for about 60 biscuits |
| --- |
| 350 g/12 oz margarine |
| 150 g/6 oz sugar |
| pinch salt |
| 1 sachet/approx. ½ oz vanilla sugar |
| 500 g/1 lb 2 oz flour |
| margarine for greasing |
| 1 egg yolk |
| 5 tbsp caster sugar |

1 Beat together margarine, sugar, salt and vanilla sugar until creamy. Add flour and knead to a smooth dough. Shape the dough into 4 cm/12 inch thick sausages, wrap in cling film and refrigerate for 30 minutes.

2 Cut the dough sausages into 4 mm/4 inch thick slices. Grease a baking sheet, lay the slices of dough on the sheet and bake in a preheated oven at 200°C/400°F/Gas mark 6 for 10-15 minutes. Leave the biscuits to cool a little.

3 Beat the egg yolk. Dredge the biscuits first in egg yolk, then in sugar. Leave to cool completely on a wire rack. Store in a tin.

# ITALIAN ALMOND BISCUITS

| Ingredients for approx. 100 biscuits |
| --- |
| 500 g/1 lb 2 oz flour |
| 3 eggs |
| 100 g/4 oz margarine |
| 400 g/14 oz caster sugar |
| 1 sachet/approx. ½ oz vanilla sugar |
| 2 tbsp grated lemon zest |
| 200 g/7 oz chopped almonds |
| 100 g/4 oz whole almonds |

1 Mix flour, eggs, margarine, sugar, vanilla sugar, lemon zest and chopped almonds to a smooth dough. Finally mix in the whole almonds. Divide the dough into 3 portions and shape each portion into a sausage approx. 3 cm/1 inch across. Wrap in cling film and refrigerate for 30 minutes.

2 Line a baking sheet with baking parchment or grease thoroughly. Remove cling film from dough, place on baking sheet and bake in a preheated oven at 175°C/350°F/Gas mark 4 for 15-20 minutes.

3 Leave to cool and cut into slices approx. 1 cm/½ inch thick. Put the almond biscuits back on the baking sheet and bake at the same temperature for a further 15-20 minutes until golden brown. The almond biscuits are done when they are very crisp.

# SHORTBREAD

**Ingredients for a large shortbread round (approx. 28 cm/approx. 11 inches diam.)**

| |
|---|
| 50 g/2 oz almonds |
| 150 g/6 oz margarine |
| 150 g/6 oz sugar |
| pinch salt |
| 25 g/1 oz cornflour |
| 200 g/7 oz flour |
| 1-2 sachets/approx. ½ -1 oz vanilla sugar |

1 Pour boiling water over the almonds, leave to stand for a little while, rinse with cold water and remove from shells. Grind in an almond mill.

2 Beat the margarine and sugar together until creamy. Mix the ground almonds with the salt, cornflour and flour and add to margarine and egg mixture. Knead all the ingredients to a smooth dough. Shape into a ball, wrap in cling film and refrigerate for 30 minutes.

3 Line a baking sheet with baking parchment. Roll out dough on sheet to form a circle approx. 28 cm/11 inches across. Mark 16 portions on the dough with the back of a knife and crimp the edge.

4 Prick all over with a fork and bake in a preheated oven at 175°C/350°F/Gas mark 4 for about 35 minutes until light golden brown. Remove from oven and sprinkle with vanilla sugar straight away.
*Makes 16 slices.*

TIP: Wrap the shortbread in cling film or place in a tin which closes tightly and store in a cool place. It will stay fresh for at least 3 weeks.

# VEGETABLE TARTS

| Ingredients for 8 tart tins |
| --- |
| (8 cm/ 3 inches diam.) |
| **FOR THE PASTRY** |
| 250 g/9 oz flour |
| 100 g/4 oz margarine |
| 1 tsp salt |
| 1 tsp vinegar |
| **FOR THE TOPPING** |
| 150 g/6 oz leeks |
| 150 g/6 oz red pepper |
| 150 g/6 oz carrots |
| 2 tbsp olive oil |
| 1 clove garlic |
| salt, pepper |
| paprika |
| margarine for greasing |
| ½ bunch thyme |

1 Mix flour, margarine, salt, vinegar and 100 ml water/approx. 3 fl. oz to a smooth dough. Shape into a ball, wrap in cling film and refrigerate for 30 minutes.

2 Meanwhile wash and clean leeks and red peppers. Cut the leeks into rings, dice the red pepper. Clean the carrots, wash and dice finely. Fry the vegetables in oil for 5 minutes. Peel the garlic, crush and add to vegetables. Season with salt, pepper and paprika.

3 Roll out pastry. Grease tin and line with pastry, drawing pastry up sides of tin. Bake in a preheated oven at 225°C/425°F/Gas mark 7 for 8-10 minutes.

4 Spread vegetables over tarts. Sprinkle with thyme and bake at 225°C/425°F/Gas mark 7 for a further 10-15 minutes.

VARIATION: You can make a large tart instead of several small ones. For this you will need a 28 cm diameter/11 inch flan tin or spring form tin, and you will have to extend the cooking time to about 25 minutes for the filled tarts.

# TUSCAN MEAT PIE

| Ingredients for a loaf tin |
| --- |
| (30 cm long, 2 l capacity/12 inches |
| long, 3½ pints capacity) |
| **FOR THE PASTRY** |
| 250 g/9 oz flour |
| 2 tsp baking powder |
| 75 g/3 oz margarine |
| ½ tsp salt |
| 100 ml/approx. 3 fl. oz milk |
| margarine for greasing |
| **FOR THE FILLING** |
| 100 g/4 oz Parma ham in strips |
| 1 large onion |
| 1 tsp margarine |
| 2 tbsp pine kernels |
| 2 cloves garlic |
| 1 apple (about 100 g/about 4 oz) |
| 500 g/1 lb 2 oz minced meat (pork, beef) |
| 1 tbsp tomato ketchup |
| 2 tbsp sultanas |
| ½ tsp grated lemon zest |
| salt and pepper |
| 1 tbsp fresh rosemary • 1 egg yolk |

1 Mix the flour, baking powder, margarine, salt and milk together. Shape dough into a ball, wrap in cling film, refrigerate for 30 minutes.

2 Grease the tin. Roll out ¾ of pastry and line tin so that the edge of the pastry covers the edge of the tin. Cover the pastry base with the slices of ham. Peel and chop onion, fry in margarine and spread over ham.

3 Chop pine kernels, peel garlic and crush. Peel, core and grate apple. Mix everything thoroughly with all other ingredients (except egg yolk) and place in tin.

4 Beat egg yolk and brush edge of pastry with half the beaten egg. Roll out rest of pastry, cut out a lid, place on top of meat mixture and fold over edges. Prick all over with a fork and brush with remaining egg yolk. Bake in a preheated oven at 200-225°C/400-425°F/Gas mark 6–7 for 45-55 minutes.
*Makes 18-20 slices.*

# FARMER'S PASTY

**Ingredients for a ring mould**
**(approx. 24 cm diam., 2.5 l capacity/**
**approx. 9 inches diam., 4¼ pints capacity)**

250 g/9 oz flour

1 tbsp herbes de Provence

250 g/9 oz low fat curd cheese or quark

½ tsp salt • 200 g/7 oz margarine

1 onion (50g)/2 oz]

1 courgette (100g)/4 oz]

2 tomatoes (150g)/6 oz]

100g/4 oz mushrooms

1 tsp margarine

salt and freshly milled black pepper

100g/4 oz firm liver paté

1 bread roll • 500 g/1 lb 2 oz veal

1 egg • ½ tsp dried marjoram

2 tbsp mild mustard • 1 bunch chives

1 Mix flour, herbs, curd cheese, salt and margarine to a smooth dough. Shape into a ball, wrap in cling film and refrigerate for 1 hour.

2 Peel onion, wash courgette and tomatoes and clean, remove seeds from tomatoes. Finely dice all 3 vegetables. Clean mushrooms and slice. Gently fry

vegetables in margarine for 5 minutes, season with salt and pepper, leave to cool.

3 Dice liver paté and mix with vegetables. Soften the bread roll in water. Finely chop or mince the meat. Squeeze liquid out of bread roll and knead together with meat and vegetable mixture.

4 Roll pastry out between cling film. Grease the tin, line with pastry so that it hangs over edges of tin. Fill tin with meat mixture. Fold excess pastry over top of meat and crimp together firmly. Prick all over with a fork. Bake in a preheated oven at 200°C/400°F/ Gas mark 6 for 55-60 minutes. Remove from tin and serve hot or cold. *Makes 16 slices.*

# PIQUANT CHEESECAKE

**Ingredients for a spring form tin**
**(26 cm/10 inches diam.)**

150 g/6 oz flour • 1 egg white

160 g/6 oz margarine • ½ tsp salt

400 g/14 oz full fat cream cheese

100 g/4 oz crème fraiche

250 g/9 oz low fat curd cheese or quark

1 egg yolk • 1 clove garlic, salt

2 bunches parsley • 1 bunch dill

1 bunch chives • 1 onion • salt • pepper

250 g/9 oz pumpernickel or other dark bread

450 g/1 lb tomatoes • 10 slices salami

12 stuffed olives

3 spicy pickled gherkins (approx. 100 g)/4 oz]

1 Mix flour, egg white, 60 g/2 oz margarine, 1 tbsp water and salt to a smooth dough. Shape into a ball, wrap in cling film and refrigerate for 30 minutes.

2 Roll out pastry and line base of tin. Prick all over with a fork and bake in a preheated oven at 200°C/400°F/Gas mark 6 for 10 minutes. Leave to cool on a wire rack.

3 Beat the remaining margarine until creamy. Add cream cheese, crème fraiche, curd cheese and

egg yolk. Finely crush garlic with salt. Finely chop herbs (reserve a few parsley leaves for garnish), dice onion and add to cheese mixture. Season with salt and pepper and mix well.

4 Make bread crumbs with pumpernickel (a food processor is best for this) and spread over the pastry base. Pile cheese mixture on top and finish with another layer of bread crumbs. Wash tomatoes, cut in 8 pieces and arrange on top of cheesecake with remaining ingredients. Refrigerate for 3-4 hours.
*Makes 10-12 slices.*

FATLESS SPONGE

# A marriage of fresh eggs and air

The secret of a successful fatless sponge is tempo. If you wield your balloon whisk with vigour and skill, eggs and air combine in an intimate relationship which is the basis for the importance of this speciality in confectionery, whether it is as the base for a fruit flan, whether filled or rolled or combined with carrots to make moist carrot cake.

Strawberry and cream gateau. Recipe on page 124.

# HOW TO MAKE SUCCESSFUL FATLESS SPONGE

Fatless sponges should be airy, simple and light – and therefore flour and fat are not so important for the preparation of this cake mixture. The main protagonists in fatless sponges are eggs and a great deal of air! Everything revolves around whisking as much air as possible into the mixture.

It is best to whisk egg yolks and egg whites separately, as this makes the resulting baking particularly light. If you are using a powerful food processor, however, then you don't need to separate the eggs but can beat them together with the sugar in one step. The sponge will then be a little more elastic and less airy.

A basic fatless sponge contains only four ingredients – 4 size 3 eggs, 125 g/5 oz caster sugar, 75 g/3 oz flour and 50 g/2 oz cornflour. A slightly richer version also requires 50 g/2 oz melted fat. If you use this recipe the sponge stays fresh a couple of days longer and tastes moister. In order to make Chocolate Sponge replace roughly a quarter of the flour with cocoa powder; for Nut Sponge use finely ground nuts instead of some of the flour. If you can manage with only a tablespoon of flour and cornflour and otherwise just use nuts, the resulting sponge will be very fine.

**1** Fatless Sponge: Whisk egg whites in a food processor until stiff. Gradually add the sugar in a trickle and continue whisking until the egg whites form very stiff peaks and are creamy.

**2** Add the egg yolks to the egg whites and mix in briefly. Don't mix for too long or the egg whites will collapse and the beaten-in air will disappear. When baked the sponge will then turn out flat and tough.

**6** Heat the margarine for the sponge mixture in a pan. Leave the fat to cool a little, then pour into the egg mixture, whisking all the time. The margarine and egg and sugar mixture will then form a smooth custard.

**7** Whisk egg whites until very stiff and place on top of the egg yolk mixture. You can also add a pinch of salt at this stage.

**3** Sieve flour and cornflour into the foaming egg mixture and lightly fold in using a plastic spatula. You shouldn't stir the mixture too hard at this stage either, as you need to retain as much air as possible in the mixture.

**4** For a Rich Sponge Mixture, using fat, place the egg yolks and 1 tbsp water per yolk in a bowl. Whisk the egg yolks with a large balloon whisk or a hand mixer until creamy.

**5** Gradually add the caster sugar, whisking mixture all the time. Continue whisking until the mixture is thick and pale.

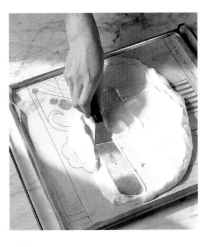

**8** Mix the flour and cornflour together and sieve onto the egg whites. If you want to make absolutely certain that the sponge will be really light, you can also add a pinch of baking powder.

**9** Gently fold in the flour and cornflour using a plastic spatula. You can also use a large balloon whisk. It is very important that you don't stir the mixture, but gently and evenly work through it until the egg whites and flour are incorporated.

**10** Pour the sponge mix onto a prepared baking sheet and spread flat using a palette knife, or pour into a prepared spring form tin. You shouldn't grease the sides of the tin, otherwise the mixture will slide off.

# FATLESS SPONGE

## GOOD TOOLS
■ The airy light structure of fatless sponge cries out for fillings and toppings. In short, fatless sponges are the ideal base for gateaux, and such works of art will turn out best with good tools.

## CAKE RING
■ If you bake a lot of cakes, you should acquire an adjustable stainless steel or plastic cake ring. Place the ring on top of the sponge base, fill with custard, whipped cream and further layers of sponge as desired, smooth over and refrigerate. Later, loosen the set fillings from around the edge of the ring, remove the ring, and you will be left with a perfectly shaped gateau with a smooth edge.

## CAKE DIVIDER
■ To divide a cake into even portions you either need a very good eye or a plastic/aluminium cake divider. A divider also helps when decorating gateaux, because if you press the plastic ribs down lightly on cream, it shows the correct portions and thus indicates where you can pipe cream rosettes. N.B.: gateaux with soft fillings should be cut into larger slices.

## CAKE BOARD
■ Use your cake board to prevent disasters overtaking your cut sponge base or finished gateau. A metal or plastic board will slip easily under the base of your cake and will keep the cake stable when you are moving it.

**Spread the sponge mixture evenly with an angled palette knife.**

## FATLESS SPONGE BASE
■ When rolled up it becomes a Swiss roll, when stacked up it is a layered cake. As a fatless sponge only takes 10 to 12 minutes to cook, it is ideal for making quick cakes, but many people avoid these recipes because the flat sheet of sponge breaks easily when layered with filling. Two simple tricks will help prevent disasters. Before baking spread the sponge mixture as evenly as possible on the baking sheet. If there are thin patches the sponge will become too hard when baked and will break easily. Also don't bake this type of sponge for a moment longer than necessary. Two or three minutes before the cake should be done, tap gently with your fingers on the surface of the cake. If it isn't sticky, take the baking sheet out of the oven. The sponge will still be sufficiently moist and elastic to roll up beautifully.

**Practical baking aids: adjustable stainless steel cake ring , round metal cake board , cake divider and angled palette knife**

## THE TRICK TO SWISS ROLLS

■ A baked sponge should be turned out onto and rolled up in a sugared tea towel so it can be shaped into a roll easily, or you can use a large sheet of baking parchment. Use paper which is coated on both sides so that nothing can stick to it. After the sponge has cooled unroll it and spread with filling desired. The paper should not be removed from underneath the sponge. Then all you have to do is pick up one edge of the sponge with both hands, lift it slightly, and the sponge will roll up on its own.

Turn the layer of fatless sponge out onto a large sheet of baking parchment, paper side uppermost. Brush the top of the paper with water and gently pull off sponge. Roll up the layer of sponge together with the bottom layer of clean paper and leave to cool.

## BASIC SWISS ROLL

If you just want to fill a Swiss roll with jam, the sponge doesn't need to be left to cool. It is quite all right to spread the hot sponge cake with jam, roll up, then leave to cool and serve immediately.

## NON-STICK

Because this type of sponge contains little or no fat, it has a tendency to stick to the tin, so the base of a spring form tin should be lined with baking parchment as a precaution. Place a piece of paper over the tin base, place the sides of the tin on top and close. In this way the paper is held tight and you can easily tear off the superfluous paper. When the sponge is baked, loosen the edges of the cake from the tin with a knife and remove sides of tin. Leave the sponge to cool a little, turn out and remove paper. Warning – never grease the sides of a spring form tin when baking fatless sponges, otherwise the mixture will slip off the sides and your lovely smooth sponge base will have a bumpy middle.

## CUTTING BASES

Crafty cake lovers use a knife with a long, thin blade which will cut evenly through fatless sponge without difficulty. The blade must be at least 25 cm/10 inches long so that it reaches right through the width of the sponge base. Alternatively you can use a cheese wire, wrapping it around the cake at the desired height and pulling both ends tight. The wire won't cut the light sponge as cleanly and with as few crumbs as a sharp knife, but the individual layers of sponge will be even in size.

Cutting sponge bases: with a long bladed knife or with a cheese wire.

## LIGHT CAKES

If you prefer gateaux which are made with little sponge, you can layer several different fillings on top of a sponge base. Use a cake ring and fill with fruit or curd cheese fillings stiffened with gelatine (see recipe on page 216, for example). Each layer must be allowed to set before the next one is added so that the individual layers don't run together.

How to make successful multi-layered cakes: leave each layer of filling to set, then add the next layer.

# CHERRY GATEAU

**Ingredients for a spring form tin (26 cm diam., 2.5 l capacity/10 inches diam., 4¼ pints capacity)**

| |
|---|
| **FOR THE SPONGE** |
| 30 g/1 oz soft margarine |
| 6 eggs |
| 150 g/6 oz caster sugar |
| 1 sachet/approx. ½ oz vanilla sugar |
| 225 g/8 oz flour |
| ¼ tsp baking powder |
| **FOR THE FILLING** |
| 8 leaves white gelatine |
| 750 g/1 lb 11 oz cherries |
| 300 g/11 oz low fat curd cheese or quark |
| 3 tbsp icing sugar |
| 1 tsp grated lemon zest |
| 3 tbsp lemon juice |
| 500 g/1 lb 2 oz double cream |
| 50 g/2 oz chopped almonds |

1 Melt margarine and leave to cool. Separate eggs. Whisk egg yolks with sugar and vanilla sugar until thick and creamy. Stir in margarine. Whisk egg whites until stiff and add to egg yolk mixture. Sieve flour and baking powder onto egg whites and fold everything into egg mixture.

2 Line the base of a spring form tin with baking parchment. Fill the tin with the sponge mixture and bake in a preheated oven at 200°C/400°F/Gas mark 6 for about 25 minutes. Leave to cool in tin. Cut the base into 3 layers.

3 Soften gelatine. Wash cherries, reserve 12. Remove stalks and stones from remaining cherries. Mix curd cheese with icing sugar, lemon zest and juice. Melt the dripping wet gelatine over a low heat and stir into cheese mixture. Whisk cream until stiff and fold into cheese mixture.

4 Remove about ⅓ of the cheese mixture. Stir the cherries into the rest of the cheese. Spread cherry cream over 2 of the sponge layers and place one on top of the other. Place the 3rd layer on top of the layer of cherry cream. Spread the remaining cheese mixture over the top and sides of the gateau, forming peaks on the top. Decorate with reserved cherries.

5 Toast the almonds, leave to cool and sprinkle over sides of gateau. *Makes 12 slices.*

# STRAWBERRY AND CREAM GATEAU

**Ingredients for spring form tin (20 cm diam., 1 l capacity/8 inches diam., 1 pint capacity)**

| |
|---|
| **FOR THE SPONGE** |
| 40 g/2 oz soft margarine |
| 4 eggs |
| 200 g/7 oz caster sugar |
| 1 sachet/approx. ½ oz vanilla sugar |
| pinch salt |
| 100 g/4 oz flour |
| 100 g/4 oz cornflour |
| ½ tsp baking powder |
| **FOR THE FILLING** |
| 600 g/1 lb 5 oz strawberries |
| 600 g/1 lb 5 oz double cream |
| 3 sachets/approx. 1½ oz vanilla sugar |

1 Melt margarine and leave to cool. Separate eggs. Whisk yolks, 4 tbsp warm water, sugar and vanilla sugar until thick and creamy. Stir margarine into egg yolks. Whisk whites together with salt until stiff and spoon onto yolk mixture. Mix together flour, cornflour and baking powder, sieve onto whites and fold everything into egg yolk mixture.

2 Line tin with baking parchment. Leave a 4 cm/1½ inch border above top of tin. Fill with mixture and bake in a preheated oven at 175°C/350°F/ Gas mark 4 for 50 minutes. Slice cake into 3 layers.

3 Wash strawberries. Reserve about 15 berries, then purée 100 g/4 oz strawberries and spread over 2 of the bases. Halve the remaining fruit. Whisk cream and vanilla sugar together until stiff. Spread about ⅓ of cream over the cake layers which have been spread with strawberry purée, then arrange halved strawberries on cream. Place layers of cake on top of each other, finishing with 3rd layer of sponge.

4 Place 5 tbsp cream in a piping bag with a round nozzle. Cover gateau with remaining cream. Pipe a cream rosette around the top of the gateau and garnish with reserved strawberries. Refrigerate for 1 hour. *Makes 8 slices.*

# INDIVIDUAL FRUIT FLANS

**Ingredients for 12 individual flan tins
(each 10 cm diam./4 inches diam.)**

**FOR THE SPONGE**

50 g/2 oz soft margarine

4 eggs

125 g/5 oz caster sugar

pinch salt

75 g/3 oz flour

50 g/2 oz cornflour

pinch baking powder

margarine for greasing

flour for dusting

**FOR THE TOPPING**

250 g/9 oz redcurrants

250 g/9 oz blueberries

250 g/9 oz raspberries

200 g/7 oz redcurrant jelly

1 tbsp raspberry brandy

1 Melt margarine in a pan and leave to cool a little. Separate the eggs. Whisk egg yolks with 4 tbsp warm water until thick and creamy, using a large balloon whisk or a hand mixer. Gradually add sugar in a trickle and continue whisking until egg mixture looks like pale custard. Slowly pour margarine into egg mixture and stir in thoroughly.

2 Whisk egg whites with salt until very stiff and spoon onto egg mixture. Mix together flour, cornflour and baking powder, sieve over the egg whites and lightly fold in all the ingredients using a plastic spatula.

3 Grease the base and sides of the flan tins with margarine and dust with flour. Fill each flan tin with about 2 tbsp sponge mixture. Bake in a preheated oven at 200°C/400°F /Gas mark 6 for 12-

15 minutes. Remove from oven, leave to stand for approx. 3 minutes, then remove from tins. Leave to cool on a wire rack.

4 For the filling sort the berries, wash carefully and pat dry with absorbent kitchen paper. Heat jelly in a small pan over a low heat until liquid. Stir in raspberry brandy. There shouldn't be any bubbles when you do this; otherwise they make the jelly look dull.

5 Brush a little jelly onto each sponge flan base so the sponge doesn't become soggy. Top each flan case generously with fruit, pour the remaining jelly over the fruit and refrigerate for about 30 minutes.

# RASPBERRY SLICES

**Ingredients for 12 slices**
**FOR THE SPONGE**
100 g/4 oz good quality bitter chocolate
20 g/1 oz soft margarine
4 eggs
125 g/5 oz caster sugar
pinch salt
100 g/4 oz flour
50 g/2 oz cornflour
½ tsp baking powder
**FOR THE FILLING**
5 leaves white gelatine
500 g/1 lb 2 oz raspberries (frozen raspberries can be used)
75-100 g/3-4 oz caster sugar
500 g/1 lb 2 oz double cream
75 g/3 oz good quality bitter chocolate
1 sachet/approx. ½ oz vanilla sugar

1 Melt chocolate and margarine and leave to cool. Separate the eggs. Whisk egg yolks, 4 tbsp water and sugar until thick and creamy. Stir in the chocolate mixture. Whisk egg whites with salt until stiff and spoon onto egg yolk mixture. Sieve flour, cornflour and baking powder onto eggs and fold in all ingredients.

2 Line a baking sheet with baking parchment. Spread the sponge mixture over the baking sheet. Bake in a preheated oven at 200°C/400°F/Gas mark 6 for about 20 minutes. Turn out sponge and remove paper immediately. Leave sponge to cool and cut in half.

3 Soften gelatine. Sort the fresh raspberries, leave frozen raspberries to thaw out. Set aside a few raspberries for decoration, purée the others through a sieve and mix with sugar. Melt wet gelatine over a low heat and stir into fruit purée.

Refrigerate. Beat 375 g/13 oz cream until stiff. Fold cream into raspberry purée as soon as it begins to set.

4 Place a piece of sponge on the baking sheet. Place a strip of foil lengthways along each side of the sponge, so that there is a border of foil above the sponge. Spread the raspberry cream over the sponge base, and lay the second layer of sponge on top. Refrigerate the baking sheet for about 30 minutes.

5 Melt the chocolate in a bowl over hot water, spread on a cold marble block and allow to set slightly. Draw a metal spatula or broad-bladed knife across the chocolate to form chocolate curls (caraque). Whisk the remaining cream and vanilla sugar until stiff and spread over raspberry slice. Remove foil borders. Cut sponge into slices and decorate with chocolate curls and remaining raspberries. *Makes 12 slices.*

# NOUGAT CAKE

**Ingredients for a spring form tin (24 cm diam., 2 l/9 inches diam., 3½ pints capacity)**

**FOR THE SPONGE**

| | |
|---|---|
| 50 g/2 oz soft margarine | |
| 75 g/3 oz nougat | |
| 4 eggs | |
| 125 g/5 oz caster sugar | |
| pinch salt | |
| 75 g/3 oz flour | |
| 50 g/2 oz cornflour | |
| 1 tsp baking powder | |
| margarine for greasing | |

**FOR THE FILLING**

| | |
|---|---|
| 500 g/1 lb 2 oz double cream | |
| 1 tbsp caster sugar | |
| 30 g/1 oz chopped walnuts | |

**FOR DECORATION**

| | |
|---|---|
| 125 g/5 oz nougat | |
| 25 g/1 oz coconut oil | |

1 Melt margarine and nougat and leave to cool. Separate the eggs. Whisk together egg yolks, 4 tbsp water and sugar until thick and creamy. Stir in the nougat mixture. Whisk egg whites and salt together until stiff and spoon onto egg yolk mixture. Sieve flour, cornflour and baking powder onto eggs and fold in all ingredients.

2 Fill a tin which has only been greased on the base with the sponge mixture. Bake in a preheated oven at 175°C/350°F/Gas mark 4 for 30-40 minutes. Cut the sponge in 2.

3 Whisk cream and sugar until stiff. Fold in nuts. Fill the cake with nut cream.

4 Melt nougat and coconut oil together and mix thoroughly. Spread ⅔ over the cake. Put the rest of the nougat in a freezer bag. Cut off a corner of the bag and pipe the nougat over the cake in a lattice pattern. *Makes 12 slices.*

# WALNUT GATEAU

**Ingredients for a spring form tin (24 cm diam, 2 l capacity/9 inches diam., 3½ pints capacity)**

**FOR THE SPONGE**

| | |
|---|---|
| 5 eggs | |
| 225 g/8 oz icing sugar | |
| 50 g/2 oz ground walnuts | |
| 50 g/2 oz flour | |
| 40 g/ 2 oz cornflour | |
| 1 tsp baking powder | |
| margarine for greasing | |

**FOR THE FILLING**

| | |
|---|---|
| 2 leaves white gelatine | |
| 375 g/13 oz double cream | |
| 50 g/2 oz caster sugar | |
| 50 g/2 oz ground walnuts | |

**FOR DECORATION**

| | |
|---|---|
| 200 g/7 oz icing sugar | |
| 3 tbsp cocoa powder | |
| 25 g/1 oz coconut oil | |
| 32 walnut halves | |
| 4 tbsp grated chocolate | |

1 Separate eggs. Whisk egg yolks, 2 tbsp water and icing sugar until thick and creamy. Whisk egg whites until thick and spoon onto egg yolk mixture. Mix together flour, nuts, cornflour and baking powder and fold everything into egg mixture.

2 Grease base of tin, fill with sponge mixture. Bake in a preheated oven at 175°C/350°F/Gas mark 4 for about 50 minutes. Slice the cake into 3 layers.

3 Soften gelatine. Whisk cream until stiff. Fold in sugar and eggs. Melt gelatine, fold into cream. Fill cake with ⅔ of cream. Cover top and sides with remaining cream.

4 Mix icing sugar and cocoa with 5 tbsp hot water. Melt coconut oil and mix with cocoa. Pour chocolate icing over top and sides of cake. Decorate with walnut halves and grated chocolate. *Makes 12 slices.*

# APRICOT GATEAU

**Ingredients for spring form tin (26 cm diam., 2.5 l/10 inches diam., 4¼ pints capacity)**
**FOR THE SPONGE**
75 g/3 oz soft margarine
6 eggs
200 g/7 oz caster sugar
pinch salt
100 g/4 oz flour
75 g/3 oz cornflour
1 tsp baking powder
**FOR THE FILLING**
200 g/7 oz marzipan mix
175 g/6 oz apricot jam
**FOR DECORATION**
4 leaves white gelatine
1 tin apricot halves (drained weight 480 g)/17 oz]
125 g/5 oz double cream
3 tbsp caster sugar
50 g/2 oz flaked almonds
a little white wine
1 sachet clear cake glaze mix or ½ oz arrowroot

1 Melt margarine and leave to cool. Separate eggs. Whisk egg yolks, 6 tbsp water and sugar until thick and creamy. Stir in margarine. Whisk egg whites and salt together until stiff, spoon onto egg yolk mixture. Sieve flour, cornflour and baking powder onto eggs and fold in.
2 Fill a spring form tin with a lined base with the sponge mix. Bake in a preheated oven at 175°C/350°F/Gas mark 4 for 30-40 minutes. Remove paper. Slice cake into 3 layers.
3 Mix together marzipan and jam. Spread marzipan mixture over 2 layers of cake and place one on top of the other. Place final sponge layer on top.

4 Soften gelatine. Drain apricots, reserving juice. Purée half the fruit. Dissolve the wet gelatine over a low heat and stir into fruit purée. Spread purée over top of cake and leave to set.
5 Slice remaining fruit. Whisk cream together with 1 tbsp sugar until very stiff. Spread cream over sides of cake and sprinkle flaked almonds on top. Arrange apricot slices on top of gateau. Make up the fruit juice to 250 ml/8 fl. oz with the wine. Mix arrowroot, if used, to a smooth paste with a little fruit juice. Bring fruit juice and wine to boil with remaining sugar, and cake glaze or arrowroot. Pour glaze over fruit and leave to set. *Makes 12 slices.*

# CARROT CAKE

**Ingredients for a spring form tin
(26 cm diam., 2.5 l/10 inches diam., 4¼
pints capacity)**

**FOR THE SPONGE**

5 eggs

250 g/9 oz caster sugar

1 tsp grated lemon zest

3 tbsp lemon juice

250 g/9 oz ground almonds

250 g/9 oz grated carrots

80 g/3 oz flour

3 tsp baking powder

margarine for greasing

flour for dusting

**FOR DECORATION**

200 g/7 oz icing sugar

4 tbsp lemon juice or 2 tbsp kirsch

4 tbsp flaked almonds

16 marzipan carrots

1 Separate eggs. Whisk together egg yolks, sugar, lemon zest and juice until thick and creamy. Now mix together almonds, carrots, flour and baking powder and add gradually to egg mixture. Whisk egg whites until stiff and fold in.

2 Dust a greased spring form tin with flour and fill with sponge mixture. Bake in a preheated oven at 175°C/350°F/Gas mark 4 for 50-60 minutes. Remove cake from tin and leave to cool.

3 Mix icing sugar, lemon juice or kirsch and 1-2 tbsp water to make icing. Spread icing over cake. Toast almonds until golden brown. Sprinkle over sides of cake. Decorate top of cake with marzipan carrots. *Makes 16 slices*.

# ALMOND RING

**Ingredients for 6 individual ring
moulds (each 175 ml/¼ pint capacity)**

6 eggs

375 g/13 oz caster sugar

1 tsp grated lemon zest

150 g/6 oz ground almonds

50 g/2 oz flour

margarine for greasing

3 tbsp flaked almonds

8 tbsp rum or almond liqueur

9 fresh figs for topping

1 Separate eggs. Beat egg yolks and 175 g/6 oz sugar until thick and creamy. Add lemon zest and stir in. Whisk egg whites until stiff and spoon onto egg yolk mixture. Sprinkle ground almonds on top of egg whites and sieve flour on top. Carefully fold in all ingredients using a plastic spatula.

2 Grease 6 small ring moulds or savarin moulds thoroughly and scatter flaked almonds in tins. Fill tins with almond sponge mixture.

3 Bake in a preheated oven at 175°C/350°F/Gas mark 4 for about 35 minutes. Remove tins from oven, turn cakes out onto a wire rack and leave to cool.

4 Meanwhile bring remaining sugar to boil with 125 ml/4 fl. oz water and leave to cool. Add rum or almond liqueur to sugar. Place the almond rings on a deep plate. Using a tablespoon, drizzle the sugar solution over the rings until all the liquid is used up. Leave to soak in for a little while.

5 Wash figs and divide into 6 slices. Arrange figs on top of almond rings and serve.

# BLUEBERRY GATEAU

| Ingredients for a spring form tin (24 cm diam., 2 1/9 inches diam., 3½ pints capacity) |
| --- |
| **FOR THE SPONGE** |
| 30 g/1 oz soft margarine |
| 2 eggs |
| 75 g/3 oz caster sugar |
| pinch salt |
| 80 g/3 oz flour |
| 1 tsp baking powder |
| **FOR THE FILLING** |
| 10 leaves white gelatine |
| 750 g/1 lb 11 oz fresh blueberries/or frozen berries |
| 1 kg/2 lb 3 oz curd cheese or quark (40% fat) |
| 2 tbsp icing sugar |
| 2 sachets/approx. 1 oz vanilla sugar |
| 1 tsp grated lemon zest |

1 Melt margarine and leave to cool. Separate eggs. Whisk together egg yolks and 1 tbsp warm water until creamy. Gradually sprinkle over sugar and whisk in until thick and creamy. Stir in margarine. Whisk together egg whites and salt until stiff and spoon onto egg yolk mixture. Sieve flour and baking powder onto egg whites and fold in all ingredients.

2 Line the base of a spring form tin with baking parchment and fill with the sponge mixture. Bake in a preheated oven at 200°C/400°F/Gas mark 6 for approx. 15 minutes. Remove paper from base of cake. Slice cake into 2 layers.

3 Soften gelatine. Wash fresh blueberries, defrost the frozen berries if used. Reserve 4 tbsp blueberries. Mix the curd cheese with icing sugar, vanilla sugar and lemon zest and divide into 2 portions. Dissolve ½ the wet gelatine over a low heat and stir into ½ the curd cheese with the remaining fruit. Put the sides of the spring form tin around the sponge layer. Spread blueberry and cheese mixture over sponge base. Place other sponge layer on top. Refrigerate for about 30 minutes.

4 Dissolve remaining gelatine and stir into other ½ of curd cheese. Spread cheese all over top and sides of gateau, forming peaks in the cheese on top of the cake. Decorate with blueberries. *Makes 12 slices.*

# TROPICAL GATEAU

**Ingredients for a spring form tin (24 cm diam., 2 l/9 inches diam., 3½ pints capacity)**

**FOR THE SPONGE**

4 eggs

125 g/5 oz caster sugar

70 g/3 oz flour

½ tsp baking powder

40 g/2 oz desiccated coconut

50 g/2 oz cornflour

**FOR THE FILLING**

3 leaves white gelatine

30 g/1 oz margarine

500 g/1 lb 2 oz bananas

5 tbsp caster sugar

3 tbsp lemon juice

4 tbsp banana liqueur, if liked

500 g/1 lb 2 oz double cream

100 g/4 oz fresh coconut

1 mango

1 kiwi fruit

250 ml/8 fl. oz maracuja juice

½ sachet clear cake glaze mix or approx. ¼ oz arrowroot

1 Separate eggs. Whisk egg yolks, 4 tbsp water and sugar until thick and creamy. Beat egg whites until stiff, spoon onto egg yolk mixture. Add flour, baking powder, desiccated coconut and cornflour and fold in.

2 Line the base of a spring form tin with baking parchment and fill with the sponge mixture. Bake in a preheated oven at 200°C/400°F/Gas mark 6 for 30-35 minutes. Slice cake into 2 layers.

3 Soften gelatine. Heat margarine. Peel bananas, slice and fry until golden brown. Remove from pan. Caramelise 3 tbsp sugar. Add 3 tbsp water, 2 tbsp lemon juice and liqueur to sugar. Dissolve gelatine in sugar solution. Add bananas and refrigerate.

4 Whisk cream until stiff. As soon as banana cream starts to set, fold in half the fresh cream. Fill gateau with banana cream mixture and spread remaining fresh cream over top and sides.

5 Peel strips from fresh coconut with a vegetable peeler. Arrange around edge of gateau. Peel fruit. Slice kiwi fruit. Cut mango into sections and arrange on top of gateau. Mix together maracuja juice, remaining lemon juice, sugar and cake glaze mix; bring to boil and pour over fruit. *Makes 12 slices.*

# LEMON OMELETTE

**Ingredients for 8 omelettes**

**FOR THE SPONGE**

4 eggs

125 g/5 oz sugar

pinch salt

75 g/3 oz flour

pinch baking powder

sugar for work surface

**FOR THE FILLING**

6 leaves white gelatine

3 egg yolks

50 g/2 oz icing sugar

125 ml/4 fl. oz dry white wine

1 tsp grated lemon zest

6 tbsp lemon juice

375 g/13 oz double cream

icing sugar for dusting

1 Separate eggs. Whisk egg yolks and 4 tbsp water with sugar until thick and creamy. Whisk egg whites, remaining sugar and salt until stiff. Spoon egg whites onto egg yolk mixture. Mix flour with baking powder, sieve onto eggs and fold in.

2 Line a baking sheet with baking parchment. Mark 8 circles of 12 cm/5 inches diameter, 2 cm/1 inch apart on the paper. Using a piping bag with a round nozzle, pipe the sponge mixture in a spiral shape onto the circles. Bake in a preheated oven at 175°C/350°F/Gas mark 4 for about 12 minutes.

3 Turn the omelettes out onto a work surface sprinkled with sugar. Brush the baking parchment with water and pull away from sponge. Fold circles over to form omelettes while still warm. Leave to cool.

4 Soften gelatine. Mix together egg yolks, icing sugar, wine, lemon zest and juice. Whisk in a bowl over a pan of hot water with a balloon whisk until thick and creamy. Drain gelatine and dissolve in custard. Refrigerate.

5 Whisk cream until stiff. As soon as lemon cream begins to set, fold in fresh cream. Fill sponge omelettes with lemon cream and dust with icing sugar.

# FRANKFURT RING CAKE

**Ingredients for a ring mould
(26 cm diam., 2 1/10 inches diam., 3½
pints capacity)**

**FOR THE SPONGE**

4 eggs

125 g/5 oz caster sugar

125 g/5 oz flour

75 g/3 oz cornflour

1 tsp baking powder

50 g/2 oz soft margarine

3 slices French toast

margarine for greasing

**FOR THE FILLING**

1 sachet vanilla blancmange mix

500 ml/¾ pint milk

2 egg yolks

1 vanilla pod

4 tbsp caster sugar

pinch salt

200 g/7 oz soft margarine

150 g/6 oz cracknel for sprinkling

1 Separate eggs. Whisk egg yolks with 4 tbsp warm water until foaming. Gradually add sugar in a trickle, whisking continuously, until the mixture is thick and creamy. Whisk egg whites until stiff and spoon onto egg yolk mixture. Mix flour with cornflour and baking powder, sieve onto egg mixture and fold in everything. Melt margarine, leave to cool and mix in carefully.

2 Crush the French toast into bread crumbs. Grease a ring mould and sprinkle French toast crumbs around mould. Fill mould with sponge mixture and bake in a preheated oven at 175-200°C/350-400°F/Gas mark 4–6 for 35-40 minutes. Remove ring mould from oven and allow to rest for 10 minutes. Turn cake out onto a wire rack and leave to cool. Slice the cake into 3 layers.

3 Using a balloon whisk, mix together blancmange mix, 4 tbsp milk and egg yolks. Cut open vanilla pod and scrape out essence. Bring remaining milk to boil with sugar, salt, vanilla essence and vanilla pod. Stir in the blancmange mix and bring to boil again. Remove from heat. Remove vanilla pod. Leave blancmange to cool, then pass through a sieve or mix briefly in a blender or food processor.

4 Beat the margarine until creamy. Stir in the blancmange 1 tbsp at a time. Spread about ⅓ of vanilla cream on the bottom layer of sponge. Place the middle layer on top. Spread another ⅓ of cream on this layer and lay the final layer of sponge on top. Spread remaining vanilla cream all over cake so that the surface is smooth. Finally sprinkle cracknel over cake (see page 223).

*Makes 16 slices.*

# MOORLAND GATEAU

**INGREDIENTS FOR SPRING FORM TIN**

**(26 cm diam., 2.5 l/10 inches diam., 4¼ pints capacity)**

**For the sponge**

50 g/2 oz margarine

4 eggs

175 g/6 oz caster sugar

pinch salt

3 tbsp cocoa powder

150 g/6 oz buckwheat flour

3 tsp baking powder

**For the filling**

5 leaves white gelatine

350 g/12 oz cranberry compote

375 g/13 oz double cream

2 sachets/approx. 1 oz vanilla sugar

**FOR DECORATION**

375 g/13 oz double cream

2 tbsp caster sugar

3 tbsp flaked almonds

150 g/4 oz good quality plain cooking chocolate

150 g/4 oz cranberry compote

1  Melt margarine and leave to cool. Separate eggs. Whisk egg yolks, 4 tbsp warm water and sugar until thick and creamy. Stir in margarine, salt and cocoa powder. Whisk egg whites until stiff and spoon onto egg yolk mixture. Mix together buckwheat flour and baking powder, sieve onto egg whites and fold in.

2  Line the base of a spring form tin with baking parchment and fill with sponge mixture. Bake in a preheated oven at 175°C/350°F/Gas mark 4 for 30-40 minutes. Remove from tin, leave to cool and cut into 3 layers.

3  Soften gelatine in cold water. Stir cranberry compote. Dissolve the wet gelatine over a low heat and stir into the cranberries. Refrigerate. Whisk together cream and vanilla sugar until stiff. As soon as the cranberry mixture begins to set, fold in the cream.

Fill the gateau with the cranberry cream mixture, refrigerate and allow to soak in for a day.

4  Whisk together cream and sugar until stiff. Put ⅓ of cream into a piping bag with a star shaped nozzle. Spread remaining cream on sides and top of gateau. Pipe a ring of cream around the top of the gateau.

5  Toast flaked almonds until golden brown and leave to cool. Melt cooking chocolate and pour into a freezer bag. Cut off the tip of one of the corners of the bag and decorate sides of gateau with piped chocolate. Sprinkle toasted almonds around base of gateau. Arrange little heaps of cranberry compote on top of gateau.
*Makes 16 slices.*

# MOOR'S HEADS

Ingredients for 18 buns (each 6.5 cm diam./2½ inches diam.)

**FOR THE SPONGE**

| |
| --- |
| 150 g/6 oz margarine |
| 3 eggs |
| 150 g/6 oz caster sugar |
| ½ sachet/approx. ¼ oz vanilla sugar |
| pinch salt |
| 150 g/6 oz flour |
| 2 tbsp cocoa powder |
| 1½ tsp baking powder |
| 2 tbsp grated chocolate |
| margarine for greasing |
| flour for dusting |

**FOR THE ICING**

| |
| --- |
| 150 g/6 oz apricot jam |
| 1 tbsp apricot liqueur |
| 1-2 tbsp caster sugar |
| 100 g/4 oz good quality bitter chocolate |
| 40 g/2 oz soft margarine |
| 1 tbsp cocoa powder for dusting |

1 Melt margarine and leave to cool. Separate eggs. Whisk egg yolks, 3 tbsp warm water, sugar and vanilla sugar together until thick and creamy. Stir in margarine. Whisk together egg whites and salt until stiff and spoon onto egg yolk mixture. Mix together flour, cocoa and baking powder; sieve onto egg whites. Sprinkle grated chocolate on top of flour and fold in everything gently.

2 Grease bun tins and dust with flour. Place 1 tbsp sponge mix in each cup. Bake in a preheated oven at 175°C/350°F/Gas mark 4 for about 20 minutes.

3 Warm the apricot jam, push through a sieve and mix with apricot liqueur. Turn buns out of tins and brush top with jam. Leave to cool on a wire rack.

4 Melt sugar, 2 tbsp water and chocolate over a low heat. Add margarine and melt also. Allow the chocolate icing to cool, stirring continuously, until the spoon leaves a clear trail in the mixture. Coat tops of buns with chocolate and leave to dry thoroughly. Dust with cocoa if desired.

# CHOCOLATE-ORANGE ROLL

**Ingredients for 16 slices**

**FOR THE SPONGE**

| |
|---|
| 4 eggs |
| 125 g/5 oz caster sugar |
| pinch salt |
| 1 sachet/approx. ½ oz vanilla sugar |
| 50 g each/2 oz flour and cornflour |
| 1 tsp baking powder |
| 2 tbsp cocoa powder |
| sugar for sprinkling |

**FOR THE FILLING**

| |
|---|
| 1 sachet vanilla blancmange powder |
| 500 ml/ pint milk |
| 2 egg yolks |
| 50 g/2 oz caster sugar |
| 1-2 tsp grated orange zest |
| 200 g/7 oz soft margarine |
| 4 tbsp grated chocolate |

1 Separate eggs. Whisk egg yolks with 4 tbsp water, sugar and vanilla sugar until thick and creamy. Whisk egg whites until stiff, spoon onto egg yolk mixture. Sieve flour, cornflour, baking powder and cocoa onto eggs; then fold in.

2 Spread the sponge mixture onto a baking sheet lined with baking parchment. Bake at 200°C/400°F/Gas mark 6 for 10-12 minutes. Turn out onto a cloth sprinkled with sugar. Remove paper. Roll up sponge with cloth. Leave to cool.

3 Mix together blancmange powder, a little milk and egg yolks. Bring remaining milk, sugar and orange zest to boil. Stir in blancmange mix, bring to boil, leave to cool.

4 Beat margarine until creamy. Stir in blancmange mix. Take sponge roll out of cloth, fill with ⅔ of cream, roll up again and coat with remaining cream. Sprinkle chocolate over roll.

# WINE CREAM ROULADE

**Ingredients for 16 slices**

**FOR THE SPONGE**

| |
|---|
| 4 eggs |
| 125 g/5 oz caster sugar |
| pinch salt |
| 1 sachet/approx. ½ oz vanilla sugar |
| 75 g/3 oz flour |
| 50 g/2 oz cornflour |
| ¼ tsp baking powder |
| sugar for sprinkling |

**FOR THE FILLING**

| |
|---|
| 6 leaves white gelatine |
| 75 g/3 oz caster sugar |
| 250 ml/8 fl. oz white wine |
| ½ tsp grated lemon zest |
| 3 tbsp lemon juice |
| 250 g/9 oz double cream |

**For decoration**

| |
|---|
| 16 grapes |
| 1 tbsp icing sugar |

1 Separate eggs. Whisk egg yolks with 4 tbsp water, sugar, salt and vanilla sugar until thick and creamy. Whisk egg whites until stiff and spoon onto egg yolks. Sieve flour, cornflour and baking powder onto eggs and fold in everything.

2 Line a baking sheet with baking parchment and fill with sponge mixture. Bake in a pre-heated oven at 200°C/400°F/Gas mark 6 for 10-12 minutes. Turn out onto a cloth sprinkled with sugar. Remove paper. Roll up sponge in cloth and leave to cool.

3 Soften gelatine. Bring sugar, wine, lemon zest and juice to boil. Drain gelatine, dissolve in wine mixture and refrigerate. Whisk cream until stiff. As soon as wine cream starts to set, fold in fresh cream.

4 Remove sponge from cloth, fill with cream, roll up again and refrigerate. Wash grapes. Dust sponge roll with icing sugar, cut into slices and garnish with grapes.

# ALMOND CREAM SLICE

| Ingredients for 16 slices |
| --- |
| 4 eggs |
| 150 g/6 oz icing sugar |
| 1 sachet/approx. ½ oz vanilla sugar |
| 1½ tsp grated orange zest |
| 40 g/2 oz each flour and cornflour |
| 1 tsp baking powder |
| sugar for sprinkling |
| FOR THE FILLING |
| 6 leaves white gelatine |
| essence from 1 vanilla pod |
| 250 ml/8 fl. oz milk |
| 50 g/2 oz caster sugar |
| 1 sachet/approx. ½ oz vanilla sugar |
| 2 drops almond essence |
| 40 g/2 oz chopped almonds |
| 4 tbsp rum |
| 125 g/5 oz double cream |
| 4 tbsp raspberry jam |
| FOR DECORATION |
| 140 g/5 oz sugar |
| 70 g/3 oz flaked almonds |
| oil for brushing |
| 500 g/1 lb 2 oz double cream |

1 Separate eggs. Whisk egg yolks with 4 tbsp water, icing sugar, vanilla sugar and orange zest until thick and creamy. Whisk egg whites until stiff and spoon onto egg yolk mixture. Sieve flour, cornflour and baking powder onto eggs and fold in everything.

2 Line a baking sheet with baking parchment and fill with sponge mixture. Bake in a pre-heated oven at 200-225°C/400-425°F/Gas mark 6–7 for 10-12 minutes. Turn out onto a tea towel sprinkled with sugar. Remove paper. Leave sponge to cool, then cut into 3 strips of equal width.

3 Soften gelatine. Bring vanilla pod essence, milk, sugar, vanilla essence and chopped almonds to boil. Drain gelatine and dissolve in vanilla milk. Stir in rum and refrigerate. Whisk cream until stiff. As soon as vanilla cream begins to set, fold in fresh cream. Spread sponge slices with jam. Layer together and refrigerate.

4 Caramelise 40 g/2 oz sugar for the cracknel (see page 223). Stir in flaked almonds. Spread over an oiled plate, leave to set and break into pieces.

5 Whisk cream with remaining sugar. Fill a piping bag with a round nozzle with ½ of the cream. Cover sponge layers with remaining cream. Decorate top of sponge with piped cream and sprinkle cracknel on top.

# MOCHA CHARLOTTE

| Ingredients for a charlotte mould or a heat-resistant bowl (20 cm diam., 1⅛ inches diam., 1¾ pints capacity) |
| --- |
| **FOR THE SPONGE** |
| 2 eggs |
| 125 g/5 oz caster sugar |
| pinch salt |
| 125 g/5 oz flour |
| 50 g/2 oz cornflour |
| 2 tbsp French toast crumbs |
| 2 tsp baking powder |
| **FOR THE FILLING** |
| 5 leaves white gelatine |
| 4 eggs |
| 100 g/4 oz caster sugar |
| 1 sachet/approx. 2 oz vanilla sugar |
| pinch salt |
| 2 tsp cocoa powder |
| 4 tbsp instant coffee |
| 250 g/9 oz double cream |
| **FOR DECORATION** |
| 50 g/2 oz good quality bitter cooking chocolate |
| 250 g/9 oz double cream |
| 1 tsp cocoa powder |

1 Separate eggs. Whisk egg yolks with 1 tbsp warm water and sugar until thick and creamy. Whisk egg whites with salt until stiff and spoon into egg yolk mixture. Mix together flour, cornflour, French toast crumbs and baking powder, sieve onto eggs and fold into egg mixture.

2 Fill a piping bag with a round nozzle with the sponge mixture. Line a baking sheet with baking parchment. Pipe finger length trifle sponges on the baking sheet. Bake in a preheated oven at 200-225°C/400-425°F/Gas mark 6–7 for 10 minutes. Remove from parchment immediately and leave to cool.

3 Soften gelatine. Separate eggs, whisk egg yolks, sugar, vanilla sugar, salt and cocoa until creamy. Warm the instant coffee with 4 tbsp water. Drain gelatine and dissolve in coffee. Stir everything into cocoa cream and refrigerate. Whisk cream until stiff. As soon as cocoa cream starts to set, fold in fresh cream.

4 Cut 3 sponge fingers in half and use to line the base of the tin in a star shape. Spread some cocoa cream on the sponge. Line the sides of the tin with sponge fingers so the ends of the fingers are in the cream on the base. Fill with remaining cream. Refrigerate the charlotte for at least 2 hours.

5 Melt cooking chocolate and spread over a cold marble slab. Allow to set a little, then draw a spatula or broad-bladed knife across the chocolate to form large chocolate curls. Turn out charlotte. Whisk cream until stiff and use to fill a piping bag with a star- shaped nozzle. Decorate charlotte with piped cream and chocolate. Finally dust with cocoa powder. *Makes 12 slices.*

# GINGER CREAM BUNS

| Ingredients for 12 buns |
| --- |
| FOR THE SPONGE |
| 50 g/2 oz soft margarine |
| 4 eggs |
| 125 g/5 oz icing sugar |
| pinch salt |
| 50 g/2 oz flour |
| 50 g/2 oz cornflour |
| 2 tbsp cocoa powder |
| 1 tsp baking powder |
| sugar for sprinkling |
| FOR THE FILLING |
| 100 g/4 oz preserved ginger (in syrup) |
| 375 g/13 oz double cream |
| 1 tbsp caster sugar |
| 200 g/7 oz good quality dark chocolate |

1 Melt margarine and leave to cool. Separate eggs. Whisk egg yolks with 3 tbsp warm water and icing sugar until thick and creamy. Gradually stir in margarine. Whisk egg whites with salt until stiff and spoon onto egg yolk mixture. Mix flour, cornflour, cocoa and baking powder together, sieve onto eggs and gently fold in everything, using a plastic spatula.

2 Spread the sponge mix on a baking sheet lined with baking parchment. Bake in a preheated oven at 200°C/400°F/Gas mark 6 for 12-15 minutes. Leave sponge base to cool. With a pastry cutter, cut out 24 small sponge circles, each about 6 cm/2½ inches in diameter.

3 Drain the preserved ginger in a sieve, reserving syrup. Chop 50 g/2 oz ginger very finely and mix with 1 tbsp reserved syrup.

Whisk cream and sugar until stiff, fold in finely chopped ginger. Spread ginger cream over 12 sponge circles and top with remaining circles.

4 Thinly slice remaining ginger. Melt chocolate in a bowl over hot water and entirely coat filled buns in chocolate. Decorate top with ginger slices. Leave to dry on a wire rack.

**Cut out mini-sponge bases using a rotating action. Press down lightly.**

# POTATO CAKE WITH HAZELNUTS

**Ingredients for a spring form tin (26 cm diam., 2.5 l/10 inches diam., 4¼ pints capacity)**
**FOR THE DOUGH**
375 g/13 oz small potatoes
4 eggs
300 g/11 oz caster sugar
1 sachet/approx. ½ oz vanilla sugar
pinch salt
100 g/4 oz chopped hazelnuts
150 g/6 oz semolina
1 tsp baking powder
margarine for greasing
flour for dusting
**FOR DECORATION**
100 g/4 oz good quality plain cooking chocolate
100 g/4 oz good quality white cooking chocolate
50 g/2 oz whole hazelnuts

1 Wash potatoes, boil for approx. 20 minutes, drain, allow to cool and remove skins. Leave potatoes to cool completely, then grate coarsely.

2 Separate eggs. Whisk together egg yolks, sugar, vanilla sugar and salt until thick and creamy. Add grated potato and stir for 5 minutes. Mix hazelnuts with semolina and baking powder and gradually add to potato mixture. Whisk egg whites until stiff and gently fold into the potato mixture.

3 Grease the base only of a spring form tin and dust with flour. Fill with sponge mixture. Bake in a preheated oven at 175-200°C/350-400°F/Gas mark 4–6 for 50-60 minutes. Turn cake out of tin and leave to cool on a wire rack.

4 Melt the dark and white chocolate over hot water in separate bowls. Spread chocolate over potato cake in a marbled pattern. Coarsely chop hazelnuts and scatter over cake. Allow chocolate coating to dry. *Makes 16 slices.*

# CHOCOLATE ORANGE MINI GATEAUX

**Ingredients for 10 individual soufflé tins (approx. 7 cm diam., 150 ml/3 inches diam., ¼ pint capacity)**
**FOR THE SPONGE**
4 eggs
125 g/5 oz caster sugar
pinch salt
1 sachet/approx. ½ oz vanilla sugar
50 g/2 oz each flour and cornflour
3 tbsp cocoa powder
margarine for greasing
flour for dusting
**FOR THE FILLING**
1 sachet vanilla blancmange powder
500 ml/¾ pint milk
1 egg yolk
2 tbsp caster sugar
2 tsp grated orange zest
200 g/7 oz soft margarine
3 tbsp orange liqueur
candied fruit for garnish
1 tbsp coarsely chopped walnuts

1 Separate eggs. Whisk together egg yolks, 2 tbsp warm water, sugar, salt and vanilla sugar until thick and creamy. Whisk egg whites until stiff and spoon onto egg yolk mixture. Mix together flour, cornflour and cocoa, sieve onto egg whites. Fold in everything.

2 Grease bases of soufflé tins and dust with flour. Divide the sponge mixture among the tins. Bake in a preheated oven at 200°F/Gas mark 6 for 15-20 minutes. Loosen cakes from sides of tins, turn out and leave to cool.

3 Mix blancmange powder with 3 tbsp milk and egg yolk. Bring remaining milk, sugar and orange zest to boil. Stir in blancmange mix, bring to boil again and leave to cool. Strain through a sieve.

4 Beat margarine until creamy. Stir in blancmange mixture a tablespoonful at a time. Add liqueur. Cut the gateaux in half and fill with ⅓ of cream. Coat gateaux all over with remaining cream. Chop candied fruit into small pieces. Decorate gateaux with fruit and nuts.

# DATE SPONGES

**Ingredients for 16 ramekins
(each 125 ml/approx. ¼ pint capacity)**
**200 g/7 oz whole hazelnuts**
**200 g/7 oz dates**
**6 eggs**
**175 g/6 oz icing sugar**
**1 tbsp rum**
**½ tsp grated lemon zest**
**2 tbsp lemon juice**
**pinch salt**
**3 slices French toast**
**margarine for greasing**
**icing sugar for dusting**

1 Toast hazelnuts for about 10 minutes on a baking sheet in an oven preheated to 225°C/425°F/Gas mark 7. Put in a sieve and leave to cool for 5 minutes. Shake the sieve so that the brown skins are loosened from the nuts, or wrap the nuts in a tea towel and using your hands vigorously rub the nuts against each other. Finely grind the roasted hazelnuts. Remove stones from dates and dice flesh.

2 Separate eggs. Whisk egg yolks, icing sugar and rum until thick and creamy. Add lemon zest and juice, stir in ground hazelnuts and diced dates. Whisk egg whites with salt until stiff and spoon onto egg yolk mixture. Carefully fold in egg whites using a plastic spatula.

3 Put the French toast in a freezer bag and crush to fine crumbs with a rolling pin. Grease ramekins with margarine and sprinkle with French toast crumbs. Divide sponge mixture among ramekins and bake in a preheated oven at 175-200°C/350-400°F/Gas mark 4–6 for 30-35 minutes.

4 Run a knife round the sides of the ramekins to loosen the date sponges and turn out. Leave to cool on a wire rack. Dust with icing sugar.

# ORANGE CREAM GATEAU

| Ingredients for spring form tin |
| --- |
| (26 cm diam., 2.5 l/10 inches diam., |
| 4¼ pints capacity) |
| FOR THE SPONGE |
| 50 g/2 oz soft margarine |
| 4 eggs |
| 120 g/5 oz caster sugar |
| 80 g/3 oz flour |
| 50 g/2 oz cornflour |
| ¼ tsp baking powder |
| sugar for sprinkling |
| FOR THE FILLING |
| 5 leaves white gelatine |
| 600 g/1 lb 5 oz double cream |
| 1 sachet/approx. ½ oz vanilla sugar |
| 6 tbsp orange marmalade |
| 1 tsp grated lemon zest |
| 1 tbsp orange liqueur |
| FOR DECORATION |
| 1 organic orange |
| 75 g/3 oz chopped pistachio nuts |

1 Melt margarine and leave to cool. Separate eggs. Whisk egg yolks, 4 tbsp warm water and sugar until thick and creamy. Stir in margarine. Whisk egg whites until stiff and spoon onto egg yolk mixture. Mix together flour, cornflour and baking powder, sieve onto egg whites and fold in lightly.

2 Line a baking sheet with baking parchment and spread sponge mix over sheet. Bake in a preheated oven at 200°C/400°F/Gas mark 6 for 10-12 minutes. Turn out onto a tea towel sprinkled with sugar and remove paper. Roll up sponge base in tea towel.

3 Soften gelatine. Whisk cream and the vanilla sugar until stiff. Stir half the marmalade and lemon zest into cream. Melt wet gelatine over a low heat and stir into orange cream.

4 Unroll sponge layer from cloth and drizzle orange liqueur on top. Spread remaining marmalade over sponge. Then spread ⅔ of orange cream over sponge. Cut sponge layer into 6 cm/2 inch wide strips. Roll up a strip and place upright on a cake plate so that from above the rolled-up sponge looks like the pattern on a snail's shell. Position the second strip against the end of the first strip and wind round in spiral. Continue until all the sponge strips are used up. Place the sides of a spring form tin around the gateau and refrigerate for 2 hours.

5 Meanwhile, wash the orange and slice thinly. Remove spring form tin. Cover gateau all over with remaining cream. Arrange slices of orange on top of gateau and sprinkle chopped pistachio nuts around sides.
*Makes 16 slices.*

# CURD CHEESE AND CREAM CHARLOTTE

| Ingredients for a heat resistant mould or bowl (about 2 l/3½ pints capacity) |
|---|
| **FOR THE SPONGE** |
| 4 eggs |
| 125 g/5 oz caster sugar |
| 1 sachet/approx. ½ oz vanilla sugar |
| 75 g/3 oz flour |
| 50 g/2 oz cornflour |
| ¼ tsp baking powder |
| sugar for sprinkling |
| **FOR THE FILLING** |
| 4 tbsp red jam (e.g. strawberry) |
| 6 leaves white gelatine |
| 500 g/1 lb 2 oz curd cheese or quark (20% fat) |
| 125 g/5 oz caster sugar |
| 1 sachet/approx. ½ oz vanilla sugar |
| 1 tsp grated lemon zest |
| 6 tbsp lemon juice |
| 250 g/9 oz double cream |

1 Separate eggs. Whisk egg yolks with 3 tbsp water, sugar and vanilla sugar until thick and creamy. Whisk egg whites until stiff, spoon onto egg yolk mixture. Sieve flour, cornflour and baking powder onto eggs and fold in.

2 Line a baking sheet with baking parchment and fill with sponge mixture. Bake in a preheated oven at 200°C/400°F/Gas mark 6 for 10-12 minutes. Turn

out onto a tea towel sprinkled with sugar. Remove paper immediately. Spread jam over sponge, roll up tightly and leave to cool.

3 Soften gelatine. Mix curd cheese with sugar, vanilla sugar, lemon zest and juice. Dissolve wet gelatine over a low heat and stir into cheese mixture. Whisk cream until stiff. As soon as curd cheese mixture begins to set, fold in cream.

4 Divide roll into about 24 slices and use to line mould. Fill mould with cheese and cream mixture and refrigerate for 2 hours. Turn out and serve.
*Makes 16 slices.*

# SPONGE ROLL WITH APPLES

| **FOR THE SPONGE** |
|---|
| 4 eggs |
| 125 g/5 oz caster sugar |
| 75 g/3 oz flour |
| 50 g/2 oz cornflour |
| sugar for sprinkling |
| **FOR THE FILLING** |
| 500 g/1 lb 2 oz double cream |
| 75 g/3 oz caster sugar |
| 500 g/1 lb 2 oz apples |
| 2 tbsp lemon juice |
| 1 green apple for garnish |
| lemon juice for drizzling |

1 Separate eggs. Whisk egg yolks with 3 tbsp water and sugar until thick and creamy. Whisk egg whites until stiff and spoon onto egg yolk mixture. Sieve flour and cornflour onto egg whites and fold in everything.

2 Spread the sponge mixture over a baking sheet lined with

baking parchment. Bake in a preheated oven at 200°C/400°F/Gas mark 6 for 10-12 minutes. Turn out onto a tea towel sprinkled with sugar. Remove paper. Roll up sponge in cloth. Leave to cool.

3 Whisk cream and sugar until stiff. Peel apples, remove cores, grate coarsely and mix with lemon juice. Mix ½ of the cream with the apples. Fill the sponge roll with apple cream. Coat sponge roll in remaining cream. Wash apple for garnish, quarter, core and slice thinly. Drizzle lemon juice over apple, then arrange as garnish on sponge roll.
*Makes 16 slices.*

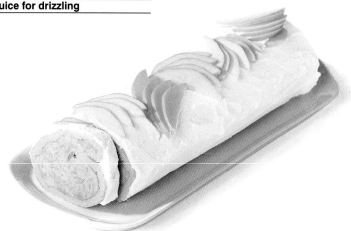

# Quick change artists from a saucepan

From its initial appearance as a lump of dough in a saucepan, you would never guess the many faces of choux pastry. When it has risen in the oven to a majestic size, it turns into a pastry puff ready to be filled with either sweet or savoury mixtures, or into an éclair filled with chocolate or mocha flavoured cream, whilst the Spanish pipe metre-long strands into hot oil to make their beloved crispy churros.

Vanilla cream puff. Recipe on page 158.

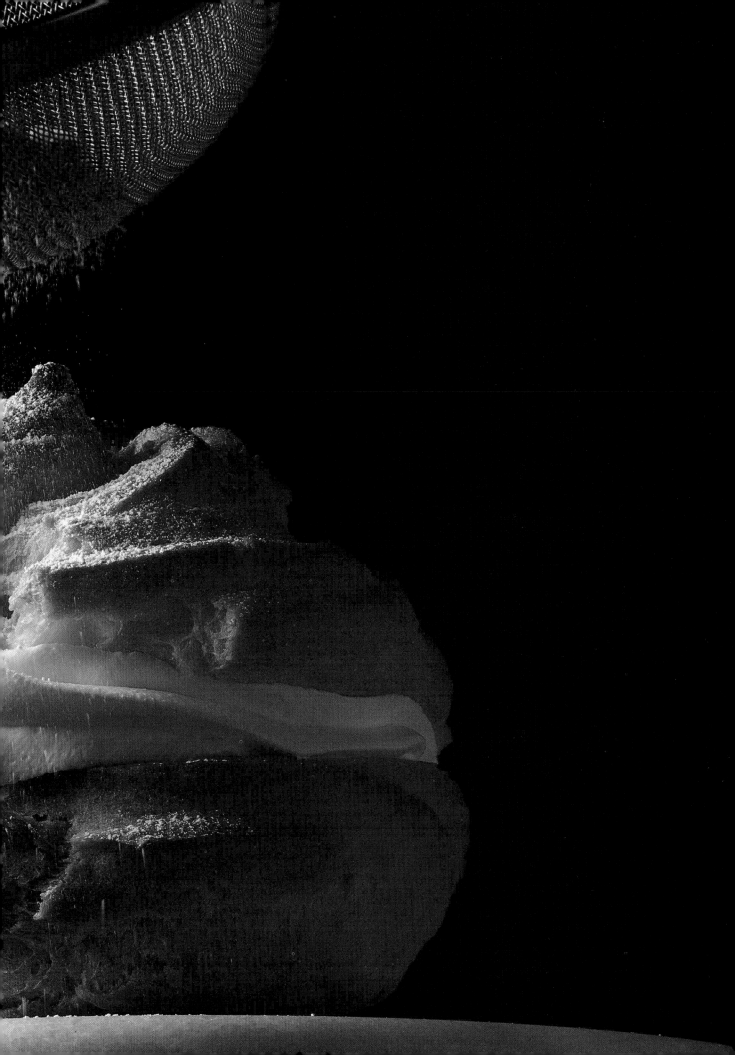

# HOW TO MAKE SUCCESSFUL CHOUX PASTRY

Airy and light choux pastry can appropriately be described as a firm crust with a cavity underneath. For example, a successful cream puff will at least triple in size during baking. The inside is then almost hollow and just waiting for a moist filling. Choux pastry itself has a neutral taste, making it ideal for both sweet and savoury fillings.

You start to make choux pastry on the stove when flour, fat and water are cooked to a thick paste. Expert cooks call this 'scouring'. Then the eggs are added – we use size 3 unless another size is stated – and the dough is ready. A reliable Basic Recipe for choux pastry requires: 250 ml/8 fl. oz water, 50 g/2 oz margarine, pinch salt, 150 g/6 oz flour, 4-5 eggs.

When baked the pastry should be cut open immediately to let the steam evaporate – this is important for the taste. For large pastries it is best to use a serrated knife, but it is easier to cut open small profiteroles with kitchen scissors.

**1** Carefully measure out the liquid. Water and milk are both suitable, or a mixture of the two. Add the margarine and salt. If you use water the pastry will be crisper, on the other hand if you use milk the pastry will be richer.

**2** Weigh the flour and sieve. Bring the fat and water mixture to the boil. As a safety precaution remove the pan from the heat.

**6** Put the ball of dough in a mixing bowl, allow to cool a little and thoroughly stir in the first egg. In this way the dough will become smooth and from now on it will be easy to work.

**7** Now you come to the tricky bit – the correct quantity of egg. There is no hard and fast rule: it depends on the quality of the flour, the size of the eggs and also how much water evaporated during cooking.

**3** Tip the sieved flour into the margarine and water all at once and mix vigorously with a wooden spoon. Continue beating the mixture so that the flour is evenly distributed and any lumps are removed.

**4** Return the pan to the heat and heat the pastry, stirring vigorously all the time (scouring). The mixture will turn into a thick paste.

**5** Continue cooking the paste until it comes away from the sides of the saucepan and forms a ball. The process is completed as soon as a pale, fine coating appears on the base of the saucepan.

**8** The best solution is to crack open the eggs and whisk them one at a time. Gradually add to the lukewarm dough. The pastry has reached the correct consistency when it is shiny and pastry pulls away from the mixture in long threads when you remove the spoon.

**9** Break off portions of the prepared pastry with two teaspoons and place on a greased baking sheet. Leave plenty of room between the portions as the pastry rises a lot.

**10** If you prefer your pastry to be attractively shaped you can put it in a piping bag. Pipe long strips for éclairs and whirls for profiteroles.

# CHOUX PASTRY

## RAISING STEAM

■ Choux pastry puffs should rise as much as possible. The pastry needs damp air in the oven to avoid a hard crust forming too quickly, as this would cause the pastry case to burst open during further cooking. Bakers have ovens with a supply of steam, and special equipment for choux pastry cases. This is why their choux pastry is so light, but you can still bake wonderfully light choux pastry puffs and éclairs at home in your own oven. Choux pastry cooks very well in fan ovens. If you have a conduction oven you can use the following trick: fill a small flat dish (a gratin dish, for example) with boiling water and place it on the floor, in a corner, at the back of your pre-heated oven. In 15 minutes the oven will be humid, thus helping the puffs to rise successfully. It also helps if you sprinkle the baking sheet with about two tablespoons of water. Sometimes just pouring a cup of water over the floor of the preheated oven will do, but take care because although this may create a lot of steam, it can also quickly ruin the enamel coating on the floor of your oven.

## CHANGEABLE

There is a limitless choice of fillings for choux pastry puffs and éclairs. You might want to serve savoury puffs with aperitifs but haven't got much time. No problem. Delicatessens stock ready-made savoury spreads such as taramasalata, pesto and tapenade which can either be used on their own, or blended with cream cheese or crème fraiche, to make interesting fillings, Ready pre-

**Decorative – mini-puffs with pastel coloured icing. Mix icing sugar with lemon juice and a drop of food colouring to a smooth paste and brush onto cooled choux pastry puffs.**

pared delicatessen salads can also be used in this way, or if it's a very special occasion you could even try a blob of crème fraiche with caviar.

## CLOSED DOOR

■ You need patience when baking choux pastry. You mustn't open the oven door before the end of the cooking time under any circumstances because the pastry will sink; the only thing which makes it rise is steam. You should only look in the oven once the puffs have risen and have had chance to develop a firm framework inside.

**Dessert idea: fill small choux pastry puffs with ice cream and dip in chocolate icing.**

## FOR EVERY OCCASION

Once the pastry has been prepared it shouldn't be left standing around for very long. When you have baked your choux pastry puffs they should be served immediately. You can't really prepare choux pastry in advance, so you will have to freeze the pastry when baked. If you bake a few extra puffs you will always have something for unexpected guests. They will keep in the freezer for 3 months and can be defrosted in the oven in 5 minutes.

## MANY NAMES

Choux pastry is popular throughout Europe. For choux pastry puffs you need to pipe large rosettes, which will then rise to a diameter of 10 cm/4 inches or more. For profiteroles, popular in southern Europe, instead of piping large rosettes you need to pipe only a small whirl on the baking sheet. If you pipe a stripe on the sheet and fill it when baked, this is an éclair.

## CROQUEMBOUCHE

The name 'croquembouche' means 'crispy in the mouth' and is the name for a decorative pyramid made of filled choux pastry balls. The pyramid is surrounded by a web of spun caramel strands. It is well worth experiencing this contrast between delicate filling, light pastry and crunchy caramel. Bake about 120 walnut-sized choux pastry balls. Fill them with fresh cream, a cream mixture (page 216) or chocolate cream (page 220). Now we come to the caramel which holds the whole thing together. Put 250 g/9 oz caster sugar in a saucepan with 2 tbsp water and boil until the mixture turns pale brown. Remove pan from heat, dip the top of each choux pastry ball in the caramel and build up layers into a pyramid on a cake board or a flat plate. Spin threads with a teaspoon from the remaining liquid caramel (see page 225) and build up into a web around the choux pastry pyramid.

## FOR DIABETICS

Choux pastry is ideal for diabetics because it doesn't contain any sugar. As you can't use sugar icing or chocolate, the next best thing is to sweeten the pastry itself with half a teaspoon of liquid sweetener. Flour which is rich in roughage is good for diabetics. Instead of using plain flour, try using a wholemeal flour, and at least 5 eggs because the flour will need more liquid. The puffs will turn out a little darker but will taste delicious. The basic recipe (page 150) makes about 12 puffs, and curd cheese or quark, fresh fruit or diabetic jam can be used as fillings.

**Choux pastry freezes very well indeed. Small profiteroles can be put straight into a freezer bag when they have cooled. For larger puffs you should first cut off a pastry lid to let the steam escape.**

# PLUMS IN CHOUX PASTRY

| Ingredients for 8 puffs |
| --- |
| 125 ml/4 fl. oz milk |
| 65 g/2 oz soft margarine |
| pinch salt |
| 1 tsp caster sugar |
| 100 g/4 oz flour |
| 2 eggs (size 2) |
| oil for greasing |
| 8 prunes (de-stoned) |
| vegetable oil for frying |
| 4 tbsp caster sugar |
| 1 tsp cinnamon for dredging |

**1** Bring milk, margarine, salt and sugar to boil. Add flour and baking powder all at once and stir until the dough comes away from the sides of the saucepan and forms a ball. Remove pan from heat and stir in 1 egg. Leave choux pastry to cool a little, then mix in 2nd egg.

**2** Using ½ the dough make 8 little heaps on oiled baking parchment or greaseproof paper. Lay a prune on top of each, then put the remaining dough on top of the prunes. Flour hands and use to shape dough into balls.

**3** Heat vegetable oil to 170°C/350°F. Slip the dough balls into the fat a couple at a time and fry for about 10 minutes until golden brown. Drain on absorbent kitchen paper. Mix the sugar and cinnamon together and dredge the baked plums in the sugar.

# FILLED CHOUX PASTRY HEARTS

| Ingredients for 3 hearts |
| --- |
| FOR THE DOUGH |
| 80 g/3 oz margarine |
| pinch salt |
| 200 g/7 oz flour |
| 4 eggs (size 2) |
| 2 tbsp flaked almonds for sprinkling |
| FOR THE FILLING |
| 2 leaves white gelatine |
| 250 g/9 oz red currants |
| 50 g/2 oz icing sugar |
| 200 g/7 oz double cream |
| 1 tbsp icing sugar for dusting |

**1** Bring margarine, 250 ml/8 fl. oz water and salt to boil. Add flour and stir until the dough comes away from the sides of the saucepan in a ball. Remove pan from heat. Add eggs one by one.

**2** Put the choux pastry in a piping bag with a star-shaped nozzle. Pipe 3 hearts onto a baking sheet lined with baking parchment. Sprinkle almonds over hearts. Bake in a preheated oven at 225°C/425°F/Gas mark 7 for 25-30 minutes, then cut open.

**3** Soften gelatine. Wash berries and strip from stalks. Reserve 1 tbsp berries. Pass the remaining berries through a sieve and mix with icing sugar. Dissolve gelatine and stir into redcurrant purée.

**4** Whisk cream until stiff and fold into redcurrant mixture. Fill hearts with cream. Decorate with reserved redcurrants and icing sugar.

# STRAWBERRY ECLAIRS

| Ingredients for 10 éclairs |
| --- |
| **FOR THE DOUGH** |
| 60 g/2 oz margarine |
| pinch salt |
| 1 sachet/approx. ½ oz vanilla sugar |
| 125 g/5 oz flour |
| 4 eggs |
| **FOR THE FILLING** |
| 4 leaves white gelatine |
| 500 g/1 lb 2 oz strawberries |
| 3 tbsp caster sugar |
| 400 g/14 oz double cream |
| 1 sachet/approx. ½ oz vanilla sugar |
| 1 tbsp icing sugar for dusting |

**1** Bring margarine, 250 ml/8 fl. oz water, salt and vanilla sugar to boil. Add all flour at once and stir until the dough comes away from the sides of the saucepan and forms a ball. Remove pan from heat and stir in 1 egg. Allow to cool a little, then add the other eggs one by one.

**2** Put the choux pastry in a piping bag with a large, star-shaped nozzle. Pipe 10 strips, each 10 cm/4 inches long on a baking sheet lined with baking parchment. Bake the éclairs in a pre-heated oven at 225°C/425°F/Gas mark 7 for about 30 minutes. As soon as they come out of the oven cut in half with a pair of scissors. Leave to cool.

**3** Soften gelatine in cold water. Wash and clean strawberries. Slice 12-15 fruit, purée the rest and mix with sugar. Drain gelatine, dissolve and stir into strawberry purée. Refrigerate.

**4** Whisk cream and vanilla sugar until stiff. As soon as the strawberry purée begins to set, fold in cream. Using a piping bag with a round nozzle fill bases of éclairs with strawberry cream. Arrange strawberry slices on top of cream. Put other half of éclair on top of strawberries and dust éclair with icing sugar.

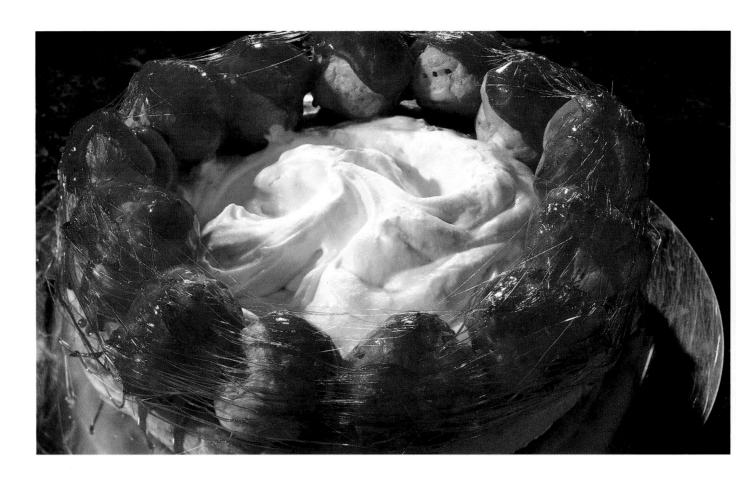

# GATEAU ST HONORÉ

**Ingredients for a spring form tin (24 cm/8 inches diam.)**
**FOR THE FILLING**
1 sachet vanilla blancmange powder
200 ml/approx. 7 fl. oz milk
½ vanilla pod
1 tbsp caster sugar
**FOR THE BASE**
150 g/6 oz frozen puff pastry
50 g/2 oz soft margarine
1 sachet/approx. ½ oz vanilla sugar
salt
150 g/6 oz flour
4-5 eggs (size 2)
200 g/7 oz caster sugar for the caramel
**FOR THE FILLING**
50 g/2 oz soft margarine
2 egg yolks
2 tbsp apricot brandy
200 g/7 oz double cream

**1** Mix the blancmange powder with 3 tbsp milk. Slit open vanilla pod and bring to boil with remaining milk and sugar. Stir in prepared blancmange mix, bring to boil again, cover with cling film and leave to cool.

**2** Defrost puff pastry. For the choux pastry bring 250 ml/8 fl. oz water, margarine, vanilla sugar and salt to boil. Add all flour at once and stir until the dough comes away from the sides of the pan in a ball.

**3** Remove saucepan from heat and stir in 1 egg. Leave to cool a little, gradually add remaining eggs and stir in.

**4** Put choux pastry in a piping bag with a round nozzle and pipe 16 walnut-sized balls on a baking sheet lined with baking parchment. Bake in a preheated oven at 225°C/425°F /Gas mark 7 for 10-12 minutes. Leave to cool.

**5** Lay the sheets of puff pastry on top of each other and roll out on a floured work surface. Cut out a circle with a 26 cm/8 inch diameter and place on a 2nd baking sheet.

**6** Pipe the remaining choux pastry as a border around the puff pastry. Pipe the centre in a spiral. Bake the base at the same temperature as the choux pastry buns for about 20 minutes.

**7** To make the caramel heat 1 tbsp water and the sugar in a saucepan. Using a tablespoon, pour caramel around the edge of the cake base. Place the choux buns on top. Pour a little caramel over each bun, and draw the rest around the edge of the cakes in spun sugar threads.

**8** Beat together margarine, egg yolks and apricot brandy until creamy. Gradually stir in the blancmange mix. Whisk cream until stiff and fold in. Fill gateau with cream and refrigerate. *Makes 10-12 slices.*

# EBERSWALD CRULLERS

**Ingredients for 15 crullers**
**FOR THE DOUGH**
60 g/2 oz soft margarine
pinch salt
1 tbsp caster sugar
1 sachet/approx. ½ oz vanilla sugar
150 g/6 oz flour
30 g/1 oz cornflour
5 eggs
oil for greasing
vegetable oil for frying
**FOR THE ICING**
200 g/7 oz icing sugar
3 tbsp lemon juice

**1** Bring margarine, 250 ml/8 fl. oz water, salt, sugar and vanilla sugar to boil. Mix together flour and cornflour and add to margarine. Stir until the dough comes away from the sides of the pan in a ball.
**2** Remove pan from heat and stir in 1 egg. Leave choux pastry to cool a little, then gradually stir in the remaining eggs one by one.
**3** Cut 15 cm/6 inch strips of greaseproof paper or baking parchment and brush with oil. Heat vegetable oil to about 170°C/350°F in a deep pan or deep fat fryer. Meanwhile put choux pastry in a piping bag with a star shaped nozzle. Pipe a ring 6-7 cm/approx. 3 inches in diameter on the paper.
**4** Lift up the dough rings with the paper and slide head first, 3 at a time, into hot fat. Fry until golden brown in these batches.

Turn after 2-3 minutes. Remove and drain well on absorbent kitchen paper.
**5** Mix the icing sugar and lemon juice to form icing. Brush crullers with icing and leave to dry.

**The crullers also taste good if dusted with icing sugar or dredged with caster sugar.**

# VANILLA CREAM PUFFS

| Ingredients for 12 puffs |
| --- |
| 50 g/2 oz soft margarine |
| pinch salt |
| 3 sachets/approx. 1½ oz vanilla sugar |
| 150 g/6 oz flour |
| 4-5 eggs (size 2) |
| 400 g/14 oz double cream |
| sugar to taste |
| icing sugar for dusting |

1 Bring margarine, 250 ml/8 fl. oz water, salt and 1 sachet/ approx. ½ oz vanilla sugar to boil. Add all flour at once and stir until dough comes away from sides of pan and forms a ball.

2 Remove saucepan from heat and stir 1 egg into dough. Leave to cool a little, then stir in the other eggs one by one, whilst beating the dough until smooth.

3 Put choux pastry in a piping bag with a star-shaped nozzle. Pipe 12 mounds of dough onto a baking sheet lined with baking parchment. Bake in a preheated oven at 225°C/425°F/Gas mark 7 for about 30 minutes.

4 Remove puffs and immediately cut open using scissors. Leave to cool on a wire rack.

5 Whisk the cream together with the remaining vanilla sugar until stiff. Put cream in a piping bag with a star-shaped nozzle. Fill the lower half of the puff with cream. Place the lid on top. Dust with icing sugar.

# CHURROS – SPANISH CRULLERS

| Ingredients for 20-22 churros |
| --- |
| 60 g/2 oz soft margarine |
| pinch salt |
| 150 g/6 oz flour |
| 4 eggs |
| 1 tsp brandy |
| olive oil for frying |
| FOR SPRINKLING |
| 2 tbsp caster sugar |
| ½ tsp cinnamon |

1 Bring margarine, 250 ml/8 fl. oz water and salt to boil. Add all flour at once and stir until dough comes away in a ball from sides of pan. Remove pan from heat and stir in 1 egg. Leave to cool a little, then stir in the remaining eggs and brandy. Continue stirring choux pastry until smooth.

2 Heat olive oil to about 170°C/ 350°F. Put choux pastry in a piping bag with a star-shaped nozzle. Pipe portions directly into oil in strips approx. 15 cm/6 inches long and fry for 4-5 minutes until golden brown. Remove with a skimmer. Drain on absorbent kitchen paper.

3 Mix cinnamon and sugar. Dredge churros in sugar and serve while still warm.
*Makes 4-6 portions.*

# PROFITEROLES

**Ingredients for approx. 50 profiteroles**
**FOR THE DOUGH**
75 g/3 oz soft margarine
1 tsp caster sugar
salt
150 g/6 oz flour
4-5 eggs (size 2)
**FOR THE FILLING**
3 leaves white gelatine
100 ml/3 fl. oz advocaat
400 g/14 oz double cream
1 tbsp caster sugar
**FOR DECORATION**
50 g/2 oz good quality bitter chocolate
5 strawberries
10 white grapes
125 ml/approx. ¼ pint white grape juice
½ sachet clear cake glaze or approx. ¼ oz arrowroot
200 g/7 oz icing sugar
2-3 tsp lemon juice
1 tbsp desiccated coconut
1 tbsp cocoa powder

**1** Bring margarine, 250 ml/8 fl. oz water, sugar and salt to boil. Add all flour at once and stir until the dough comes away from the base of the pan in a ball. Stir in 1 egg. Leave to cool. Stir in remaining eggs.

**2** Put choux pastry in a piping bag with a round nozzle. Pipe approx. 50 buns on a baking sheet lined with baking parchment. Bake in a preheated oven at 225°C/425°F/Gas mark 7 for 12-15 minutes.

**3** Soften gelatine, drain and stir into advocaat. Whisk cream until stiff. As soon as advocaat begins to set, fold in cream. Put advocaat cream in a piping bag with a small round nozzle, pierce each choux ball underneath and pipe full of cream.

**4** Melt the chocolate in a bowl over hot water and use to fill a freezer bag. Cut off a tiny corner of the bag and pipe chocolate stripes over 8 balls.

**5** Wash fruit and slice. Decorate 8 balls with grapes and 8 with strawberries. Bring grape juice, cake glaze or arrowroot, and 1 tsp icing sugar to boil. Spoon over fruit profiteroles using a tablespoon.

**6** Mix together 100 g/4 oz icing sugar and lemon juice. Decorate 8 profiteroles with lemon icing, then sprinkle with desiccated coconut. Decorate another 8 profiteroles with icing and dust with cocoa.

**7** Caramelise the remaining icing sugar, pour over remaining profiteroles and draw spun sugar threads around them. Place the profiteroles in small paper cases.

# NUT BALLS

| Ingredients for 16 balls |
| --- |
| 125 ml/4 fl. oz milk |
| 30 g/1 oz soft margarine |
| ¼ tsp salt |
| ¼ tsp white pepper |
| 50 g/2 oz flour |
| 50 g/2 oz ground hazelnuts |
| 2 tsp baking powder |
| 2 eggs |
| 1 bunch chives |
| vegetable oil for frying |

**1** Bring margarine, milk, salt and pepper to boil. Add flour, hazelnuts and baking powder all at once and stir until the dough comes away from the base of the pan in a ball.

**2** Remove pan from heat and stir in 1 egg. Leave dough to cool a little and add 2nd egg. Wash chives, chop finely and stir into dough.

**3** Heat vegetable oil in a deep pan or deep fat fryer to about 170°C/350°F. Form small dumplings out of the dough using 2 teaspoons and float a few at a time in the oil to fry for 3-4 minutes until golden brown. Drain well on absorbent kitchen paper.

# PARIS-BREST RING

| Ingredients for 1 ring (approx. 30 cm diam./approx. 12 inches diam.) |
| --- |
| FOR THE DOUGH |
| 90 g/4 oz soft margarine |
| pinch salt |
| 150 g/6 oz flour |
| 5 eggs |
| margarine for greasing |
| 2 tbsp flaked almonds |
| 3 tbsp icing sugar for dusting |
| FOR THE FILLING |
| 375 g/13 fl. oz. milk |
| pinch salt |
| 2 tsp instant coffee |
| 5 egg yolks |
| 100 g/4 oz caster sugar |
| 45 g/2 oz flour |
| 250 g/9 oz soft margarine |

**1** Bring margarine, 250 ml/8 fl. oz water and salt to boil. Add flour and stir until dough comes away from base of pan in a ball. Stir in eggs one by one.

**2** Fill a piping bag with pastry. Pipe a 30 cm/12 inch diameter ring on a greased baking sheet. Sprinkle with almonds and bake in a preheated oven at 200°C/400°F/ Gas mark 6 for about 30 minutes, then slice into 2 layers.

**3** Bring milk, salt and coffee to boil. Whisk together egg yolks, sugar and flour. Pour milk onto egg yolks, stirring all the time. Return custard to pan, bring to boil. Strain through a sieve and leave to cool.

**4** Whisk the margarine until creamy and stir in the coffee custard a spoonful at a time. Put the custard in a piping bag with a star-shaped nozzle and use to fill the ring. Dust with icing sugar.

# THYME PUFFS

| Ingredients for 6 puffs |
| --- |
| **FOR THE DOUGH** |
| **30 g/1 oz soft margarine** |
| **salt** |
| **70 g/3 oz flour** |
| **2 eggs** |
| **1 bunch thyme** |
| **FOR THE FILLING** |
| **30 g/1 oz peeled almonds** |
| **2 small tomatoes** |
| **1 small clove garlic** |
| **100 g/4 oz mayonnaise or salad cream** |
| **1 tbsp wine vinegar** |
| **salt** |
| **white pepper** |
| **cayenne pepper** |

**1** Bring margarine, 125 ml/4 fl. oz water and salt to boil. Add all flour at once and stir until dough comes away from sides of pan and forms a ball.

**2** Remove pan from heat and stir in 1 egg. Leave dough to cool a little and stir in 2nd egg. Reserve a few thyme stalks for garnish. Strip leaves from stalks, chop and add to dough.

**3** Using 2 teaspoons make 6 little mounds of dough on a baking sheet lined with baking parchment. Bake in a preheated oven at 225°C/425°F /Gas mark 7 for about 30 minutes. Using scissors, cut open the cooked puffs straight away and leave to cool.

**4** Toast almonds until golden brown, then chop finely. Plunge the tomatoes into boiling water, blanch, remove skins and seeds, and dice. Reserve 1 tbsp for garnish.

**5** Peel and finely chop garlic. Mix together with mayonnaise, diced tomato, almonds and vinegar. Season with salt and pepper.

**6** Fill lower half of puffs with almond mayonnaise. Decorate with diced tomato and thyme leaves, place lid on top of puff and dust lightly with cayenne pepper.

# CHEESE GOUGERE

| Ingredients for approx. 40 gougères |
| --- |
| 500 ml/16 fl. oz milk |
| 125 g/5 oz soft margarine |
| 1-2 tsp salt |
| freshly ground white pepper |
| freshly ground nutmeg |
| 250 g/9 oz flour |
| 7 eggs (size 2) |
| 125 g/5 oz gruyère cheese |
| 2 tbsp double cream |

1 Bring milk, margarine, salt, pepper and nutmeg to boil. Add all flour at once and stir until the dough comes away from the sides of the pan and forms a ball. Remove pan from heat and stir in 1 egg. Leave dough to cool a little and stir in the remaining eggs one by one. Finely chop the cheese and mix into dough with the cream.
2 Break off small pieces of dough with 2 tablespoons and place on a baking sheet lined with baking parchment.
3 Bake in a preheated oven at 225°C/425°F/Gas mark 7 for 25-30 minutes.

TIP: This hearty cheese pastry comes from Burgundy in France, where it is served as an accompaniment to wine.

# SAVOURY ALMOND RINGS

| Ingredients for 8-10 rings |
| --- |
| 50 g/2 oz soft margarine |
| pinch salt |
| 75 g/3 oz flour |
| 2 eggs |
| 30 g/1 oz Emmental cheese |
| 1 egg yolk |
| 3 tbsp flaked almonds |
| 200 g/7 oz blue cheese |
| 2-3 tbsp double cream |
| 1 stick celery |
| 1 bunch chives |
| 10 cherry tomatoes |

1 Bring margarine, 125 ml/4 fl. oz water and salt to boil. Add all flour at once and stir until dough comes away from sides of pan and forms a ball. Remove pan from heat and stir in 1 egg. Leave dough to cool a little and add 2nd egg.
2 Finely grate cheese and stir into dough. Put dough in a piping bag with a round nozzle. Pipe 8-10 rings, each 5 cm/2 inches in diameter, on a baking sheet lined with baking parchment. Brush with beaten egg yolk and sprinkle flaked almonds on top.
3 Bake in a preheated oven at 225°C/425°F/Gas mark 7 for about 20 minutes. Cut open immediately with scissors and leave to cool.
4 Mash the blue cheese with a fork and stir in cream. Wash and clean celery, dice finely and mix with cheese. Put cheese in a piping bag with a large round nozzle and use to fill bottom half of ring.
5 Wash and finely chop chives. Wash cherry tomatoes and slice. Arrange tomatoes on top of cheese and sprinkle with chopped chives. Place upper half of ring on top.

## WHOLEGRAIN INGREDIENTS

# Wholemeal and granary – healthy through and through

Rye alone spurs sourdough to great heights. This time-honoured method of raising dough works on its own, but the right temperature in the kitchen and a patient cook will help. Whole wheat and buckwheat also combine happily with yeast, whether in granary bread, substantial rolls or delicious cakes and pastries.

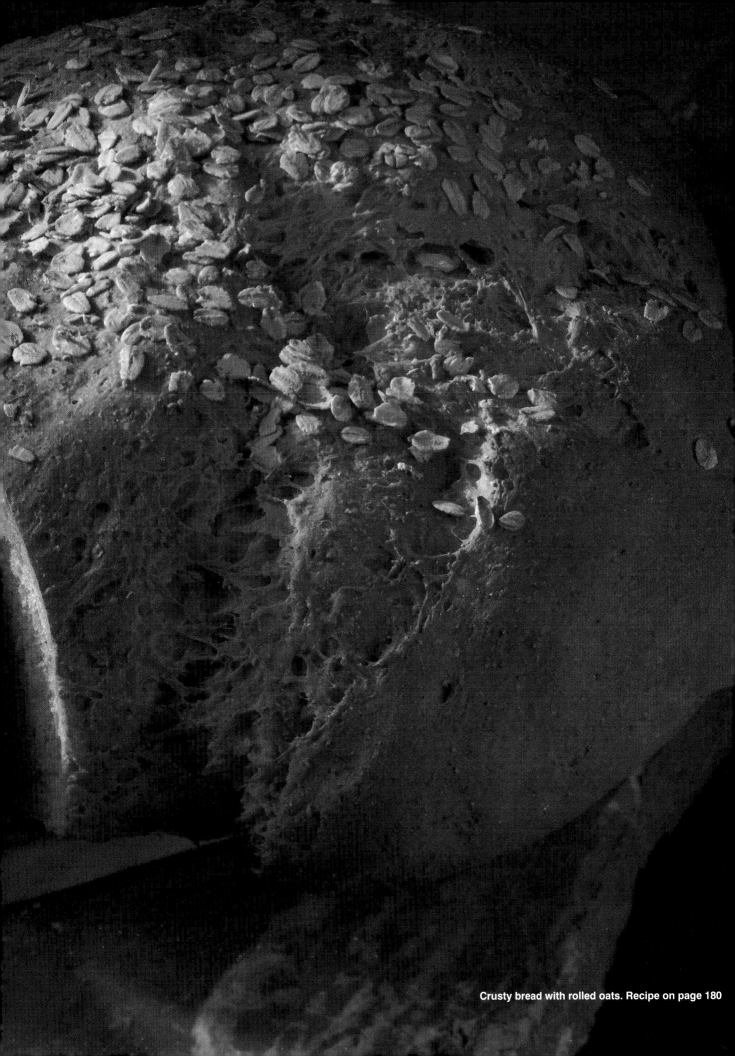

Crusty bread with rolled oats. Recipe on page 180

# HOW TO MAKE SUCCESSFUL SOURDOUGH BREAI

If you like making wholegrain bread sooner or later you will have to use leaven. For dough with a high rye content, yeast alone is not enough to lighten the mixture. Only the acid in the leaven can unlock the protein in the rye which is so important to the success of bread. Then the dough will be light and the delicious aroma of the bread will develop fully. But what is leaven? Basically it is the ancient predecessor of yeast. Nowadays the hard-working bacteria in baker's yeast is carefully cultured, but with sourdough you simply wait until wild yeasts, acetic acid and malolactic acid bacteria colonise the dough, souring it and lightening it by their action. The tried and tested Basic Recipe for leaven requires 10 g/2 oz yeast, 250 ml/8 fl. oz warm water, 150 g/6 oz medium grain rye flour. If you mix these ingredients and leave them at room temperature you will be able to bake with the leaven after 3 days.

**1** To start the leaven working mix the yeast with water and rye flour. Loosely cover the bowl with a cloth and leave to work in a warm room for 3-5 days.

**2** You will need about 100 g/4 oz fermented leaven to 1 kg/2 lb 3 oz flour or wholegrain flour. Depending on the recipe you are using, you will have to mix the leaven with yeast and the appropriate quantity of water. It is better if all the ingredients are at room temperature.

**6** Leave the dough to rise for 6-12 hours in a cool room or in the refrigerator. It is ready when deep cracks appear on the surface. If the dough gets too warm whilst rising it will turn out too sour and won't rise when baked.

**7** Knead the dough thoroughly with your hands on a floured work surface. This takes quite a lot of strength and a little patience.

**3** For sourdough bread you can use any mixture of rye flour, wheat flour and whole grains. Combine with spices and don't forget salt, or the bread won't turn out well.

**4** Pour the liquid leaven and yeast mixture into the flour and knead to a smooth dough. You can either use muscle power on a floured work surface, or a large food processor, to knead the dough until it is smooth and elastic.

**5** Shape the dough into a ball on a floured work surface and leave to rise in a bowl covered with a cloth.

**8** Shape into smooth loaves, brush with salt water and sprinkle rolled oats, whole grains or flour on top. Or if you want a shiny crust, brush the loaf with coffee substitute made from malted barley. Leave to rest for an hour before baking.

**9** An alternative method is to place the dough in a large greased loaf tin and make a cut along the length of the loaf. Brush with salt water and leave to rest for an hour.

**10** Bake the bread in a preheated oven for 20 minutes at 225°C/425°F/Gas mark 7, then a further 60-90 minutes, depending on size, at 200°C/400°F/Gas mark 6. To test if the bread is done, tap firmly on top of the loaf. If it sounds dull and hollow, then the bread is ready.

# WHOLEGRAIN INGREDIENTS

## FRESHLY GROUND

If you like baking with freshly ground wholemeal flour because of the pleasant, nutty aroma, you are spoilt for choice when it comes to flour mills. A hand-powered mill is usually sufficient for a small household. They are

**Hazelnuts or walnuts can usually be replaced by oily seeds, which make the baking particularly moist. Pictured above are pumpkin seeds (top), sesame seeds (centre) and sunflower seeds (bottom).**

**Corn mill: the housing is made of wood but the grinding mechanism may be made of steel, china or even stone to achieve finely ground grains.**

relatively cheap and can cope with up to 50 g/2 oz flour or grains per minute. They are particularly suitable for households with several members, or families who particularly like freshly baked bread. Your best buy is a table-top machine, or buy a milling attachment for your food processor. If you want to grind nuts and seeds in the mill, such as linseed or poppy seeds, you should pay special attention to the grinding mechanism. Only mills with a steel or china mechanism will be able to grind oily seeds.

## QUALITY OF FLOUR

Mills regularly test the flour they produce for its baking qualities,

which may vary greatly depending on the weather and the conditions at the time the grain was harvested. A branded flour will therefore always be about the same quality, but this is not always true of flour which you have ground yourself. Sometimes it will need less liquid than at other times, sometimes the baking will be light, sometimes more solid. For this reason you should not add all the liquid at once, but should stop adding liquid as soon as the dough achieves the correct consistency. If wholemeal dough is too wet, don't add more flour straight away as the dough may soak up the liquid and become firmer.

## MANY KINDS

If our recipes just state 'flour', then we mean normal white wheat flour for general baking. It is a basic grind, which means that only a small part of the whole grain, the so-called flour hull, goes into the bag of flour. Depending on how much of the vitamin-rich outer layers of the grain are included in flour, the greater the roughage content. Wholemeal flour contains the most roughage at around 12 g/½ oz per 100 g/4 oz flour.

## RYE FLOUR

If you use half rye flour for your bread, but you don't want to use leaven, you will need to add a little acid to the dough. Replace the water with buttermilk or whey, or add 1 or 2 tablespoons of wine vinegar.

## MILLET AND BARLEY

Both these grains, when finely ground, are ideally suited to short-crust pastry. On the other hand yeast dough and sponge mixtures should only contain a maximum of one quarter of these types of flours, otherwise they will be too tough.

## SOYA FLOUR

Soya flour and soya grains are excellent for baking. The high content of the natural emulsifier, lecithin, in soya improves the resulting cakes and pastries and increases the nutritional value. You can replace up to 20 percent wheat flour with soya flour in biscuit and cake recipes without any problems. If you use more than this, however, it alters the taste of the baking.

## OATMEAL

The subtle, nutty aroma of oats harmonises well with both sweet and savoury cakes and pastries. However, don't expect cakes baked with oatmeal to turn out light and airy. You can replace up to one quarter of white wheat flour with oat flakes or oatmeal.

**Dried fruits can be used partly to replace sugar in baking. They also make the cake beautifully moist and impart a fruity tang.**

## SWEET MATTERS

You can't bake cakes without sweetening ingredients. However the 80 percent sugar content in honey makes it very sweet, and it contains so much liquid that it is unsuitable for many recipes. The same applies to syrup and fruit sugar. If you want to use a natural product instead of normal refined sugar, try using cane sugar. It is available from health food shops. It comes in pale brown crystals, so it can be sprinkled and used just like sugar.

**Abundance of corn: when finely ground the end product is hearty, aromatic cakes. When coarsely ground the grains turn up in sourdough breads.**

# SPICY WHOLEGRAIN BAPS

| Ingredients for 16-18 baps |
| --- |
| 10 g/½ oz yeast |
| 150 g/6 oz whole rye flour |
| 1 cube/2 oz yeast |
| 1 tbsp apple juice or sugar beet syrup |
| 100 g/4 oz whole rye flour |
| 500 g/1 lb 2 oz rye flour |
| 350 g/12 oz wheat flour |
| 1 tbsp salt |
| 1 tbsp caraway |
| 1 tsp ground coriander |
| flour for work surface |

**1** To make the leaven dissolve yeast in 250 ml/8 fl. oz warm water. Mix with whole rye flour and cover with a cloth. Leave to ferment for 3-5 days at room temperature.

**2** Mix together yeast, 100 g/4 oz leaven, 1 tbsp apple juice or sugar beet syrup and 600 ml/1 pint water. Knead in flours, salt, caraway and ground coriander and leave to rise for 2 hours at room temperature.

**3** Knead the dough on a floured surface and divide into 16-18 pieces. Shape the pieces of dough into flat bread rolls. Leave to rest for 1 hour at room temperature.

**4** Bake in a preheated oven at 225°C/425°F/Gas mark 7 for the first 5 minutes, then at 175°C/350°F/Gas mark 4 for a further 30-35 minutes. Leave baps to cool.

# RYE SOURDOUGH BREAD

| Ingredients for a large loaf |
| --- |
| 10 g/½ oz yeast |
| 150 g/6 oz whole rye flour |
| 1 cube/2 oz yeast |
| 250 g/9 oz whole rye flour |
| 300 g/11 oz rye flour |
| 350 g/12 oz wheat flour |
| 100 g/4 oz sunflower seeds |
| 1 tbsp salt |
| 1 tsp sugar |
| ½ tsp ground caraway |
| 1 tsp ground coriander |

**1** To make the leaven, dissolve yeast in 250 ml/8 fl. oz lukewarm water. Mix with whole rye flour and cover with a cloth. Leave to ferment for 3-5 days at room temperature.

**2** Mix together yeast, 100 g/4 oz leaven, 600 ml/1 pint water, flours, sunflower seeds, salt, sugar, caraway and coriander. Leave the dough to rise for 3-4 hours at room temperature.

**3** Knead vigorously again and put into a round wicker basket. Leave to rest for 1-2 hours.

**4** Remove dough from basket and brush with water. Place on a baking sheet and bake for 5 minutes at first in an oven preheated to 225°C/425°F/Gas mark 7, then at 200°C/400°F/Gas mark 6 for 10 minutes. Finally bake for 1 hour at 175°C/350°F/Gas mark 4 until done.

# SOYA ROLLS

**Ingredients for 16 rolls**
**300 g/11 oz wheat flour**
**200 g/7 oz rye flour**
**1 cube/2 oz yeast**
**250 g/9 oz full fat yoghurt**
**2 tsp salt**
**40 g/2 oz soft margarine**
**flour for work surface**
**50 g/2 oz soya meal**
**margarine for greasing**
**soya meal for sprinkling**

**1** Put the wheat flour and rye flour in a bowl. Crumble yeast and sprinkle over flour. Mix together yoghurt, salt and 100 ml/approx. 3 fl. oz water and heat gently in a pan. Add margarine to pan and allow to melt.

**2** Add yoghurt mixture to flour. Knead to a smooth dough using the dough hook of a hand mixer. Cover with a cloth and leave to rise in a warm place until doubled in size.

**3** Knead the dough vigorously on a floured surface with your hands and knead in the soya meal. Roll the dough out into a sausage shape. Divide into 16 equal portions and shape each portion into a roll.

**4** Grease a baking sheet with margarine. Place the rolls on the sheet and brush with warm water. Sprinkle a little soya meal over each roll and cut a cross in the top of each roll with a knife. Leave to rest for a further 20 minutes.

**5** Bake in a preheated oven at 200°C/400°F/Gas mark 6 for about 20 minutes. Remove rolls from baking sheet and leave to cool on a wire rack.

# RYE BREAD WITH NUTS

**Ingredients for a loaf tin
(25 cm long, 1.5 l capacity/10 inches
long, 2 ½ pints capacity)**

| |
|---|
| 275 g/10 oz wheat flour |
| 200 g/7 oz rye flour |
| 25 g/1 oz wheat bran |
| 1 tsp salt |
| 250 g/9 oz full fat yoghurt |
| 1 cube/2 oz yeast |
| 40 g/2 oz soft margarine |
| 30 g/1 oz whole hazelnuts |
| 20 g/1 oz pistachio nuts |
| flour for work surface |
| 50 g/2 oz sunflower seeds |
| margarine for greasing |
| wheat or oat flakes for sprinkling |

**1** Put wheat flour, rye flour, wheat bran and salt in a bowl and mix together. Mix the yoghurt with 100 ml/approx. 3 fl. oz lukewarm water. Crumble yeast and dissolve in yoghurt and water mixture. Put the margarine in a saucepan, melt, and allow to cool again. Add the yeast mixture and margarine to the flour.

**2** Knead everything to a smooth dough with the dough hook of a hand mixer. Cover with a cloth and leave to rise in a warm place until doubled in size.

**3** Meanwhile coarsely chop the hazelnuts and pistachios. Vigorously knead the bread dough on a floured surface with your hands, kneading in the hazelnuts, pistachios and sunflower seeds.

**4** Shape the dough into a long loaf. Grease tin with margarine. Lay the dough in the tin, brush lightly with salted water and sprinkle wheat or oat flakes on top.

**5** Leave bread dough to rest for a further 20 minutes in a warm place. Bake in a preheated oven at 175°C/350°F/Gas mark 4 for about 55 minutes. Run a knife round edge of tin to loosen loaf, turn out and leave to cool on a wire rack.

# FOUR GRAIN FLAT BREAD

**Ingredients for 4 flat loaves**
**300 ml/½ pint buttermilk**
**½ cube/1 oz yeast**
**200 g/7 oz wholemeal wheat flour**
**100 g/4 oz maize flour**
**75 g/3 oz soya flour**
**100 g/4 oz whole rye flour**
**1 tsp salt**
**flour for work surface and for dusting**
**margarine for greasing**
**50 g/2 oz salted peanuts**
**50 g/2 oz pumpkin seeds**

1 Heat the buttermilk in a pan. Crumble yeast and dissolve in buttermilk. Put wheat flour, maize flour, soya flour, whole rye flour and salt in a mixing bowl and mix together. Add the yeast mixture and knead to a smooth dough using the dough hook of a hand mixer.

2 Cover with a cloth and leave to rise in a warm place until doubled in size.

3 Vigorously knead the dough on a floured surface by hand. Divide into 4 portions and roll out each one to a flat loaf approx. 1 cm/½ inch thick.

4 Grease a baking sheet with margarine and lightly dust with flour. Lay the flat loaves on the sheet and brush with water. Sprinkle peanuts and pumpkin seeds on top. Press them lightly down into the dough.

5 Leave to rest for a further 20 minutes. Prick the loaves all over with a fork. Bake in a preheated oven at 200°C/400°F/Gas mark 6 for about 30 minutes.

TIP: If the loaves are to be served for breakfast or brunch, prepare the dough cold the day before and refrigerate overnight. Next morning, shape as described in step 3, leave to rise and bake for about 30 minutes.

# RAISIN DANISH PASTRIES

| Ingredients for 12-15 pastries |
| --- |
| 200 ml/8 fl. oz milk |
| 200 g/7 oz cane sugar |
| ½ cube/1 oz yeast |
| 200 g/7 oz wheat flour |
| 300 g/11 oz wholemeal wheat flour |
| 1 tsp salt |
| 130 g/5 oz soft margarine |
| 2 eggs |
| 250 g/9 oz dried apricots |
| 200 g/7 oz raisins |
| 100 g/4 oz runny honey |

1 Warm 100 ml/approx. 3 fl. oz milk. Dissolve 1 tsp cane sugar in milk. Crumble yeast and dissolve in milk. Leave mixture to work for 15 minutes.

2 Mix flours, 100 g/4 oz cane sugar and salt in a bowl. Heat the remaining milk and melt 80 g/ 3 oz margarine in milk. Add eggs, yeast mixture and margarine to flour. Knead everything to a smooth dough.

3 Cover the yeast dough and leave to rise in a warm place until doubled in size. Then knead again and roll out to a 5 mm/¼ inch thick rectangle, approx. 30 x 35 cm/approx. 12 x 14 inches.

4 For the filling, chop the apricots into small dice. Melt the remaining margarine and mix with the apricots, remaining cane sugar and raisins. Spread the mixture over the dough and, starting from the shortest side, roll up loosely.

5 Cut the roll into slices approx. 2 cm/1 inch thick. Place on a baking sheet lined with baking parchment so that the cut side is uppermost. Leave to rest for 20 minutes.

6 Bake at 175°C/350°F/Gas mark 4 in a preheated oven for about 60 minutes. Brush the warm pastries with honey.

# PUMPKIN SEED SLICES

| Ingredients for 40-50 slices |
| --- |
| 150 g/6 oz pumpkin seeds |
| 150 g/6 oz rolled oats |
| 100 g/4 oz soft margarine |
| 80 g/3 oz cane sugar |
| 3 tbsp honey |
| pinch salt |
| 1 tsp ground cinnamon |
| pinch ground cloves |
| 2 tsp lemon juice |
| margarine for greasing |

1 Roast the pumpkin seeds and rolled oats in a frying pan, turning all the time, until pale gold. Put them in a bowl and leave to cool. Add margarine, cane sugar, honey, salt, cinnamon, cloves and lemon juice and stir.

2 Lay out a square 20 cm x 20 cm/8 x 8 inches on a greased baking sheet, using an adjustable baking tin, greaseproof paper or foil. Fill square with mixture and spread out until approx. 1.5 cm/½ inch thick.

3 Bake in a preheated oven at 175°C/350°F/Gas mark 4 for about 15 minutes. Remove from oven, allow to cool a little. While still warm cut into small diamonds.

# STUFFED CHICKEN

| Ingredients for 3 chickens |
| --- |
| **FOR THE DOUGH** |
| **500 g/1 lb 2 oz wholemeal wheat flour** |
| **500 g/1 lb 2 oz wheat flour** |
| **500 ml/3/4 pint milk** |
| **60 g/2 oz yeast** |
| **150 g/6 oz cane sugar** |
| **150 g/6 oz soft margarine** |
| **pinch salt** |
| **1 egg** |
| **FOR THE FILLING** |
| **250 g/9 oz freshly ground poppy seeds** |
| **100 g/4 oz raisins** |
| **50 g/2 oz desiccated coconut** |
| **100 g/4 oz honey** |
| **2 egg whites** |
| **margarine for greasing** |
| **FOR DECORATION** |
| **1 egg yolk** |
| **poppy seeds** |
| **pumpkin seeds** |

1 Mix the different types of flour and make a well in the centre. Heat 50 ml/approx. 2 fl. oz milk, dissolve yeast in milk and pour into well with 2 tsp cane sugar and stir until the consistency is similar to porridge. Cover and leave to work for 10 minutes.

2 Melt margarine and leave to cool. Add to the flour with the remaining cane sugar, milk, salt and egg, and knead everything to a smooth dough. Cover and leave to rise in a warm place until doubled in size.

3 Cut out a hen shape approx. ⅔ size of the baking sheet. Bring the poppy seeds and 200 ml/6 fl. oz water to boil and leave seeds to swell for 8 minutes. Drain and leave to cool. Mix with raisins,

desiccated coconut, honey and 1 egg white.

4 Roll out the yeast dough until approx. 5 mm/¼ inch thick and cut out 6 hens (make 3 hens approx. 2 cm/4 inch larger). Place the 3 smaller hens on a greased baking sheet. Put the filling on the dough and spread, leaving a 1-2 cm/½-1 inch edge all around. Brush the edges with remaining egg white. Place the larger hens on top and crimp edges tightly together.

5 Beat together egg yolk and 1 tbsp water. Brush hens with egg wash. Decorate the combs, tail and feet with poppy and pumpkin seeds. Bake in a preheated oven at 200°C/400°F/Gas mark 6 for 15-20 minutes.

# SEA BUCKTHORN CAKE WITH QUINCE

**Ingredients for a spring form tin (20 cm diam., 1 l capacity/8 inches diam., 1 pints capacity)**
**FOR THE DOUGH**
2 eggs
75 g/3 oz cane sugar
75 g/3 oz soft margarine
pinch salt
1 tsp grated lemon zest
2 tbsp lemon juice
75 g/3 oz wholemeal wheat flour
1 level tsp baking powder
**FOR THE FILLING**
125 ml/4 fl. oz white wine
3 tbsp honey
1 tsp grated lemon zest
2 tbsp lemon juice
3 quinces
6 leaves white gelatine
250 g/9 oz sea buckthorn purée with honey
300 g/11 oz whipped cream
1 tsp pistachio nuts for sprinkling

**1** Separate eggs. Whisk together egg yolks, cane sugar, margarine, salt, lemon zest and juice until creamy. Mix together flour and baking powder and stir in. Beat egg whites until stiff and fold in.
**2** Line the spring form tin with baking parchment and fill with mixture. Bake in a preheated oven at 175-200°C/350-400°F/Gas mark 4–6 for 25-30 minutes
**3** Bring wine, 125 ml/4 fl. oz water, 2 tbsp honey, lemon zest and juice to boil. Peel 2 quinces, cut into 8 sections and core. Wash and slice 3rd quince. Cook the quince sections in the liquid for 15 minutes, and the quince slices for about 5 minutes, then leave to cool.

**4** Soften gelatine and melt wet gelatine over a low heat. Stir into buckthorn purée. Refrigerate. Whisk cream until stiff. As soon as purée begins to set, fold in whipped cream.
**5** Spread ½ of buckthorn cream over base. Drain quinces, reserving liquid. Spread quince sections over cream. Spread remaining cream on top of quinces. Decorate buckthorn cake with quince slices and refrigerate.
**6** Heat together remaining honey and 4 tbsp liquid from quinces. Brush over quinces. Cut the pistachio nuts into quarters lengthways and sprinkle over cake.
*Makes 8 slices.*

# BUCKWHEAT COOKIES

**Ingredients for 18 bun tins or 6-8 brioche moulds (brioche moulds each 175 ml capacity/each approx. ¼ pint capacity)**
100 g/4 oz buckwheat meal
250 ml/8 fl. oz milk
50 g/2 oz soft margarine
pinch salt
4 eggs
100 g/4 oz cane sugar
1 tsp ground cinnamon
pinch ground cardamom
200 g/7 oz ground hazelnuts
1 tsp lemon juice
margarine for greasing
**For sprinkling**
100 g/4 oz cashew nuts
cane sugar

**1** Bring buckwheat meal, milk, margarine and salt to boil. Simmer for 2 minutes, stirring constantly. Remove pan from heat and leave buckwheat meal to swell for 20 minutes. Stir occasionally.
**2** Separate eggs. Mix together egg yolks and cane sugar, leave to rest for 1-2 minutes, then whisk until creamy. Add cinnamon, cardamom and ground hazelnuts to egg yolks and stir in. Stir in the cooled buckwheat.

**3** Whisk together egg whites and lemon juice until stiff. Stir ⅓ of egg whites into buckwheat, then lightly fold in rest of egg whites with a balloon whisk. Grease tins with margarine. Fill with mixture. Cut cashew nuts in half and sprinkle on top of cookies with cane sugar.
**4** Bake in a preheated oven at 200°C/400°F/Gas mark 6 for 30 minutes if mixture is in bun tins, and for 60 minutes if in brioche moulds. Remove cookies from oven and turn out onto a wire rack. Leave to cool.

# MARBLED YOGHURT GATEAU

| Ingredients for a spring form tin (26 cm diam., 2.5 l capacity/10 inches diam., 4¼ pints capacity) |
| --- |
| **FOR THE DOUGH** |
| 200 g/7 oz wholemeal wheat flour |
| pinch salt |
| pinch baking powder |
| 75 g/3 oz cane sugar |
| 100 g/4 oz soft margarine |
| 1 egg |
| 2 tbsp sour cream (24% fat) |
| **FOR THE TOPPING** |
| 12 leaves white gelatine |
| 450 g/1 lb full fat yoghurt |
| ½ tsp grated lemon zest |
| 5-6 tbsp lemon juice |
| 150 g/6 oz maple syrup or |
| runny honey |
| 200 g/7 oz double cream |
| 500 g/1 lb 2 oz strawberries |
| 3 mangoes (each approx. 300 g/11 oz) |

**1** Knead together ingredients for dough. Cover and refrigerate for 30 minutes, roll out and use to line the base of a spring form tin. Prick the base all over and bake in a preheated oven at 200°C/400°F/ Gas mark 6 for about 20 minutes.

**2** Soften gelatine. Mix together yoghurt, lemon zest, and 3 tbsp lemon juice and sweeten to taste with maple syrup. Dissolve 6 leaves of wet gelatine over a low heat, stir into yoghurt and refrigerate. Whisk cream until stiff. As soon as yoghurt begins to set, fold in whipped cream. Spread yoghurt over base. Refrigerate until yoghurt is set.

**3** Wash, clean and purée the strawberries, reserving 10 berries. Sweeten with maple syrup. Peel mangoes and cut away from stone in slices. Purée the flesh of 2 mangoes, adjust taste with lemon juice and maple syrup.

**4** Dissolve remaining wet gelatine over a low heat. Stir ½ gelatine into strawberry purée and ½ into mango purée. Spread fruit purées over yoghurt. Using a spoon make marbled patterns in purée. Refrigerate gateau until purée sets.

**5** Slice strawberries and garnish yoghurt gateau with remaining fruit. *Makes 12 slices.*

# WHOLEMEAL BISCUITS

| Ingredients for 60-80 biscuits |
| --- |
| **FOR THE DOUGH** |
| 350 g/12 oz wholemeal flour |
| ¼ tsp baking powder |
| ½ tsp ground cinnamon |
| pinch salt |
| 1 tsp grated lemon zest |
| 150 g/6 oz cane sugar |
| 150 g/6 oz ground almonds |
| 3 eggs |
| 175 g/6 oz soft margarine |
| 1 tsp lemon juice |
| wholemeal flour for work surface |
| a little cane sugar for sprinkling |

**1** Mix together wholemeal flour, baking powder, cinnamon, salt, lemon zest, cane sugar and almonds. Separate 1 egg. Add egg white, remaining eggs, margarine and lemon juice to flour and knead everything to a smooth dough. Refrigerate for 30 minutes.
**2** Roll out dough on a floured surface to approx. 3 mm/approx. ¼ inch thick. Cut into shapes, e.g. triangles, as liked. Now place the biscuits on a baking sheet lined with baking parchment.
**3** Beat together egg yolk and 1 tbsp water. Brush biscuits with egg wash and sprinkle with cane sugar. Then bake in a preheated oven at 200°C/400°F/Gas mark 6 for 18-20 minutes and leave to cool.

# HONEYCOMB CAKE

| Ingredients for a baking sheet (30 x 40 cm/12 x 16 inches) or a flan tin (30 cm diam./12 inches diam.) |
| --- |
| **FOR THE DOUGH** |
| 200 ml/approx. 7 fl. oz buttermilk |
| 125 g/5 oz cane sugar |
| essence from 1 vanilla pod |
| 4 eggs |
| ½ tsp grated orange zest |
| 300 g/11 oz wheat flour |
| 100 g/4 oz chopped hazelnuts |
| 1 sachet/approx. ½ oz baking powder |
| margarine for greasing |
| **FOR THE TOPPING** |
| 150 g/6 oz soft margarine |
| 50 g/2 oz cane sugar |
| 2 tbsp honey |
| 3 tbsp milk |
| 75 g/3 oz each whole hazelnuts and walnuts |

**1** Beat together buttermilk, cane sugar, vanilla essence and eggs until creamy. Add orange zest. Mix together flour, hazelnuts and baking powder and stir into egg mixture.
**2** Spread the mixture over a greased baking sheet or use to fill a greased flan tin. Bake in a preheated oven at 200°C/400°F/Gas mark 6 for 15 minutes.
**3** Meanwhile bring margarine, cane sugar, honey, milk, hazelnuts and walnuts to boil, stirring continuously, and leave to cool.
**4** Spread topping over base and bake at the same temperature as before for a further 10-15 minutes. *Makes 24 slices.*

# CURD CHEESE PASTIES

| Ingredients for 18-20 pasties |
| --- |
| 250 g/9 oz wheat flour |
| 150 g/6 oz wholemeal wheat flour |
| 175 g/6 oz cane sugar |
| 1 tsp grated lemon zest |
| 200 ml/approx. 6 fl. oz milk |
| 1 cube/2 oz yeast |
| 150 g/6 oz soft margarine |
| 500 g/1 lb 2 oz curd cheese or quark (20% fat) |
| 1 sachet vanilla blancmange powder |
| 2 eggs |
| 75 g/3 oz ground almonds |

1 Mix together flours, 75 g/3 oz cane sugar and ½ tsp grated lemon zest. Warm milk, crumble yeast and dissolve in milk. Add yeast and milk mixture, and 75 g/3 oz margarine, to flour. Knead to a smooth dough using the dough hook of a hand mixer. Cover and leave to rise in a warm place for about 30 minutes.

2 Melt remaining margarine and mix to a smooth paste with curd cheese, blancmange mix, remaining cane sugar and lemon zest, 1 egg and almonds.

3 Vigorously knead the dough again and roll out until 3 mm/ approx. ¼ inch thick. Cut out circles with a diameter of 12.5 cm/5 inches]. Put 1 tbsp of cheese mixture on each circle.

4 Separate egg. Brush edges of dough with egg white and fold in half. Press together pastry edges with the tines of a fork to create a wave pattern. Beat together egg yolk and 1 tbsp water with a fork. Brush pasties with egg wash and place on a baking sheet lined with baking parchment. Bake in a preheated oven at 175°C/350°F/ Gas mark 4 for 10-15 minutes.

# CRUSTY BREAD WITH ROLLED OATS

| Ingredients for 1 loaf |
| --- |
| 750 g/1 lb 11 oz wheat flour |
| 200 g/7 oz rye flour |
| 30 g/1 oz wheat bran |
| 2 tsp salt |
| 600 ml/1 pint buttermilk |
| 1 cube/2 oz yeast |
| 25 g/1 oz soft margarine |
| 2 tbsp rolled oats for sprinkling |

1 Mix together wheat flour, rye flour, wheat bran and salt in a bowl. Heat buttermilk. Crumble yeast into buttermilk and dissolve. Add buttermilk and margarine to flour and knead everything to a smooth dough. Cover and leave to rise in a warm place until doubled in size.

2 Vigorously knead dough again. Shape into a loaf and place on a baking sheet lined with baking parchment. Brush loaf with water and sprinkle with rolled oats.

3 Leave to rest in a warm place for a further 20 minutes. Then bake in a preheated oven at 200°C/400°F/Gas mark 6 for about 40 minutes. Remove bread from baking sheet and leave to cool.

MERINGUES, STRUDEL AND HONEY CAKE

# White as snow, wafer thin and sweet as honey

Meringues made of beaten egg whites and sugar are fabulously sweet. Spicy ginger biscuits and dark honey cake are popular at any time of year. Practice makes perfect when it comes to making strudel. Strudel pastry is perfect, so the saying goes in Vienna, when you can read the newspaper through it.

Classic apple strudel. Recipe on page 195.

# HOW TO MAKE SUCCESSFUL STRUDEL

If you make successful strudel even experienced cooks will be lost in speechless admiration, because strudels are thought to be difficult to make. This simply isn't true. You can't go wrong if you just rely on our instructions for the method and a tried and tested basic recipe comprising 250 g/9 oz flour, 50 g/2 oz melted margarine, 1 egg, pinch of salt, approx. 125 ml/4 fl. oz lukewarm water.

You can omit the egg and add more water if you wish (approx. 150 ml/¼ pint). Now all you need is patience when kneading the pastry and a little courage when drawing out the sheet of strudel.

**1** Heap flour, margarine, salt and egg together on the work surface. Gradually add lukewarm water. Knead to a smooth dough using 2 palette knives or mix in a bowl.

**2** Put the pastry on a floured work surface and knead for at least 10 minutes (!) by hand. To be certain that you knead the pastry for the correct length of time, set your kitchen timer.

# HOW TO MAKE SUCCESSFUL CURD CHEESE PUFF PASTRY

Curd cheese puff pastry is similar to real puff pastry or flaky pastry, and its short, flaky texture is just as attractive, but the best thing about it is that it is much easier to make. The ingredients for the basic recipe are as follows: 250 g/9 oz flour, ½ tsp salt, 1 tsp baking powder, 250 g/9 oz low fat curd cheese or quark, 250 g/9 oz margarine.

Curd cheese puff pastry is very adaptable and is ideal for all kinds of small pastries. It tastes best fresh from the oven.

**1** Put the curd cheese in a sieve lined with muslin and leave to drain for several hours. Alternatively you can twist the muslin and wring it out.

**2** Put the flour in a heap on the work surface. Add the drained cheese, margarine and salt to the flour.

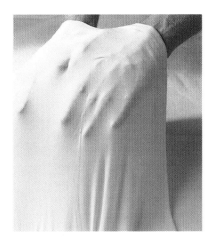

**3**  The pastry should now be elastic and should shine like silk. Shape into a ball, brush with oil and cover with a warmed ceramic basin. Leave to rest for at least 30 minutes.

**4**  Spread out a large cloth, such as a tablecloth, and dust with flour. Roll out the strudel pastry on the cloth until it is as thin as possible.

**5**  Run the backs of your hands under the pastry, slowly stretching it. Continue doing this until the dough is so thin that you can see the pattern of the cloth underneath. Cut off the thick edges.

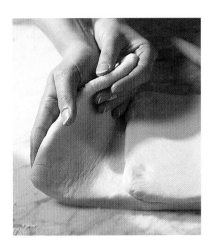

**3**  Chop all the ingredients into each other using two palette knives or table knives until a smooth, soft dough is produced. You can also use the dough hook of a hand mixer. Leave to rest for an hour.

**4**  To obtain the flaky texture, roll out the pastry into a long rectangle, approx. 20 x 40 cm/8 x 16 inches. Starting at the narrow side, first fold 1/3 into the centre of the rectangle, then fold the other section over the top. Wrap in cling film and leave to rest for 30 minutes.

**5**  Turn the closed side of the pastry envelope towards you and roll out again. Fold together again and refrigerate for 30 minutes. Repeat this process twice more.

# HOW TO MAKE SUCCESSFUL MERINGUES

You only need 2 ingredients for these light, sweet treats – egg whites and caster sugar. Whether the meringue is successful or not will depend on the ratio of these ingredients. This easy recipe requires 50 g/2 oz sugar per egg white or 400 g/14 oz sugar per 250 ml/8 fl. oz egg whites. To help you to judge the quantity, 8 size 3 eggs contain approx. 250 ml/8 fl. oz of egg white. When the egg whites are beaten until stiff and slowly baked in the oven, this quantity will make a mountain of small meringues or 4 gateau bases of 24 cm/10 inches diameter each.

**1** Whisk the egg white until it looks like cotton wool and is no longer shiny. Egg whites can be whisked until very stiff in a food processor, by starting slowly and gradually increasing the speed.

**2** The egg whites are sufficiently stiff when they stick to the whisk or when you can clearly see a cut made by a knife.

# HOW TO MAKE SUCCESSFUL HONEY CAKE

Honey cake is similar to another age-old recipe – sourdough bread. Sweet honey cake doesn't just get its aroma and light texture from traditional raising agents such as bicarbonate of soda, but also from wild yeast and malolactic acid bacteria in the atmosphere which colonise the dough when it is left to stand for a long time. A typical Recipe for honey cake is 250 g/9 oz honey, 100 g/4 oz caster sugar, 50 g/2 oz margarine, 100 g/4 oz chopped nuts, 350 g/12 oz flour, ½ sachet bicarbonate of soda (7.5 g/approx. 2 oz), 2 tbsp rum, 1 sachet mixed spice or own mix of spices.
Cover the mixture and leave to rest in the kitchen for several days or even weeks. The aroma will then be particularly fragrant.

**1** Heat the honey, sugar and margarine in a pan until fat and sugar are dissolved. Leave to cool, stirring occasionally, until mixture reaches blood heat.

**2** Dissolve the bicarbonate of soda in the rum so that the raising agent will be distributed evenly throughout the mixture. Add ground spices such as cinnamon, cloves, ginger, aniseed, cardamom and coriander to taste and mix together.

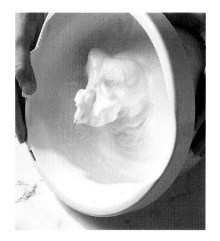

**3** Another way to test whether the egg whites are stiff enough is to tip the mixing bowl upside down. The egg whites should not fall out. Gradually add the sugar in a trickle and continue beating.

**4** You can also add all the sugar at once and fold in evenly using a plastic spatula. Both methods work but the result will be slightly different.

**5** Either fill a piping bag with meringue and pipe rosettes onto a baking sheet lined with baking parchment, or use 2 teaspoons to form little mounds.

**3** Mix the flour in a bowl with the spices and nuts. Mix in the honey and fat mixture and bicarbonate solution, then knead. Large quantities can be processed in a food processor, but the mixture may then be rather heavy.

**4** Knead the dough once again by hand, then put into a covered container or in a bowl covered with cling film and leave to stand at room temperature for at least 3 days, preferably 2 weeks.

**5** Knead dough again and roll out until thin. Cut out Christmas shapes or cut the dough into strips. Bake at 175°C/350°F/Gas mark 4 for 12-15 minutes.

# SPECIALITIES

## MERINGUES

■ Must meringues always be snow white? Or is it acceptable for them to have a golden brown hue? Different people have different opinions but one thing is certain – you only get the golden brown colour if the oven is very hot. Temperatures between 120 and 150°C/250-300°F are ideal in an electric oven. The appropriate setting for gas ovens would be mark ½-1. As a general rule, the lower the temperature, then the whiter the meringue and the longer it will take to dry out. Some people,

however, particularly like the delicate caramel flavour which develops when a meringue browns slowly, and so they set their oven temperature at 10°C higher.

## COLOURING MERINGUES

■ Meringues which have already been mixed can easily be coloured. Either use a few drops of food colouring, or use natural colours such as cocoa powder for brown and turmeric for yellowy-orange, or achieve a delicate shade of green with finely ground pistachio nuts.

**Weighing honey: put the honey or syrup jar on the scales and spoon out honey until the scales show that the required amount has been removed.**

## JAPONAIS

■ This is what confectioners call meringues which have been mixed and which have roasted ground hazelnuts or almonds added before baking. If you want to try this, take 25 g/1 oz of nuts per egg white and use the mixture to make a flat base. All you need to do is spread the meringue mixture over a circle cut out of baking parchment, or pipe the meringue in a circle, and bake at 160-170°C/350°F/Gas mark 3, for about 30 minutes. The Japonais gateau is well known in Germany. It consist of 3 layers of nut meringue filled with mocha cream and sprinkled with roasted nuts or almonds.

## STRUDEL

■ You hardly dare touch strudel pastry, it's so transparent and tears so easily. You don't need strength to stretch strudel pastry, just time and patience, and the

**There must not be any trace of fat on the kitchen utensils when making meringues or the egg whites won't stiffen. The egg whites will be even firmer if you add a pinch of cream of tartar (available from chemists) when whisking.**

**Strudel pastry which has been rolled out thoroughly should appear transparent and wafer thin.**

right kind of flour. Use an extra strong plain flour. It is a little coarser than cake flour, but just as white. It absorbs liquid well, the pastry expands and becomes very elastic. The volume of extra strong flour differs from ordinary flour, so it is best to weigh out the quantity precisely rather than using a measuring jug. An ordinary tea cloth isn't big enough for rolling out strudel pastry. You really need to use a table-cloth.

## HONEY CAKE

■ You shouldn't be mean with spices for honey cake. They are typical of this type of cake, which smells very Christmassy when baked. If you like spicy flavours, choose your favourite mix from nutmeg, cardamom, aniseed, cinnamon, cloves, ginger and coriander and add to the mixture a teaspoonful at a time. You can do this instead of using the ground spice mix recommended in the recipe.

## HARD OR SOFT?

■ If honey cake mixture turns out too soft you can always add a little more flour. If it is too stiff, add a little rum or water. The consistency of the mixture may vary because it is often very difficult to measure out honey or syrup accurately. You can also use wholemeal flour to make honey cake. If the mixture seems to be too soft using wholemeal

flour, wait a little before you add any more flour, as wholemeal flour takes longer to absorb liquid.

## BICARBONATE OF SODA

■ Bicarbonate of soda is used as a raising agent in honey cakes, which are supposed to stand for several days before baking.

**Colouring meringues, with food colouring or a little cocoa powder, for example.**

Bicarbonate of soda works in the same way as baking powder. It doesn't start to work at once but develops slowly while the mixture is standing. Bicarbonate of soda dissolves best in alcohol, so you should mix the powder with rum or brandy before adding it to the mixture.

## BAKING POWDER

■ If you don't want to leave honey cake mixture to stand, use baking powder, which works immediately, as the raising agent, instead of the 'slow' raising agent, bicarbonate of soda. For 500 g/1 lb 2 oz flour you need at least 1 sachet/approx. 2 oz of baking powder.

**Honey cake will keep for weeks in a tin. If it does become hard, add a slice of bread or a couple of apple slices to the tin for a few days.**

# BOHEMIAN CABBAGE STRUDEL

**FOR THE PASTRY**
**50 g/2 oz soft margarine**
**250 g/9 oz flour**
**pinch salt**
**1 tbsp oil**
**flour for rolling out**
**FOR THE FILLING**
**1.5 kg/3¼ lb white cabbage**
**1 onion**
**150 g/6 oz smoked streaky bacon**
**50 g/2 oz margarine**
**1 tbsp caraway**
**salt, freshly ground pepper**

**1** Melt margarine. Mix with flour, salt, and 125 ml/4 fl. oz lukewarm water. Work to a dough, then knead by hand for about 10 minutes until the dough is soft and elastic. Brush with oil and wrap in cling film. Leave to rest for at least 30 minutes at room temperature.

**2** Wash cabbage, divide into quarters and cut into thin ribbons. Peel and dice onion. Dice bacon. Heat 1 tbsp margarine, fry bacon in margarine, sweat onions in fat until transparent. Add cabbage and ½ tbsp caraway and sweat vegetables until just done. Season with salt and pepper. Leave to cool.

**3** Roll out pastry on a floured cloth and stretch over back of your hands until very thin. Melt remaining margarine and brush over pastry. Spread filling over pastry. Fold in edges of pastry over filling, then roll up strudel.

**4** Line a baking sheet with baking parchment and place the strudel on the sheet, seam side down. Sprinkle with remaining caraway and bake in a preheated oven at 200°C/400°F/Gas mark 6 for 40-45 minutes.
*Makes 6-8 portions.*

# APRICOT PINWHEELS

**Ingredients for approx. 8 pinwheels**
**250 g/9 oz low fat curd cheese or quark**
**250 g/9 oz flour**
**pinch salt**
**250 g/9 oz soft margarine**
**flour for work surface**
**8 tinned apricot halves**
**100 g/4 oz apricot jam**

**1** Put the curd cheese in a cloth and squeeze out the liquid. Mix flour, salt, margarine and curd cheese to a smooth dough using the dough hook of a hand mixer. Refrigerate for 30 minutes.

**2** Roll out pastry on floured surface to form a rectangle 20 x 40 cm/8 x 16 inches and fold over 3 times to form an envelope. Refrigerate for about 30 minutes. Repeat process 3 times, folding as described in basic recipe.

**3** Roll out pastry until thin and cut out squares with sides 15 cm/6 inches long. Make a 5 cm/2 inch long cut in the middle of all 4 sides of the square. Fold over a corner on each side to form a pinwheel. Press down gently. Put an apricot half in the middle of each pinwheel.

**4** Pass the jam through a sieve, mix to a smooth consistency with 2 tbsp hot water and brush over pastries. Bake in a preheated oven at 200°C/400°F/Gas mark 6 for 12-15 minutes.

# CHERRY STRUDEL

**FOR THE PASTRY**

| |
|---|
| 50 g/2 oz soft margarine |
| 250 g/9 oz flour |
| pinch salt |
| flour for rolling out |
| 100 g/4 oz margarine for brushing |
| margarine for greasing |

**FOR THE FILLING**

| |
|---|
| 1 kg/2 lb 3 oz cherries |
| 150 g/6 oz crème fraiche |
| 50 g/2 oz double cream |
| 3 tbsp chopped hazelnuts |
| 3 tbsp caster sugar |
| 100 g/4 oz soft margarine |
| 2 tbsp flaked hazelnuts |
| 2 tbsp icing sugar for dusting |

**1** Melt margarine. Mix flour, salt and 150 ml/¼ pint warm water together and knead for 10 minutes. Wrap in cling film and leave to rest for 30 minutes.

**2** Wash cherries and remove stones. Mix with crème fraiche, cream, 2 tbsp hazelnuts and sugar.

**3** Roll out pastry on a floured cloth and stretch until very thin. Melt margarine, brush half over pastry. Sprinkle remaining nuts over pastry. Spread cherries down one side of pastry in a strip.

**4** Roll up strudel, place in a heat resistant greased dish or tin and brush with remaining melted margarine. Sprinkle with flaked nuts. Bake in a preheated oven at 200°C/400°F/Gas mark 6 for 30-35 minutes. Dust with icing sugar. The cherry strudel goes well with vanilla custard. *Makes 6-8 portions.*

# CURD CHEESE STRUDEL

**FOR THE PASTRY**

| |
|---|
| 60 g/2 oz margarine |
| 350 g/12 oz flour |
| pinch salt |
| 1 egg |
| flour for rolling out |

**FOR THE FILLING**

| |
|---|
| 100 g/4 oz raisins |
| 3 tbsp brandy |
| 75 g/3 oz soft margarine |
| 2 eggs |
| 125 g/5 oz double cream |
| 125 g/5 oz sour cream |
| essence from 1 vanilla pod |
| 500 g/1 lb 2 oz curd cheese or quark (10% fat) |
| 1 tsp grated lemon zest |
| 100 g/4 oz caster sugar |
| 1 tbsp ground walnuts |
| 125 ml/4 fl. oz milk for pouring |
| 3 tbsp powder sugar for dusting |

**1** Melt margarine. Mix with flour, salt, egg and 125 ml/4 fl. oz warm water to form a dough and knead for 10 minutes. Wrap in cling film and leave to rest for 30 minutes.

**2** Soak the raisins in brandy. Mix together 60 g/2 oz margarine, eggs, cream, sour cream, vanilla essence, curd cheese, lemon zest, 80 g/3 oz sugar and raisins.

**3** Roll out pastry on a floured cloth and stretch until very thin. Melt remaining margarine and brush over pastry. Sprinkle walnuts on pastry. Put the cheese mixture in a strip down one side of the pastry. Roll up strudel, place in a tin and sprinkle remaining sugar on top.

**4** Bake in a preheated oven at 200°C/400°F/Gas mark 6 for 10 minutes. Pour milk over strudel and bake for a further 35-40 minutes. Dust with icing sugar. *Makes 8-10 portions.*

# BRIK – MOROCCAN PASTRY PARCELS

**Ingredients for 8 parcels**
**FOR THE PASTRY**
25 g/1 oz soft margarine
125 g/5 oz flour
½ level tsp salt
flour for rolling out
**FOR THE FILLING**
200 g/7 oz celery
200 g/7 oz carrots
200 g/7 oz leeks
40 g/2 oz soft margarine
salt, freshly ground pepper
3 tbsp capers
1 egg white
8 egg yolks
oil for frying

1 Make strudel pastry out of melted margarine, flour and salt; knead and leave to rest.
2 Thinly slice celery and cut carrots and leeks into thin strips. Melt margarine. Sweat vegetables in margarine until just cooked. Season with salt and pepper. Add capers to vegetables and leave to cool.
3 Roll out dough, then stretch to a very thin rectangle measuring approx. 30 x 60 cm/12 x 24 inches. Divide into 8 15 cm/6-inch squares. Brush edges with egg white.
4 Put ½ the vegetables in the centre of the pastry squares. Make a small well in the centre of the vegetables and put an egg yolk in each. Cover with remaining vegetables. Fold the corners of the pastry in to the centre, covering the vegetables. Press the edges of the pastry tightly together with a fork and draw up the pastry borders.
5 Heat the oil to approx. 180°C/350°F. Fry the pastry parcels in the oil for 2-3 minutes on each side until golden brown.

**Taste best served hot.**

# ORIENTAL STRUDEL PIE

**Ingredients for 1 flan tin or spring form tin (22 cm diam./9 inches diam.)**

**FOR THE PASTRY**

| | |
|---|---|
| 1 tbsp soft margarine | |
| 350 g/12 oz flour | |
| pinch salt | |
| 3 tbsp oil | |
| flour for rolling out | |
| 80 g/3 oz margarine for brushing | |

**FOR THE FILLING**

| | |
|---|---|
| 100 g/4 oz whole walnuts | |
| 100 g/4 oz candied figs | |
| 1 tsp ground cinnamon | |
| pinch ground cloves | |
| 2 tbsp soft margarine | |
| 1 tbsp icing sugar | |

**FOR THE SYRUP**

| | |
|---|---|
| 75 g/3 oz caster sugar | |
| 1 tbsp honey | |
| 1 stick cinnamon | |
| 3 cloves | |
| ½ tsp grated lemon zest | |
| 2 tsp lemon juice | |
| 50 g/2 oz margarine for brushing | |

**1** Melt margarine. Mix with flour, salt, 2 tbsp oil and 150 ml/¼ pint lukewarm water to form a dough. Knead dough by hand for about 10 minutes until soft and elastic. Brush with remaining oil. Wrap in cling film and leave to rest for 1 hour at room temperature.

**2** Coarsely chop nuts and figs. Mix with cinnamon, cloves, margarine and icing sugar.

**3** Bring sugar, honey and 75 ml/approx. 2 fl. oz water to boil. Add cinnamon stick, cloves, lemon zest and juice. Simmer gently, uncovered, for about 15 minutes. Remove cloves and cinnamon stick. Refrigerate.

**4** Roll out dough on a floured cloth and stretch over back of hands until very thin, forming a square. Melt margarine and brush onto pastry.

**5** Cut pastry into 10 cm/4 inch wide strips. Put 1 tbsp filling on the end of each strip of pastry. Fold over pastry to form a triangle. Fold the triangle over again and, using a knife, separate from pastry strip.

**6** Put the pastry parcel in a greased tin so that the opening is uppermost and the filling is visible. Make 11 more parcels in the same way.

**7** Bake in a preheated oven at 200°C/400°F/Gas mark 6 for about 30 minutes. Pour syrup over pie.

**The parcels should be packed tightly together in the tin.**

# CLASSIC APPLE STRUDEL

**FOR THE PASTRY**
| |
|---|
| 1 tbsp soft margarine |
| 350 g/12 oz flour |
| pinch salt |
| 3 tbsp oil |
| flour for rolling out |

**FOR THE FILLING**
| |
|---|
| 120 g/5 oz soft margarine |
| 80 g/3 oz packet bread crumbs |
| 1.5 kg/34 lb apples (e.g. Cox or Worcester) |
| 100 g/4 oz caster sugar |
| 1 tsp ground cinnamon |
| 2 tbsp icing sugar for dusting |

**1** Melt margarine. Mix with flour, salt, 2 tbsp oil and 150 ml/¼ pint lukewarm water, and knead for 10 minutes until pastry is soft and elastic. Brush with remaining oil. Wrap pastry in cling film and leave to rest for at least an hour at room temperature.

**2** Melt 50 g/2 oz margarine and brown the bread crumbs in the margarine. Peel apples and remove cores. Cut apples into small pieces.

**3** Roll out pastry on a floured cloth, then stretch over backs of hands until very thin. Cut off thick pastry edges. Sprinkle roasted bread crumbs over pastry. Spread chopped apple, sugar and cinnamon over pastry.

**4** Fold edges of pastry in over filling. Carefully roll up strudel and place on a baking sheet lined with baking parchment.

**5** Melt remaining margarine. Brush ⅔ of margarine onto strudel. Bake in a preheated oven at 175°C/350°F/Gas mark 4 for about 45 minutes.

**6** Brush strudel with remaining margarine and dust with icing sugar. Serve whilst still warm. Strudel tastes best served with vanilla custard or ice cream. *Makes 8-10 slices.*

MICROWAVE TIP: Strudel which has been made the day before can easily be reheated in the microwave, for 1 minute at 600 watts.

TIP: You can also put strudel in a baking dish and pour over a mixture of beaten eggs and milk before baking. For this you will need 500 ml/approx. ¾ pint milk with 1 egg and 2-3 tbsp caster sugar, beaten together. Pour over the strudel so that ⅔ of the pastry is covered.

# LEMON MERINGUE PIE

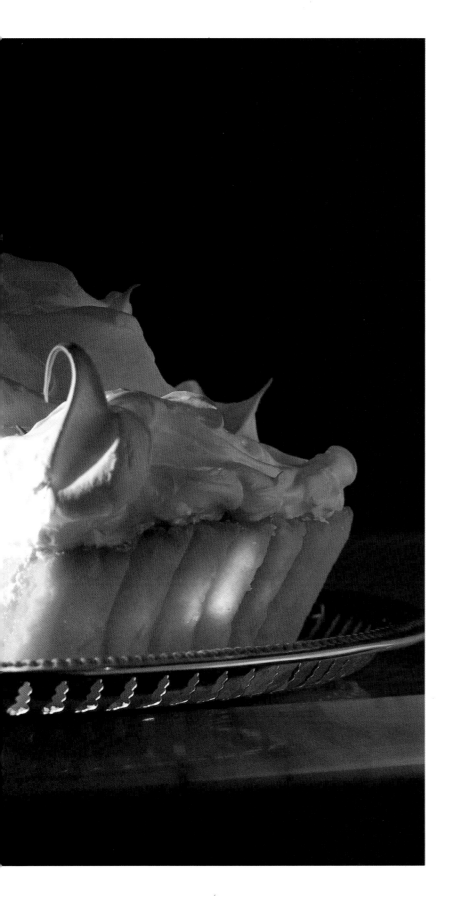

**Ingredients for a pie dish or spring form tin (24 cm diam./10 inches diam.)**

**FOR THE PASTRY**

| |
|---|
| 250 g/9 oz flour |
| 200 g/7 oz chilled margarine |
| 2 tbsp caster sugar |
| pinch salt |
| 3 tbsp lemon juice |
| flour for work surface |
| dried peas for baking blind |

**FOR THE LEMON FILLING**

| |
|---|
| 6 eggs |
| 350 g/12 oz caster sugar |
| 1 heaped tbsp cornflour |
| 250 g/9 oz soft margarine |
| 2 tsp grated lemon zest |
| 6 tbsp lemon juice |
| pinch salt |

**1** Mix flour, 175 g/6 oz margarine, sugar, salt and lemon juice to a smooth dough. Cover and refrigerate for 30 minutes. Roll out pastry on a floured work surface until 4 mm/approx. ¼ inch thick, and use to line tin, drawing pastry about 3 cm up sides of tin.

**2** Melt remaining margarine and brush onto pastry. Line pastry case with greaseproof paper or baking parchment and fill with dried peas. Bake in a preheated oven at 200°C/400°F/Gas mark 6 for 15 minutes. Remove peas and paper and bake for a further 10-15 minutes. Remove from tin and leave to cool.

**3** Separate eggs. Mix together egg yolks, cornflour and 125 g/5 oz sugar in a pan. Add the margarine in small pieces, the lemon zest and 5 tbsp lemon juice and stir. Whisk the lemon custard with a balloon whisk over a medium heat until the custard thickens. Leave to cool a little, pour over prepared pastry case and leave to cool thoroughly.

**4** Whisk together egg whites, salt and lemon juice until stiff, gradually adding the remaining sugar. Pile the egg whites on top of the lemon custard and form into peaks. Bake in a preheated oven at 225°C/425°F/Gas mark 7 for 8-10 minutes until golden brown. *Makes 12 slices.*

# COCONUT KISSES

| Ingredients for approx. 60 kisses |
| --- |
| 125 g/5 oz coconut flakes |
| 4 egg whites |
| pinch salt |
| 125 g/5 oz caster sugar |
| 75 g/3 oz ground almonds |

**1** Put the coconut flakes in a frying pan and roast, stirring occasionally, until golden brown. Remove from pan and leave to cool.

**2** Whisk egg whites and salt together until very stiff, gradually adding the sugar. Lightly fold in coconut flakes and ground almonds using a balloon whisk.

**3** Using 2 teaspoons, take little mounds of meringue and place on a baking sheet lined with baking parchment. Bake in a preheated oven at 125°C/250°F Gas mark ½-1 for about 30 minutes.

**4** Remove coconut kisses from baking sheet, leave to cool on a wire rack and place in paper cases.

# MACAROONS

| Ingredients for approx. 30 macaroons |
| --- |
| 3 egg whites |
| 150 g/6 oz caster sugar |
| 250 g/9 oz ground hazelnuts or walnuts |
| about 15 glacé cherries |
| 2 tbsp icing sugar for dusting |

**1** Whisk egg whites until very stiff. Gradually add ½ the sugar. Continue whisking until mixture shines. Lightly fold in remaining sugar and ground nuts, using a balloon whisk.

**2** Using 2 tablespoons, shape the macaroon mixture into round or oval heaps and place on a baking sheet lined with baking parchment. Slice the glacé cherries in half and put half a cherry on top of each of the macaroons.

**3** Leave macaroons to dry naturally for 1-2 hours, then bake in a preheated oven at 225-250°C/425-475°F/Gas mark 7–8 for about 5 minutes. Leave to cool on a wire rack, then dust with icing sugar.

# GINGER MERINGUES WITH CHOCOLATE CREAM

| Ingredients for 8 meringues |
| --- |
| **FOR THE MERINGUE** |
| 3 egg whites |
| 150 g/6 oz caster sugar |
| 50 g preserved ginger (in syrup) |
| **FOR THE TOPPING** |
| 100 g/4 oz good quality bitter chocolate |
| 200 g/7 oz double cream |
| 50 g/2 oz chocolate flake |
| 2 tsp cocoa powder for dusting |

**1** Whisk egg whites until very stiff. Gradually add ½ the sugar. Continue beating until the mixture shines. Add the remaining sugar and fold in.

**2** Drain ginger, chop finely and fold into meringue mixture. Put the meringue in a piping bag with a round nozzle. Draw 8 circles, each 6 cm/2 inches in diameter on baking parchment. Place the parchment on a greased baking sheet and pipe circles of meringue, working in a spiral.

**3** Leave meringues to dry naturally for 1-2 hours. Then bake in a preheated oven at 100°C/200°F/ Gas mark ½ for 2 hours. Remove meringues from paper and leave to cool on a wire rack.

**4** Finely grate ½ the chocolate, chop the rest. Whip cream until stiff. Fold grated and chopped chocolate into whipped cream. Place 2 tbsp cream on top of each meringue base. Decorate with crumbled chocolate flake, and dust with cocoa powder.

# CINNAMON STARS

**Ingredients for approx. 60 biscuits**
**500 g/1 lb 2 oz whole almonds with skins**
**3 egg whites**
**400 g/14 oz icing sugar**
**1½ tsp ground cinnamon**
**2 tbsp kirsch or lemon juice**
**icing sugar for rolling out**

**1** Grind almonds. Whisk egg whites until very stiff. Sieve icing sugar and gradually whisk into the egg whites, a little at a time. Remove ⅓ of meringue mixture and reserve.

**2** Mix almonds with remaining meringue mixture, cinnamon and kirsch or lemon juice.

**3** On a work surface thoroughly dusted with icing sugar, roll out the meringue mixture until 5 mm/approx. ¼ inch thick. Plunge a pastry cutter into ice cold water, then use to cut out star shapes.

**4** Carefully place the cinnamon stars on a baking sheet lined with baking parchment and brush with reserved meringue mixture. Knead together pastry scraps, roll out again, cut out more stars and brush with left-over meringue mix.

**5** Leave biscuits to dry naturally in a warm place, overnight if possible, Bake in a preheated oven at 175-200°C/350-400°F/Gas mark 4–6 for 5-10 minutes. The meringue glaze should stay white. Remove cinnamon stars from baking parchment and leave to cool on a wire rack.

TIP: You should buy good quality cinnamon for this labour intensive Christmas treat. The flavour of cheap cinnamon often isn't strong enough because it is comes from less flavourful types of cinnamon and parts of the plant that don't contain much essential oil.

# PAVLOVA

**FOR THE MERINGUE**
**3 egg whites**
**pinch salt**
**175 g/6 oz caster sugar**
**1 tsp cornflour**
**1 tsp lemon juice**
**FOR THE TOPPING**
**1 tbsp margarine**
**30 g/1 oz oat flakes**
**500 g/1 lb 2 oz strawberries or raspberries**
**400 g/14 oz double cream**
**sugar for sweetening to taste**

**1** Whisk egg whites and salt until very stiff. Gradually add 100 g/4 oz caster sugar. Continue whisking until mixture shines. Gently fold in remaining sugar, cornflour and lemon juice using a balloon whisk.

**2** Line a baking sheet with baking parchment and draw a circle 26 cm/10 inches in diameter on the paper. Put meringue in a piping bag with a round nozzle, and using ⅔ of the mixture, pipe a meringue circle, working in a spiral. Pipe rosettes around the edge of the circle with remaining ⅓ of meringue mixture.

**3** Bake in a preheated oven at 100°C/200°F/Gas mark ½ for about 2 hours. Remove meringue base from paper and leave to cool on a wire rack.

**4** Melt margarine in a frying pan. Fry oat flakes in margarine until crisp and brown, turning occasionally. Remove and leave to cool on a plate. Sort the raspberries if used, or carefully wash strawberries and drain on absorbent kitchen paper. Then hull and slice in half.

**5** Whip cream until stiff and mix with ½ of prepared fruit. Sweeten to taste with sugar. Spread fruit and cream over meringue base. Sprinkle remaining fruit and roasted oat flakes on top of cream. Refrigerate pavlova for about 1 hour.
*Makes 12 slices.*

# HONEY CAKE

**Ingredients for a baking sheet (approx 27 x 35 cm/approx. 11 x 14 inches)**

**FOR THE MIXTURE**

| | |
|---|---|
| 250 g/9 oz honey | |
| 100 g/4 oz soft margarine | |
| 2 eggs | |
| 125 g/5 oz caster sugar | |
| 10 g/approx. ½ oz bicarbonate of soda | |
| 375 g/13 oz flour | |
| 2 tbsp mixed spice | |
| 1 tsp grated lemon zest | |
| 2 tbsp rum | |
| 1 tbsp cocoa powder | |
| 100 g/4 oz diced candied lemon peel | |
| 50 g/2 oz diced candied orange peel | |
| 80 g/3 oz chopped almonds | |
| margarine for greasing | |

**FOR DECORATION**

| | |
|---|---|
| 75 g/3 oz whole almonds | |
| 60 g/2 oz red glacé cherries | |
| 1 egg white | |

**1** Melt margarine and honey and leave to cool. Whisk eggs and sugar until foamy. Stir in honey and fat mixture. Mix together bicarbonate of soda and 1 tbsp water and mix with flour, mixed spice, lemon zest, rum, cocoa, lemon peel, orange peel and almonds.

**2** Grease baking sheet with margarine. Spread honey cake mixture onto sheet and smooth off. Plunge almonds into boiling water, blanch and remove skins. Cut glacé cherries into halves or quarters.

**3** Using a ruler and knife, mark 7 x 9 cm/3 x 4 inch squares on the mixture. Decorate slices with cherries and almonds. Beat together egg white and 1 tbsp water and brush onto honey cake. Bake in a preheated oven at 175°C/350°F/Gas mark 4 for about 20 minutes.
*Makes 15 slices.*

# HONEY COOKIES

**Ingredients for approx. 30 cookies**
450 g/1 lb honey
75 g/3 oz good quality rock candy
100 g/4 oz sugar
75 g/3 oz candied orange peel
1 sachet/approx. ½ oz vanilla sugar
2 tsp ground cinnamon
½ tsp each grated lemon zest, ground aniseed, ginger, coriander and cardamom
1 tsp cocoa powder 475 g/17 oz flour
15 g/approx. ½ oz bicarbonate of soda
3 tbsp brandy
100 g/ 4 oz flaked almonds
200 g/7 oz dark chocolate for coating

**1** Melt honey with 3 tbsp water and remove from heat. Add rock candy and sugar and leave to cool, stirring frequently.
**2** Finely chop candied orange peel. Mix with vanilla sugar, cinnamon, lemon zest, aniseed, ginger, coriander, cardamom and cocoa powder in a bowl and add 450 g/1 lb flour. Mix bicarbonate of soda with brandy. Mix honey solution, flour mixture and bicarbonate of soda and knead together thoroughly with hands.

**3** Dust dough with remaining flour and cover with cling film. Leave to stand for at least 1 week at room temperature.
**4** Roll out dough on a work surface sprinkled with flaked almonds to approx. 5 Mm/¼ inch thick. Cut into 3 x 8 cm/1 x 3 inches strips. Place on a baking sheet lined with baking parchment and bake at 175°C/350°F/ Gas mark 4 for 12-15 minutes. Leave cookies to cool on a wire rack.
**5** Melt the chocolate in a bowl over hot water and allow to cool a little, then heat again, stirring constantly, and use to coat cookies thickly. Make ripples in the top of the chocolate and leave to dry.

# LEBKUCHEN WITH NUTS

**Ingredients for approx. 40 lebkuchen**
375 g/13 oz honey
100 g/4 oz soft margarine
500 g/1 lb 2 oz flour
75 g/3 oz chopped walnuts
125 g/5 oz each candied lemon and orange peel
125 g/5 oz chopped almonds
3 tbsp mixed spice
½ tsp ground cinnamon
½ tsp bicarbonate of soda
2 tbsp rose water
200 g/7 oz good quality plain cooking chocolate
halved walnuts, hazelnuts and chopped pistachio nuts for decoration

**1** Melt margarine and honey, stirring all the time. Mix together flour, walnuts, candied orange peel, lemon peel, almonds, mixed spice and cinnamon in a bowl. Add honey. Mix bicarbonate of ammonia with rose water and also add to mixture. Mix and knead to a smooth dough. Cover and leave to stand overnight.

**2** Roll out mixture to just 1 cm/½ inch thick and cut out circles 6-8 cm/2-3 inches in diameter. Place lebkuchen on a baking sheet lined with baking parchment and bake in a preheated oven at 200-225°C/400-425°F/Gas mark 6–7 for about 12 minutes. Remove from baking parchment and leave to cool on a wire rack.
**3** Melt chocolate in a bowl over hot water and leave to cool a little. Warm up again, stirring all the time, and use to coat lebkuchen. Garnish with nuts and leave to dry.

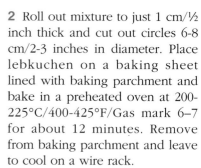

# FATHER CHRISTMAS

| Ingredients for 5 Father Christmases |
| --- |
| **FOR THE PASTRY** |
| **100 g/4 oz soft margarine** |
| **250 g/9 oz honey** |
| **125 g/5 oz caster sugar** |
| **1 tbsp ginger** |
| **1 egg** |
| **1 pinch salt** |
| **1 tsp cocoa powder** |
| **500 g/1 lb 2 oz flour** |
| **1 tsp baking powder** |
| **flour for rolling out** |
| **FOR DECORATION** |
| **200 g/7 oz icing sugar** |
| **1 egg white** |
| **red food colouring** |

**1** Melt margarine, honey and sugar together, stirring all the time, until the sugar has dissolved. Remove pan from heat.

**2** Add ginger, egg, salt and cocoa to margarine mixture. Mix flour and baking powder together, add to margarine and mix. Knead by hand until dough is smooth. Leave dough in bowl and allow to stand for 3-4 hours at room temperature.

**3** Roll out dough on a floured work surface to a rectangle approx. 1 cm/½ inch thick and measuring 20 x 42 cm/8 x 17 inches. Cut out 4 triangles of equal size. Knead together pastry cuttings, roll out again and make a 5th triangle.

**4** Place the triangles on a baking sheet lined with baking parchment and bake in a preheated oven at 200°C/400°F/Gas mark 6 for 12-15 minutes.

**5** Mix together icing sugar and egg white to form icing. Take ¼ of the icing and colour deep red with food colouring. Put the remaining icing in a piping bag with a small round nozzle, or you can use a freezer bag with a small corner cut off.

**6** Decorate triangles with red and white icing to make Father Christmases. Leave to dry.

# BASLE LECKERLI

| Ingredients for 1 baking sheet |
|---|
| **FOR THE MIXTURE** |
| 300 g/11 oz honey |
| 200 g/7 oz caster sugar |
| 1 tbsp ground cinnamon |
| pinch ground cloves |
| ¼ tsp freshly grated nutmeg |
| 150 g/6 oz chopped almonds |
| 1 tsp grated lemon zest |
| 75 g/3 oz diced candied orange peel |
| 75 g/3 oz diced candied lemon peel |
| 8 tbsp kirsch |
| 400 g/14 oz flour |
| 1 tsp baking powder |
| **FOR THE ICING** |
| 100 g/4 oz icing sugar |
| 3 tbsp kirsch or water |

**1** Melt honey and sugar, stirring all the time, until the sugar dissolves. Stir in cinnamon, cloves and nutmeg. Remove pan from heat and allow honey mixture to cool a little.

**2** Add almonds, lemon zest, lemon and orange peel and kirsch one by one to warm honey mixture. Add flour and baking powder and mix to a smooth dough.

**3** Line a baking sheet with baking parchment. Roll out dough to approx. 5mm/¼ inch on baking sheet and leave to stand for a few hours, or overnight if possible. Then bake in a preheated oven at 225°C/425°F/Gas mark 7 for 18-20 minutes.

**4** Mix the icing sugar with the kirsch or water and brush onto hot cake as soon as it comes out of the oven. Cut away any crusty edges from the cake and cut into strips 3 x 6 cm/1 x 3 inches. *Makes 60 leckerli.*

TIP: The cake must be decorated while it is still warm and cut straight away, otherwise it will be too hard. You can replace some of the almonds with hazelnuts if wished.

# LEIGNITZ BOMBS

| Ingredients for 12 bombs |
|---|
| **FOR THE DOUGH** |
| 200 g/7 oz honey |
| 100 g/4 oz cane sugar |
| 75 g/3 oz soft margarine |
| 2 tbsp milk |
| 2 eggs |
| 1 tbsp rum |
| 300 g/11 oz flour |
| 2 tbsp cocoa powder |
| 1 sachet/approx. ½ oz baking powder |
| 3 tsp ginger |
| 75 g/3 oz raisins |
| 40 g/2 oz chopped almonds |
| 40 g/2 oz chopped walnuts |
| margarine for greasing |
| 200 g/7 oz apricot jam |
| 150 g/6 oz good quality bitter chocolate |
| 100 g/6 oz good quality white chocolate |

**1** Heat together honey, cane sugar, margarine and milk to form a smooth mixture. Leave to cool. Mix together eggs and rum. Mix with flour, cocoa, baking powder, ginger, raisins and nuts.

**2** Grease 12 moulds and fill with mixture, or cut out foil circles (15 cm diam./6 inches diam.), place circles over an upturned glass with a diameter of 5 cm/2 inches and press down. Remove foil and fill the resulting mould with mixture. Bake in a preheated oven at 175°C/350°F/Gas mark 4 for 40-45 minutes. Turn cakes out of moulds.

**3** Warm jam, pass through a sieve and mix with 2 tbsp water. Brush cakes with jam.

**4** In separate bowl melt chocolate over hot water. Spread ⅓ of bitter chocolate onto a marble board, allow to set a little. Draw a spatula across the hardened chocolate to make chocolate curls. Pour the rest of the chocolate over the cakes. Then pour white chocolate over cakes and decorate with chocolate curls.

# GINGER COOKIES

| Ingredients for approx. 45 biscuits |
| --- |
| FOR THE MIXTURE |
| 300 g/11 oz honey |
| 125 g/5 oz sugar |
| 125 g/5 oz soft margarine |
| ½ tsp each ground cloves and ginger |
| 2 tsp ground cinnamon |
| 525 g/1 lb 3 oz flour |
| 150 g/6 oz ground walnuts |
| 15g/approx. ½ oz bicarbonate of soda |
| 4 tbsp rum |
| 1 egg |
| FOR THE ICING |
| 150 g/6 oz icing sugar |
| 1-2 tbsp lemon juice |

1 Heat together honey, sugar and margarine, stirring all the time, until sugar dissolves. Leave to cool until lukewarm, stirring occasionally. Mix together cloves, ginger, cinnamon, 500 g/1 lb 2 oz flour and walnuts in a bowl. Mix together rum and bicarbonate of soda. Add honey mixture, bicarbonate of soda and egg to flour; mix, and knead to a firm dough.

2 Put the dough in a bowl, dust with remaining flour and cover with cling film. Leave the bowl to stand for at least 1 week at room temperature.
3 Thoroughly knead the dough again and break off walnut sized pieces. Roll into balls and place 4 cm/1½ inches apart on a baking sheet lined with baking parchment. Bake at 175°C/350°F/ Gas mark 4 in a preheated oven for 12-15 minutes. Remove ginger cookies from baking sheet and leave to cool on a wire rack.
4 Mix together icing sugar and lemon juice to form a smooth icing. Fill a freezer bag with icing, cut off a tiny corner of the bag. Pipe the icing over the cookies in narrow stripes. Leave to dry.

# FILLED LEBKUCHEN HEARTS

| Ingredients for approx. 12 hearts |
| --- |
| 125 ml/4 fl. oz milk |
| ½ tbsp bicarbonate of soda |
| 500 g/1 lb 2 oz flour |
| 2 tbsp mixed spice |
| 1 tsp grated orange zest |
| 85 g/3 oz caster sugar |
| 125 g/5 oz runny honey |
| 125 g/5 oz light syrup |
| 400 g/14 oz marzipan |
| 1 egg white |
| 150 g/6 oz icing sugar |

1 Mix together milk and bicarbonate of soda. Add milk to flour, mixed spice, orange zest, sugar, honey and syrup; mix, and knead to a smooth dough. Refrigerate overnight.
2 Roll out dough between cling film to approx. 5 mm/approx. ¼ inch thick and cut out hearts 9 cm/3-4 inches across. Roll out marzipan between cling film to

3 mm/approx ¼ inch thick and cut out slightly smaller hearts.
3 Place a marzipan heart on top of a lebkuchen heart. Dampen the edges of the dough, and lay another pastry heart on top. Press together edges of dough with a fork. Line a baking sheet with baking parchment. Bake in a preheated oven at 200°C/400°F/Gas mark 6 for 12-15 minutes.
4 Beat together egg white and icing sugar and decorate hearts with icing.

## THE ART OF DECORATION

# Making magic with a piping bag

The piping bag and nozzle are to the confectioner what the hammer and chisel were to Michelangelo: the tools of the trade with which he gives shape to his artistic visions. A confectioner's masterpiece appeals to four senses – you can smell it, see it, and touch it; and you can also taste it, an exquisite delight, as ephemeral as a flower.

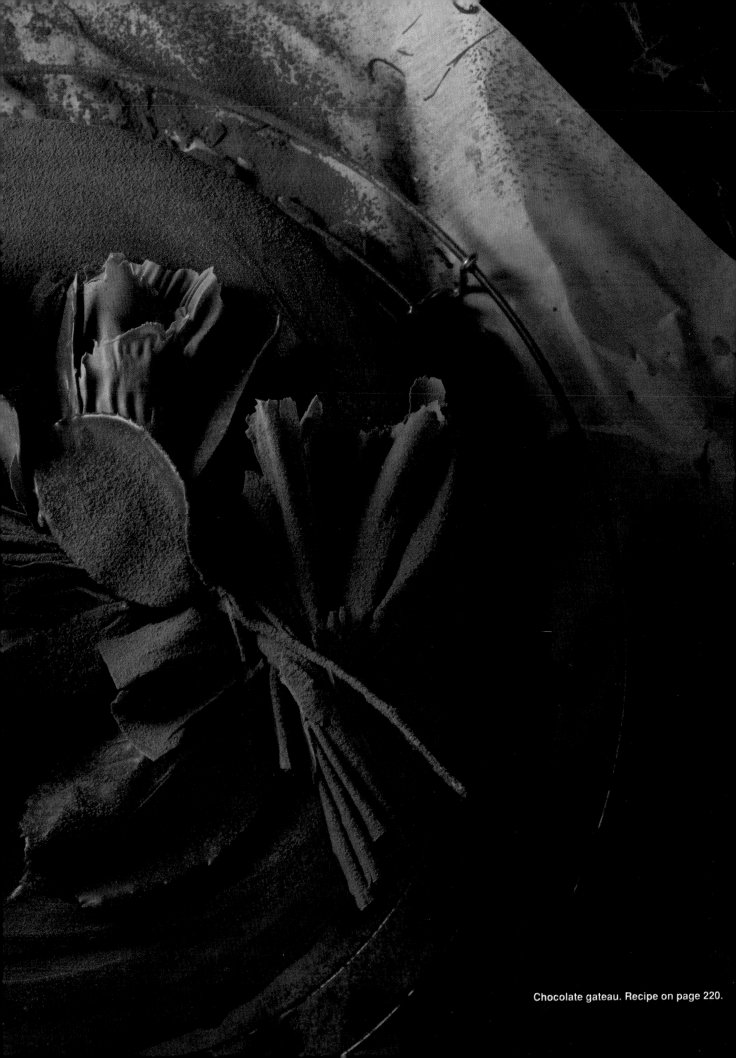

Chocolate gateau. Recipe on page 220.

# HOW TO DECORATE CAKES AND PASTRIES

Chocolate is a refined mixture of cocoa, sugar and the oil from the cocoa bean, known as cocoa butter. We recommend that you use couverture, if possible, in these recipes rather than ordinary chocolate because it contains a greater proportion of cocoa butter, making it especially suitable for moulding, spreading and piping. Couverture also sets quickly, which helps it to retain a shiny surface. However, couverture is expensive, especially if you do a lot of baking and cake decorating, and not always easily available. In our recipes we have therefore suggested that you use a good quality cooking chocolate, which is less expensive and widely available, and can be used in exactly the same way as couverture.

Whether you use couverture or cooking chocolate, it is important to melt it properly. Professional cooks call this process 'tempering'. The method described opposite shows how to melt chocolate over hot water. You can also melt chocolate in a microwave oven. It takes between 30 seconds and 2 minutes. Work in stages – switch the microwave on for a few seconds, then switch it off, stir the chocolate thoroughly, then switch on the microwave again. This way the chocolate melts evenly and retains its texture and appearance. White couverture and chocolate usually contain a higher proportion of solid ingredients and therefore are not so easy to work with. If you stir a little melted coconut oil, which should be warm but not hot, into the chocolate, the melted chocolate will then be more fluid and easier to spread.

**1** Couverture is sold in big square blocks and must be coarsely chopped before melting. The more even in size the chopped-up pieces, the better the chocolate will melt. Cooking chocolate should be broken into individual squares before melting.

**2** Put half the required amount in a pan or bowl and place over a pan of hot, not boiling, water. Melt the chocolate, stirring frequently.

## DECORATING WITH CHOCOLATE

**6** You can make attractive decorations using small cutters. Spread the chocolate onto a sheet of baking parchment and chill until set. Use the decorative cutters to cut out the shapes and lift them carefully from the paper.

**7** You can make very individual decorations if you draw the outline of a decorative shape, or letters of the alphabet, on a sheet of plain paper. Lay a sheet of greaseproof paper over the top so the shapes can be seen underneath and pipe out the shapes in chocolate.

**3** If the first batch of chocolate has melted, remove pan from heat and add remaining chocolate. Melt this chocolate, again stirring frequently, and leave to cool a little.

**4** Return the pan of chocolate to the bowl of hot water and heat gently. The couverture should be viscous and about 32°C/60°F in temperature. If the temperature exceeds 32°C/60°F, the chocolate will lose its shine.

**5** If you don't have a thermometer to measure the temperature, heat the chocolate very slowly. To test whether it has reached the right temperature, dip the tip of a knife into the chocolate. If the chocolate sets in a minute and is shiny, then it has reached the correct temperature.

**8** Fresh fruit can be used to make wonderful decorations for gateaux if the individual fruits are dipped into melted chocolate. You can also dredge them in a little sugar afterwards.

**9** Anyone can make chocolate leaves. Brush melted chocolate onto flexible, attractively shaped leaves. Chill, then carefully peel leaf away from chocolate.

**10** To make chocolate caraque, or curls, you need to work quickly. Spread a little chocolate onto a marble board. Take a spatula – the type used for stripping wallpaper is ideal – and push it across the surface of the chocolate, forming curls.

# DECORATING WITH CREAM

If you want to make your gateaux look attractive, you need a piping bag. Good quality piping bags are made of glazed cotton or other materials which can be boiled. They come with plastic or metal nozzles, with different shaped apertures which create patterns when the filling is piped, but you will need to practise first. Try using mashed potato, rather than cream, to practice your rosettes, wavy lines and garlands. This will help you to get a feel for the amount of pressure you need to exert to produce perfect rosettes and stripes.

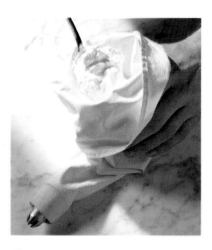

**1** Before filling the piping bag, push the nozzle down into the bag so that it rests firmly in the little hole. Fold back the edge of the bag so that it doesn't get messy, then fill the bag with the whipped cream.

**2** Don't fill the piping bag too full. Twist together the top of the bag so that the filling is pushed down. Use your left hand to guide the piping nozzle and your right to press the filling gently down the bag.

# DECORATING WITH ICING AND GLAZES

Sugar icing and glazes are used to sweeten biscuits, cakes and gateaux and to keep them fresh for longer. If you are short of time, use popular, simple Glacé icing, which is made of icing sugar mixed with a small amount of liquid such as lemon juice, rum or coffee, and which dries naturally. For stiffer Royal icing you need to mix the white of an egg with 125 g/5 oz icing sugar until the mixture is creamy and shines. Boiled glazes are usually applied hot to baking which has just come out of the oven. Bring 250 g/9 oz caster sugar and 125 ml/4 fl. oz water to the boil and continue to boil until the glaze has achieved a syrupy consistency and large bubbles appear on the surface. To test if the glaze is ready, try spinning a drop of syrup into a thread, using two fingers.

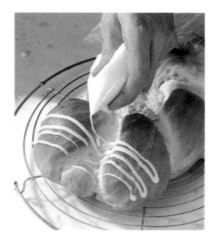

**1** Glacé icing: Fill a polythene freezer bag with basic glacé icing, made from icing sugar mixed with a little liquid, and cut a tiny corner off of the bag. Use the icing to decorate cooled cakes or biscuits.

**2** Marbled effect: First coat cakes or biscuits in glacé icing. Colour a little icing with food colouring, drip onto damp layer of icing and draw patterns in the icing with a wooden cocktail stick.

**3** Different nozzles give different piped effects. If you use a rose-shaped nozzle you will get peaked rosettes, spiral rosettes, borders and chains.

**4** A star-shaped nozzle makes similar shapes to a rose nozzle. It is good for making star-shaped rosettes, garlands and straight lines.

**5** A basic round nozzle makes round, even rosettes and thick chains with smooth edges, as shown here.

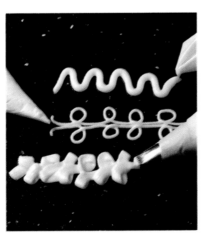

**3** Cracked icing: Boiled glaze is also known as cracked icing because when it dries, fine cracks appear in the surface. Warm glaze should be brushed onto honey cake, yeast cakes and biscuits which have just come out of the oven.

**4** Royal icing: To pipe this icing use a freezer bag (above, top), or a home-made paper icing bag (above, centre). If you use a piping bag with a flat nozzle you can make broad ribbons.

**5** Royal icing is very suitable for colouring. Allow coloured surfaces to dry before adding the next colour. To decorate, sprinkle hundreds and thousands or sugar balls on the damp icing.

# CUSTARD FILLINGS

Many classic gateaux use custard fillings. Confectioner's custard is used as the basis for these fillings by professional cooks, but we have used vanilla blancmange mix with margarine or butter added to form the custard filling.

Here is a basic recipe which can be used in many different ways. Take 1 sachet vanilla blancmange mix, 500 ml/¾ pint milk, 2 tbsp caster sugar, pinch salt, 2 egg yolks, 200 g/7 oz margarine, and 2 tbsp icing sugar. This quantity is suitable for a gateau with a 26 cm/10 inch diameter. The method opposite shows you exactly how to incorporate the ingredients.

**1** Mix the blancmange powder with a little cold milk, until smooth. Bring remaining milk, sugar and salt to boil. Add the blancmange mix and bring to the boil, stirring constantly. Remove from heat. Stir in the egg yolks.

**2** You can vary the flavour of the cream using grated lemon zest, grated chocolate, instant coffee or alcohol. To make frangipani cream, flavour the mixture with finely crushed almond macaroons.

# FRUIT AND CURD CHEESE FILLINGS

Fruit and curd cheese fillings are more refreshing and lighter than custard fillings. Gelatine produces the firm consistency for cutting, and egg whites and whipped cream make the filling light and mousse-like.

Here is a basic recipe which can be used as a filling for a fatless sponge base 26 cm/10 inches in diameter: 6 leaves white gelatine, 4 eggs, 4-5 tbsp icing sugar, 250 ml/8 fl. oz fruit juice or 250 g/9 oz fruit purée, curd cheese or yoghurt, 125 g/5 oz double cream, flavourings or alcohol if desired.

NOTE: Kiwi fruit and papaya are not suitable for fillings which use gelatine.

**1** Soften the gelatine in cold water. Separate the eggs. Whisk the egg yolks with the icing sugar until a thick, almost white custard results.

**2** Add the fruit juice or purée. Freshly squeezed citrus fruit juice or puréed berries are very good for this. Flavour the yoghurt or curd cheese with vanilla or lemon.

**3** Pass the cooled custard through a sieve. If the custard contains solid ingredients such as grated chocolate or nuts, mix the custard using a potato masher.

**4** Beat the margarine, using a food processor or a hand mixer, until light, creamy and airy. Continue beating, adding the icing sugar.

**5** Add the custard to the margarine, mixing in a spoonful at a time. The prepared cream filling is firm enough to be used in sponge gateaux, but can also be used in light fatless sponges and choux pastry.

**3** Dissolve the drained gelatine over a gentle heat. Add a little of the custard to the warm gelatine, then stir the gelatine mixture into the custard. In this way the gelatine and custard won't separate out.

**4** Refrigerate the custard until it begins to set. To test if it is ready, draw a spoon through the custard. If the trail can be clearly seen then the custard is sufficiently set.

**5** Pile whipped cream and beaten egg whites onto the custard and fold in. To do this draw a balloon whisk gently through both mixtures, don't stir.

# DECORATING BISCUITS AND COOKIES

No other baking carries the same connotations of quality and loving care as 'home-made' biscuits. However, most of the work is not involved in producing the biscuit mix, but in devotedly shaping and decorating the biscuits. A well-filled cookie jar will be a year-round attraction for children and adults alike, and many an unexpected guest will be delighted by fine, home-made biscuits with a cup of tea or coffee.

Short-crust pastry is a wonderful base for many types of biscuit (basic recipe page 86). If you knead cocoa powder or finely grated bitter chocolate into a portion of the dough, you will be able to prepare attractive dark and light biscuits.

Finely chopped or ground almonds and other nuts add 'bite' to basic short-crust pastry. Replace part of the quantity of flour with nuts, or flavour the basic dough with grated lemon or orange zest, a pinch of cinnamon or nutmeg, or knead in finely chopped candied lemon peel.

Hollowed-out cookies can be filled with jam which has been passed through a sieve, and a coating of chocolate will elevate the most basic cookie to the level of a special treat.

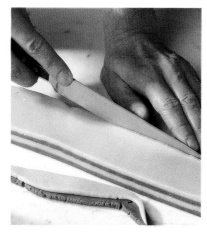

**1** To make layered dark and light cookies, thoroughly chill dark and light short-crust pastry. Roll pastry out to 1 cm/approx. ½ inch thick, lay the sheets of pastry on top of each other and cut into 1 cm wide strips. Layer together to form a chess-board pattern.

**2** Wrap the chess-board pastry in a layer of light-coloured pastry. Refrigerate. Slice and bake. Knead together the pastry cuttings, shape into a sausage and cut into slices.

**6** Round cookies look particularly nice when the base is coated in chocolate. Simply dip the lower half of the cookie in melted chocolate.

**7** Filled short-crust cookies or lebkuchen hearts look wonderful if coated completely in chocolate. Using a fork, dip the cookie in melted chocolate until it is coated all over, then place on a wire rack to drain. If you put a sheet of greaseproof paper under the rack you can scrape off cooled chocolate and use it again.

**3** For children's biscuits use large cutters or cut out shapes free-hand. If you add pastry decorations the shapes become more exciting. For example, a piece of dough pushed through a garlic press will produce fine strands which can be used for a person's hair or a horse's mane and tail.

**4** Terraced biscuits: While biscuits are still warm from the oven, dust circular and ring-shaped biscuits with icing sugar and layer together with jam.

**5** A quick method of decoration is to shape short-crust pastry into little balls. Press whole walnuts or hazelnuts into the dough, or drill a hole using a wooden cocktail stick and fill with nougat.

**8** Round short-crust pastry biscuits look nice if decorated with a piped praline rosette. Make sure biscuits are completely cool before dipping in melted chocolate.

**9** As long as melted chocolate is still damp. decorations made of candied fruit, chopped pistachios or other nuts, and chopped chocolate will stick to the biscuits.

**10** Biscuits look especially attractive if white chocolate decorations are piped onto the dark chocolate coating. To achieve a marbled effect, draw a wooden cocktail stick through the wet chocolate. This decorative idea can also be used on gateaux.

# CHOCOLATE GATEAU

**Ingredients for a spring form tin (22 cm diam., 1.5 l capacity/9 inches diam., 22 pints capacity)**

| | |
|---|---|
| **FOR THE FILLING** | |
| 500 g/1 lb 2 oz double cream | |
| 380 g/13 oz good quality plain cooking chocolate | |
| **FOR THE MIXTURE** | |
| 150 g/6 oz soft margarine | |
| 7 eggs | |
| 175 g/6 oz caster sugar | |
| 100 g/4 oz flour | |
| 100 g/4 oz drinking chocolate | |
| 3 tbsp cocoa powder | |
| 2 tsp baking powder | |
| 6 tbsp cold black coffee for soaking | |
| **FOR THE MARZIPAN LAYER** | |
| 300 g/11 oz marzipan | |
| 4 tbsp icing sugar | |
| 250 g/9 oz good quality milk cooking chocolate for coating | |
| **FOR DECORATION** | |
| 150 g/6 oz good quality plain cooking chocolate | |
| 1 tsp oil | |
| 5 rose leaves with stalks | |
| 2 tbsp cocoa powder | |

**1** A day in advance, bring the cream to the boil, melt the plain chocolate in the cream, cool and refrigerate.

**2** Line a spring form tin with baking parchment, leaving a 3 cm/1 inch border above the top of the tin. Melt margarine, sepa- rate eggs. Whisk together egg yolks, 2 tbsp warm water and sugar until thick and creamy. Stir in the margarine.

**3** Whisk egg whites until stiff and pile onto margarine and sugar mixture. Sieve flour, drink- ing chocolate, cocoa and baking powder onto egg whites, gently fold in all ingredients and pour into tin. Bake in a preheated oven at 175°C/350°F/Gas mark 4 for 35 minutes. Leave to cool.

**4** Slice the sponge cake into 3 lay- ers. Soak each layer in 2 tbsp black coffee. Whisk chocolate cream until very stiff and spread ⅔ of cream over 2 layers of cake. Put the cake layers together and spread the remaining chocolate cream all over the gateau. Refrigerate.

**5** For the coating knead together the marzipan and 2 tbsp icing sugar. Sprinkle remaining icing sugar over work surface and roll out marzipan until 2-3 mm/approx. ¼ inch thick. Using the spring form tin, mark a circle on the marzipan and cut out. Roll out remaining marzipan to form a strip 70 x 5 cm/28 x 2 inches, then roll up.

Unwrap the marzipan roll, working around the sides of the cake.

Pour the melted chocolate into the middle of the cake.

Spread the chocolate using a palette knife.

Straighten the edges. Place the marzipan circle on top of the cake, gradually unroll the marzipan strip around the sides of the cake, and press down gently. Place the cake on a wire rack and put grease- proof paper under the rack.

**6** To make the chocolate coating, melt the milk chocolate in a bowl over hot water, stir until smooth and pour onto centre of cake. Spread evenly with a palette knife and leave to cool.

**7** Melt the plain chocolate in a bowl over hot water and stir until smooth. Add the oil.

**8** Wash the rose leaves, pat dry and brush with melted chocolate.

First place the marzipan topping on top of the cake coated in chocolate cream.

Leave to dry. Carefully peel away rose leaves.

**9** To make the chocolate caraque, spread the remaining melted chocolate onto a marble surface and leave to set a little. Using a broad-bladed spatula, draw along the chocolate to produce wide chocolate curls. Decorate the cake with chocolate curls and leaves. Dust with cocoa powder. *Makes 12 slices.*

**When the chocolate is dry the rose leaves can be peeled away.**

**Chocolate cream can be used for many things.**

**Finally, decorate the chocolate cake with chocolate caraque (see also page 213) and chocolate leaves.**

# THREE-BASE CAKE

**Ingredients for a spring form tin
(24 cm diam., 2 l capacity/9 inches
diam., 3½ pints capacity)**

| | |
|---|---|
| **FOR THE MERINGUE** | |
| 2 egg whites | |
| 100 g/4 oz sugar | |
| **For the short-crust pastry** | |
| 125 g/5 oz flour | |
| 80 g/3 oz soft margarine | |
| 2 tbsp caster sugar | |
| pinch salt | |
| 1 egg yolk | |
| **FOR THE SPONGE** | |
| 3 eggs | |
| 100 g/4 oz caster sugar | |
| 70 g/3 oz flour | |
| 15 g/2 oz cornflour | |
| 4 tsp baking powder | |
| **FOR THE FILLING** | |
| 200 g/7 oz praline | |
| 3 tbsp double cream | |
| 4 leaves white gelatine | |
| 250 g/9 oz Cape gooseberries (physalis) | |
| 3 tbsp icing sugar | |
| 600 g/1 lb 5 oz double cream | |
| 400 g/14 oz raspberries | |
| 75 g/3 oz hazelnut cracknel for decoration | |

**1** To make the meringue, whisk the egg whites until stiff, fold in the sugar. Draw a circle 24 cm/9 inches in diameter on a sheet of baking parchment. Use baking parchment to line a baking sheet. Spread the meringue over the circle and bake at 75°C/200°F/Gas mark ¼ for about 4 hours. Trap a spoon handle in the oven door so it does not close fully. This will help the meringue to dry.

**2** To make the short-crust pastry, mix together flour, margarine, sugar, salt and egg yolk and knead to a smooth dough. Refrigerate for about 30 minutes. Roll out on a floured work surface until 3-4 mm/approx. ¼ inch thick. Using the spring form tin mark a circle on the pastry and cut it out. Place on a baking sheet lined with baking parchment and bake in a preheated oven at 200°C/400°F/Gas mark 6 for 15-20 minutes.

**3** To make the sponge base, separate the eggs, whisk together egg yolks, 3 tbsp warm water and sugar until thick and creamy. Whisk egg whites until stiff and add to egg yolk mixture. Mix together flour, baking powder and

Spread praline over short-crust pastry base.

Spread fruit cream on top of meringue.

Sprinkle cracknel over sides of gateau.

cornflour, sieve onto egg mixture and fold in. Fill a spring form tin lined with baking parchment with the sponge mixture. Bake in a preheated oven at 200°C/400°F/Gas mark 6 for 10-12 minutes. Remove paper and leave sponge to cool.

**4** Place a spring form tin or gateau mould around short-crust pastry base. Gently heat together praline and cream and mix until smooth. Spread praline cream on pastry base. Put the meringue base on top and press together gently.

**5** Soften gelatine. Reserve 12 Cape gooseberries. Remove casing from other gooseberries, chop finely and mix with 2 tbsp icing sugar.

A cake with 3 layers, short-crust (bottom), meringue (middle) and fatless sponge (top).

**Cracknel made of sugar and almonds.**

**Crush with a rolling pin.**

**6** Drain gelatine, melt over a low heat and mix with fruit. Whip 400 g/14 oz cream until stiff. As soon as the fruit mixture begins to set, fold in the whipped cream. Wash the raspberries and pat dry. Fold ½ of raspberries into fruit and cream.

**7** Spread the fruit cream over the meringue base. Finally, place the sponge base on top of the cream and press down lightly. Refrigerate the gateau for 2 hours.

**8** Remove mould from gateau. Whisk icing sugar and remaining cream until stiff and spread all over cake. Using a spoon press little wells in the cream on top of the cake.

**9** Sprinkle cracknel over sides of gateau. If you want to make the cracknel yourself, melt 100 g/4 oz caster sugar over a medium to high heat, remove pan from heat and stir in 50 g/2 oz chopped almonds or hazelnuts. Then spread the mixture onto a greased wooden board using a wooden spoon and leave to cool. Make the cracknel by crushing the sugar and nuts with a wooden rolling pin.

**10** Decorate the gateau with Cape gooseberries and remaining raspberries. *Makes 12 slices.*

**Carefully peel back the gooseberry leaves.**

**You can't tell by looking but you can certainly taste it – three types of cake hidden under a delicious layer of cream.**

# BRANDYSNAP BASKETS WITH GINGER TEA CREAM

| Ingredients for 8 baskets |
| --- |
| **FOR THE DOUGH** |
| 50 g/2 oz marzipan |
| 1 egg white |
| 1 egg |
| 60 g/2 oz icing sugar |
| 50 g/2 oz flour |
| 1 tsp cocoa powder |
| margarine for greasing |
| flour for dusting |
| **FOR THE CREAM** |
| 4 leaves white gelatine |
| 1 walnut-sized piece root ginger |
| 4 tbsp Earl Grey tea |
| (approx. 30 g/approx. 1 oz) |
| 100 g/4 oz caster sugar |
| 3 egg yolks |
| 100 ml/3 fl. oz milk |
| 200 g/7 oz double cream |
| **FOR THE CARAMEL** |
| 100 g/4 oz caster sugar |
| oil for brushing |

**1** Crumble the marzipan, mix with egg white and egg to form a smooth mixture. Mix in icing sugar and flour. Mix 1 tbsp of mixture with 1 tsp cocoa and use to fill a small piping bag made out of greaseproof paper or foil.

**2** Grease the baking sheet and dust with a little flour. Take a thin piece of cardboard, approx. 15 x 20 cm/6 x 8 inches, and cut out a circle 12 cm/5 inches in diameter. Lay the template on the baking sheet and thinly spread the basket mixture within the circle template. Using the small piping bag, pipe decorations on the circles.

**3** Bake in a preheated oven at 200°C/400°F/Gas mark 6 for 5-6 minutes. The edges of the mixture should be golden brown.

**4** As soon as they come out of the oven, lift the circles from the baking sheet using a palette knife or broad-bladed knife, position over an upturned glass or small bowl and press down around sides of glass to form the basket shape. Leave to cool. Bake the remaining mixture in the same way. If the baskets cool too quickly and start to

**Spread the mixture very thinly.**

**Pipe a pattern onto the mixture.**

**As soon as the circles come out of the oven, clamp down over an upturned bowl.**

set, return them to the oven for a few minutes to soften them.

**5** Soften the gelatine. Peel the ginger root and slice. Make the tea with 125 ml/4 fl. oz boiling water. Leave to brew for 5 minutes, strain, and measure off 50 ml/approx. 2 fl. oz.

**6** Now whisk the sugar and egg yolks until creamy. Bring milk, tea and ginger to boil, strain and beat into egg mixture. Return mixture to pan and cook over a low heat, whisking all the time with a balloon whisk, until the custard is just about to boil.

**7** Drain the gelatine, add to the custard and refrigerate. Whip cream

**Carefully lift the circles off the baking sheet using a spatula, palette knife or broad-bladed knife.**

Melt the sugar over a moderate heat. Draw spun sugar threads using 2 forks.

until stiff. As soon as the custard begins to set, fold in the whipped cream and refrigerate again.

**8** Caramelise the sugar until golden brown in a cast-iron pan or a pan without a non-stick coating. Remove the pan from the heat and, using 2 forks, spin sugar threads. Leave spun sugar webs to set.

**9** Fill the baskets with scoops of ginger tea cream using a teaspoon. Decorate with spun sugar threads.

The ginger tea cream should be firm enough to stand a spoon upright in it.

Brandy snap baskets break easily so they should be shaped as soon as they come out of the oven.

# WEDDING CAKE

**Ingredients for 2 spring form tins (16 and 22 cm diam./6 and 9 inches diam.)**

**FOR THE CAKE MIXTURE**

500 g/1 lb 2 oz soft margarine

500 g/1 lb 2 oz caster sugar

10 eggs

2 tsp grated lemon zest

2 tbsp rum

pinch salt

150 g/6 oz nibbed almonds

250 g/9 oz flour

250 g/9 oz cornflour

margarine for greasing

**FOR THE MARZIPAN LAYER**

400 g/14 oz apricot jam

400 g/14 oz marzipan

2 tbsp icing sugar

icing sugar for rolling out

**FOR THE ICING**

250 g/9 oz icing sugar

3 tbsp lemon juice

**FOR THE FLOWERS**

2 leaves white gelatine

500 g/1 lb 2 oz icing sugar

1 egg white

2 tsp glycerine (available from chemists)

food colouring as desired

**FOR PIPING ICING**

1 egg white

250 g/9 oz icing sugar

silver balls for decoration

**1** To make the cake mixture whisk together margarine, sugar and eggs until creamy. Stir in lemon zest, rum, salt, almonds, flour and cornflour.
**2** Grease the spring form tins. Fill each with cake mixture to 3 mm/approx. ¼ inch in depth, smooth out, and bake for about 2 minutes under the grill until golden brown. Fill each tin with another layer of mixture, on top of the cooked layer, and bake again. Continue with this method until all the cake mixture is used up. Leave the layers of cake to cool.
**3** To make the marzipan layer warm the jam and purée it. Brush both cakes all over with jam. Knead together marzipan and icing sugar. Roll out thinly on a surface lightly dusted with icing sugar. For the sides of the cake cut two strips, both 5 cm/2 inches wide and 50 cm and 70 cm/20 inches and 28 inches respectively in length and roll them up into coils.
**4** Cut circles for the tops of the cakes from the remaining marzipan, using each spring form tin as a template. Place the marzipan circles on top of the cakes. Unroll the marzipan strips, working round the sides of the cake. Press down gently to fix marzipan in place.

Bake each layer of cake until golden brown

Icing made from sugar and lemon juice.

Pour the glacé icing over the cakes.

Unroll the strip of marzipan for the side of the cake, gradually working around it.

**5** To make the glacé icing mix together icing sugar, lemon juice and 2-3 tbsp water to form a thick icing. Put the cakes on a wire rack, coat with icing and leave to dry. Then put the small cake on top of the large one.
**6** To make the flowers, soften gelatine. Dissolve wet gelatine over a low heat. Mix the icing sugar with the egg white and glycerine. Add the gelatine and mix to a smooth paste. If the mixture is a bit wet, add a little icing sugar. Colour part of the icing with food colouring if wished.
**7** Fill a piping bag with the icing. Pipe out a small amount, shape into

Handicraft skills: Beautiful flowers made from icing sugar and gelatine.

a petal or leaf shape and position several together to form flowers.

**8** To make the icing for piping, briefly whisk the egg whites with a hand mixer. Add the icing sugar and beat together until the icing is shiny. Make a small piping bag out of greaseproof paper and fill with ½ of the icing. Put the rest of the icing in a piping bag with a star-shaped nozzle. Decorate the wedding cake with piped icing, flowers and silver balls.

Decorate the cake with piped icing.

Not difficult, but time-consuming – a richly decorated 2-tier wedding cake.

# GLOSSARY

## Almond essence
This colourless essential oil is distilled from apricot or peach kernels, or from bitter almonds. It has a strong almond smell and is used to intensify the smell of almond flavoured cakes and biscuits, nut fillings and marzipan.

## Almonds
Almonds which are still in their skins are not only cheaper; they have a stronger flavour. It is easy to remove the skins. Simply pour boiling water over the almonds and allow to stand for 2-3 minutes. Then drain in a sieve, and press the almonds between thumb and forefinger to press them out of the skins.

## Aniseed
The dried seeds of the *Pimpinella anisum L.* are one of the oldest spices in the world. This plant, which grows up to 50 cm/20 inches high, is supposed to have originated in Egypt. Nowadays aniseed mainly comes from Spain and Italy.

Attractive star anise, which contains shiny, reddish-brown seeds in a star-shaped husk, comes chiefly from China and Indo-China.

## Artificial flavourings
These flavourings, which come in concentrated form, are either produced from plants (natural flavours) or are manufactured, synthetic flavours which can be made from natural products, or which are artificial. They impart lemon, vanilla, almond or rum flavours to baking and are stable when heated.

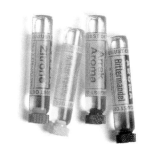

# B

## Baking blind
Short-crust pastry flan bases or individual tarts are 'baked blind' if they are going to be filled at a later stage with an uncooked topping or filling, such as in fruit flans. Dried pulses or rice replace the proper filling during baking and are removed as soon as the pastry is sufficiently cooked, which is usually halfway through the cooking time.

## Baking parchment
Some cake mixtures and doughs will stick to even a well-greased baking sheet. This is due to the high sugar content in the mixture, such as meringues. If you are baking this type of mixture, line your baking sheet or tin with baking parchment. Unlike greaseproof paper it is coated on both sides and doesn't have to be greased.

## Baking powder
This white powder, which is almost essential for sponge cake mixes, consists of sodium and an acid. In the presence of moisture and warmth the two form carbon dioxide gas which causes the mixture to rise. Only very rich sponge mixtures which contain a lot of eggs, sugar and fat will succeed without baking powder. Using baking powder in less calorie-laden mixtures will ensure that your cake is light and airy.

## Bicarbonate of soda
Bicarbonate of soda is the oldest known raising agent, but it causes mixtures to expand widthways rather than vertically. For this reason you should always leave a gap between portions of dough on a baking sheet. Bicarbonate of soda doesn't smell of anything but does taste slightly of soda.

## Bun cases
These come in multiple packs; each case holds about 1 tbsp cake mixture. The baked buns

can be served in the cases and the paper is removed before eating.

# C

## Cake dividers

You can get plastic or aluminium cake dividers which divide into 12-18 slices, so cakes and gateaux can be easily sliced into equal portions. As a general rule of thumb you should assume that the richer the cake, the smaller the slice. Flat cakes, such as fruit flans, are divided into 12 portions, deep cakes and gateaux into 14 and cream or custard filled gateaux into 16 slices.

## Candied lemon peel

The lemons used to produce candied peel can weigh up to 2 kg/4½ lb and grow in sub-tropical regions. The lemons are harvested before they are ripe, then peeled, and the thick peel is preserved in a salt solution. The peel is then blanched and candied in a sugar solution to form candied lemon peel.

## Caramel

Caramel is made from boiled sugar. As soon as the liquid starts to boil the melted sugar takes on an amber colour. Page 225 tells you how to spin sugar threads from caramel.

## Cardamom

The Greeks and Romans used cardamom as a perfume. This Asian spice adds a sharp note to spice mixes. You should always buy cardamom seeds rather than ground cardamom because it loses its essential oil very quickly.

## Cinnamon

Thin sticks of cinnamon come from the rind of the cinnamon tree which is 2 mm/⅛ inch thick. The quality of flavour depends on where the cinnamon comes from – cinnamon from Sri Lanka is particularly good.

## Cocoa powder

Cocoa contains 25 percent less fat than chocolate and is also suitable for rich cake mixtures which already contain a high proportion of fat.

## Coconut

This is the biggest of all nuts and the oil is rich in saturated fats. The white flesh, from which coconut oil and cocoa butter are produced, can be eaten raw. Grated coconut is mainly used in baking. It can be quickly and easily toasted in a microwave oven. Simply scatter 75 g/3 oz desiccated coconut on a plate and cook for 1-12 minutes at 600-700 watts.

## Coriander

Coriander is available fresh as a green herb, whilst the dried seeds are popular in spicy baking.

## Cornflour

If you don't want gluten in flour to take full effect in a particular recipe, part of the quantity of flour can be replaced with cornflour. This makes the cake especially fine textured and delicate.

## Couverture

Couverture is a type of chocolate enriched with at least 35 percent cocoa butter. It is greatly valued for cake baking because it melts evenly and is smooth textured.

## Cracknel

Sugar is slowly heated until it turns golden brown. Then chopped nuts or almonds are added and the mixture is spread over a greased baking sheet. When cooled and set the layer of sugar is crushed with a rolling pin to form cracknel.

# D

## Diabetics

Bakery products for diabetics are expensive, which makes home baking worthwhile. Replace the quantity of sugar stated in the recipe with fruit sugar or special diabetic sugar. If you use diabetic sugar, refer to the manufacturer's instructions on the packet. It is also a good idea to use wholemeal flour if possible, because refined white flour affects blood sugar levels more quickly.

## Dried fruit

Dried fruit such as apple rings, prunes, dates, figs, grapes and apricots are among the oldest and

most traditional ingredients in baking. They are used increasingly in health-conscious baking, because their sweetness can be used to replace a proportion of sugar and at the same time they provide roughage.

## Dried yeast
Dried yeast is practical because it doesn't have to work first, the granules can be added directly to the flour – but it isn't quite such a powerful raising agent. Dried yeast comes in sealed foil sachets. A 7 g/approx. ¼ oz sachet of dried yeast corresponds to about 25 g/1 oz fresh yeast.

# E

## Eclairs
These popular, finger-length pastries are made of choux pastry and contain a filling, such as strawberry cream, as shown in our strawberry éclairs on page 155.

## Egg whites
If you whisk egg whites in a food processor they will be particularly stiff and fine textured. Start the machine off on a low

setting, then increase the speed, reducing it again at the end. If you are whisking egg whites by hand you will need patience, a bowl with a rounded bottom and a large balloon whisk. You can also whisk egg whites successfully over a bowl of hot water.

# F

## Flan bases
The base of a fruit flan can easily turn soggy. To prevent this, sprinkle the base with ground nuts or French toast crumbs before adding the filling, or if you like you can brush the base of the flan with melted chocolate.

## Food colourings
Just a couple of drops suffice to colour icing and glazes. Food colourings are available in yellow, orange, red, blue and green. These artificial colourings are quite safe, although some people do have an allergic reaction to them.

# G

## Gelatine
Many cake fillings use gelatine, which is made from cow's bones and cartilage, to achieve the correct consistency. It can be either colourless (white) or red and comes in leaf form (6 leaves per pack) or as a powder in small sachets (9 g)/approx. ½ oz). Gelatine does not smell of anything. It must be softened in cold water before use. However instant gelatine (30 g/1 oz sachets), does not have to be softened first as it dissolves immediately.

## Ginger
Whether fresh ginger or preserved in syrup, whether dried or ground, ginger lends a sharp, aromatic flavour to spicy baking. Peeled root ginger can also be preserved in brandy or sherry.

## Glacé cherries
These are candied cherries in which the natural juice has been replaced by a strong sugar solution. Glacé cherries can be red, yellow or green and are suitable for decorating cakes and gateaux.

## Glycerine

Glycerine is a syrupy, sweetish liquid, which has no smell or colour, and is found in all natural fats. In the chapter on cake decoration it is used to 'soften' icing made from egg white, sugar and gelatine, for making icing flowers. Glycerine is available from chemists.

## Greaseproof paper

Transparent greaseproof paper, unlike baking parchment, does not have a non-stick coating and must always be greased thoroughly if used in baking.

## Greasing

Even non-stick baking tins should always be greased, preferably with margarine. You should never use oil. Not only does it leave behind an unpleasant yellowish film at high temperatures, it also burns into the tin, which means you won't be able to use the tin again because any cakes you bake in it in future will stick.

## Gum drops

These are either round, hard pastilles or soft, chewy sweets. They are made from purified rubber (the sap of tropical acacia trees), gelatine, cornflour, sugar, syrup and flavourings. Children love picking these sweet decorations off any cake.

# H

## Hazelnuts

Contain a high proportion of oil and quickly go bad at room temperature, so hazelnuts should be stored in a cool, dark place, especially chopped and ground nuts. If you toast nuts in a frying pan before adding them to the baking the flavour will be stronger.

## Honey

Don't use expensive comb honey for baking. Good quality honey should only be heated to a maximum of 40°C/80°F to preserve the flavour. but much higher temperatures are used during baking. Honey which has crystallised out can easily be melted in a microwave oven. Take the lid off the jar and warm for 2-3 minutes on the lowest defrost setting at 150-180 watts.

## Honey cake

Honey cake is very popular in Germany at Christmas. If the mixture is prepared using bicarbonate of soda it will easily keep for up to 4 weeks and will become softer and spicier. If you only bake a small amount at a time you will have a constant supply of fresh honey cake.

## Hundreds and thousands

These small, hard, brightly coloured sugar beads are used to decorate cakes and gateaux.

# I

## Icing sugar

Ideal for use in icing and glazes because the sugar crystals are no longer visible.

# J

## Jellied fruits

Jellied fruits usually come in raspberry, orange and banana flavours and are coated in sugar. Inside they are clear and transparent. Jellied fruits have a sharp, fruity taste, smell of the appropriate fruit and can be used as decoration for cakes and biscuits if cut into slices or pieces.

# M

## Mace
This is the dried husk of the nutmeg. The flavour is more delicate than that of the nut itself and thus it is a popular spice for use in cakes.

## Maple syrup
This sweet syrup with a delicate caramel flavour is harvested from North American maple trees which are 40-80 years old and processed to form a thick syrup on site. It takes 40 litres/70 pints of maple sap to make 1 litre/1¾ pints of syrup. Maple syrup is a popular alternative to sugar as a sweetener in baking.

## Margarine
Margarine is made from vegetable oil, water and milk. It contains between 40 percent and 80 percent unsaturated fat, depending on the type of margarine, together with vitamins A, D, E and beta carotene.

## Marzipan
Marzipan makes a delicious filling and coating for classic cakes. It is based on a mixture of ground almonds and icing sugar, to which a little grated lemon zest and rose water is added.

## Measuring beakers
If you want your baking to turn out successfully then precise measuring of ingredients is essential. You should use kitchen scales, because measuring beakers are too imprecise.

## Mixed spice
You can buy ground, ready-mixed spice for baking, which usually contains a mixture of aniseed, ginger, cardamom, coriander, nutmeg, cloves and cinnamon. If you don't do much baking then it is a good idea to use such a mix rather than buying the individual spices, because if spices are stored for a long time they lose their flavour.

# N

## Nuts
Whenever possible buy nuts in the shell and shell them shortly before you want to use them. This way the flavour and essentials oils will be preserved for as long as possible.

# P

## Pastry brush
There are various sizes of pastry brushes. They have safe, natural bristles, and can be washed, or even put in the dishwasher without problems. Also, they don't shed hairs. With the help of a pastry brush you can grease any kind of tin, or quickly brush glazes and egg washes onto cakes and pastries.

## Pastry wheel
There are two types of pastry wheel – a smooth wheel with a sharp edge for cutting pastries such as pizza, and a smaller wheel with a wavy edge for cutting out uncooked short-crust pastry or curd cheese pastry. The pastry wheel leaves a nice pattern and is suitable for making pastry decorations.

## Piping bags
For fine lettering or small decorations in icing you can easily make a piping bag from greaseproof paper. Take a rectangular sheet of paper (20 x 35 cm)/8 x 14 inches and fold it diagonally in half. Cut along the fold. Roll up to form a cornet. Tuck in the end of the paper, which will help to strengthen the cornet.

## Puff pastry

Airy, delicate and crispy – this is how puff pastry should be. It must be prepared carefully, using a specific method, and requires a great deal of experience to make it, which is why this type of pastry is usually left to the experts. You can buy frozen ready-made puff pastry which is just as good as home-made, so for this reason we have not included recipes which show you how to make it.

# R

## Raisins

Grapes which are air-dried in their country of origin. If sulphur is used in the production process, that must be stated on the packaging. The best raisins come from Australia, South Africa and Afghanistan.

## Rolling pin

We have nothing against the tried and tested wooden rolling pin, but for particularly sticky doughs you should use a non-stick rolling pin. Some plastic rolling pins are particularly handy. The centre of these is hollow so they can be filled with warm or cold water, depending on the type of pastry, so that the dough stays at the correct working temperature.

## Rose water

A drop of rose oil mixed with 125 ml/4 fl. oz water makes the best rose water, as used in marzipan. Rose oil is distilled from various types of rose petals: 4,000-5,000

kg/9-11,000 lb of rose petals make 1 kg/2 lb 3 oz rose oil.

## Rubber spatula

This is composed of a wooden or plastic handle and a smooth, bendable blade made from rubber which bends into the sides and bottoms of bowls, making it easy to scrape out pans and dishes. A rubber spatula is very useful when preparing mixtures and cream fillings.

# S

## Scissors

When baking, scissors come in useful for yeast doughs and strudel. They can be used to cut shapes out of yeast dough, and the thick edges on strudel pastry are easily cut off using kitchen scissors.

## Sugar

Whether sugar comes from sugar cane or sugar beet, it still contains 99 percent carbohydrates and 1 percent water. There are various types of sugar: caster sugar, ordinary household sugar, light brown and demerara sugar. Caster sugar is most frequently used for sprinkling in baking. Icing sugar is made from finely ground caster sugar.

## Sugar balls

These are used for decorating cakes and desserts. They are made of crystallised sugar, and are now available without artifi-

cial colours. Natural colourings which are used are turmeric and beetroot.

## Sugar decorations

Colourful hearts and bright hundreds and thousands, sugar balls and flowers are attractive edible cake decorations which do not contain artificial colourings. You can also find many different types of chocolate decorations, such as leaves.

## Sugar icing

Unlike chocolate, sugar icing is fat-free and is either made from icing sugar and liquid, or sugar and water boiled together.

## Sugar thermometer

If you do a lot of cooking using sugar syrups, such as making caramel or jam, then a sugar thermometer is ideal. The temperature scale goes up to 180°C, so you can easily see which stage the sugar has reached.

## Sweetener

Cakes need sweet ingredients. Honey and syrup are very sweet but contain too much moisture for many recipes. However, if you would rather use a natural product than refined sugar, you should use cane sugar. These pale brown crystals can be sprinkled and used in exactly the same way as ordinary sugar.

# T

**Tartar**
This is the salt from tartaric acid, which for years formed the acidic component in baking powder. However, in the last 10 years it has been replaced increasingly by different types of phosphate. Because it has a mildly acidic taste it can also be used as a flavouring.

# V

**Vanilla**
The long pod of a tropical climbing plant is harvested before it is ripe, fermented and dried. The strong vanilla aroma only devel-

ops during the drying process. The part of the plant which contains the flavour is the outside of the pod. If you use the essence from inside the pod during baking you will get a faint vanilla flavour.

**Vanilla sugar**
You can easily make vanilla sugar yourself. Put 10-12 vanilla pods in a jar and cover with caster or icing sugar. Then close the jar tightly. After 3 months the vanilla pods will have completely transferred their flavour to the sugar. Vanilla sugar can be bought ready made, and contains at least 5 percent ground vanilla pod and sugar.

# W

**Wire rack**
Most cakes should be left to cool on a wire rack, as this enables the cake to cool evenly on all sides and underneath, so that condensation cannot form. If the cake or pastry is left to cool on a baking sheet it will stay slightly damp.

# Y

**Yeast**
This biological raising agent consists of living bacteria which, in the right conditions (warmth, sugar and moisture) rapidly multiply, converting sugar into alcohol and carbon dioxide in the process. During baking the gas bubbles expand and cause the dough to rise. Fresh yeast smells pleasantly sharp and isn't greasy. Old yeast loses its power as a raising agent.

# INDEX